HOW TO BE A SUCCESSFUL TRUSTEE

HOW TO BE A SUCCESSFUL TRUSTEE

by

Peter Curbishley

PETER CURBISHLEY
HOW TO BE A SUCCESSSFUL TRUSTEE

Published in partnership with Riverside Publishing Solutions

ISBN-13: 978-1-913012-61-8

Printed and bound in the United Kingdom

Contents

List of Figures

A Note on Language

There are many types of not-for-profit organisations. Some are small organisations which are not charities. Some are provident associations or companies limited by guarantee. There are also community interest companies and social enterprises. 'Not-for-profit' is a useful omnibus word but is rather clumsy. Accordingly, in this book I use the word 'charity' to describe them all, recognising that some are *not* actual charities.

I also use the word 'trustee' throughout. There are a number of titles used in addition to trustee: managing trustee; committee member; board member; officers; governors or directors. I will stick to trustee for simplicity.

The common thread running through these organisations is that they are not working to make a profit. Such surpluses as are made are retained in the organisation and not distributed. The trustee – or whatever title is used – has a range of responsibilities to manage the organisation prudently and with due regard to the relevant legislation applicable to that organisation type.

Introduction

This book is intended to help anyone who is, or is thinking of becoming, a trustee of a small charity. I have tried to give practical advice based on my own experience, the experience of others and the results of academic research in this area. Despite the fact that there are around 166,000 charities in the UK,[1] 80% of which have incomes below £100,000, there is little in the way of practical guidance available. If we assume that each of them has six or seven trustees, then there are around a million people actively engaged in the business of running a small charity. Whereas the shelves of a reasonably sized bookshop will have many titles of advice on setting up and running businesses of various sizes, books to help charity trustees are rare. I have written this book to correct that.

When I retired I quickly became a trustee of two local charities and started attending board meetings. The meetings were well organised and we had a full set of papers before the start, and sometimes others tabled during the meeting itself. After a year or so, I left one of these meetings and as I walked to the car park, I asked myself, how much did I actually know about the organisation I was supposed to be a trustee of? I did not know how many clients we had, for example, nor did I know what the turnover of clients was. I did not know any hard facts about employee or volunteer numbers. I was ignorant of key facts around areas such as staff training or staff development. In fact, there was a wide range of essential information about the charity and its operations I had little or no idea about.

It would not be true to say there was *no* information: the accountant, for example, provided two pages of accounts. He told us the electricity bill month by month, what the phone bill was each month and a stack of other quite detailed information. But there were no percentages at all and no comparative statistics telling us what had gone on in previous quarters or during the year just gone. There was, in short, a mass of data which was difficult to make sense of. The distinction is between *data* and *information*. This was true of all the information before us. There was nothing to enable us to compare the current situation with what had gone before. There was no information about *trends*.

Some years before retiring, I had been a business adviser helping small firms with turnovers generally below £2m per annum – perhaps worth about double that now. They were still recognisable small businesses, often owned and run by an individual or a family. The discussion would often start with a tour of the workshop or factory to display what was being made and to show me any machines, particularly some early examples of computer-controlled equipment. The firms had various problems to do with finding premises, securing sufficient capital, marketing, or employing qualified staff. Sometimes I or one of my colleagues could help, sometimes not.

I was at one such meeting when I came across a vivid example of a small firm owner not fully understanding what was taking place in his business from a financial point of view. I was visiting a small engineering business with around half a dozen employees. Engineering businesses are often physically grubby affairs since everything has a patina of oil or grease. The owner's desk was no exception. The chair, the desk itself, the phone and all the paperwork was the colour of oil. The mug of coffee he gave me was also grubby. As the conversation moved on I asked about his financial situation, whereupon he opened a drawer in his grimy desk and drew out a pristine, white envelope. It was his accounts. It was the only thing in the whole workshop which was clean of grease and oil. He had obviously not looked at them, which I proceeded to do. They consisted of eleven pages of detailed accounts and notes.

With the aid of last year's figures – also in a pristine white envelope deeper in the same drawer – I was able to do a few simple calculations and work out his margin and ratios like wages to sales, which were not worked out or displayed in the accounts. These showed a worrying decline. Although his sales were increasing, his margin was getting smaller and smaller. The details do not matter; what does matter is that here was a businessman who had received a significant amount of financial information which showed, when you looked at it, a steadily deteriorating position. However, it was presented in a form he did not understand and he said the accountant had not explained the situation to him.

Both examples illustrate the problem not of an *absence* of information but how it was presented. Did it tell a story? Did it show how things were changing over time? Did the recipient understand what was being conveyed? A key feature of this book, therefore, is a discussion of information and how it is presented to a trustee board. I will discuss matters of context and the use of ratios and percentages. None of it is rocket science, but its absence in all the places I have worked has resulted in a lack of understanding of the organisation. This will go some way to enabling you as a trustee to make a contribution.

It was also during my time helping small firms that I began to acquire an interest in marketing. This is a crucial subject in the commercial world. An excellent product or service is unlikely to survive without it. An indifferent product or service properly marketed will probably prosper. Ralph Waldo Emerson famously said, 'Build a better mousetrap and the world will beat a path to your door.' Regrettably that is not true. Ultimately, I studied for a postgraduate diploma in marketing and became a member of the Chartered Institute of Marketing. Later, I did the specialist Open University course on marketing for not-for-profit organisations.

Marketing is one of the topics which feature in this book. There is a widespread belief that marketing skills – as developed for the commercial world – can be relatively easily transposed to the work of a charity. I have attended several meetings where the suggestion of getting someone in with marketing experience – and by inference from a commercial background – has been made. Some of the few books with advice on marketing for the not-for-profit sector also seem to assume a simple transfer of ideas and techniques. It is a seductive idea, as much commercial marketing is impressive, slick and professional. We can all point to impressive marketing campaigns on the TV or in print. There are problems, however – the principle one being that in the commercial world, there is usually a direct relationship between the firm and the customer. This is a direct buyer/seller transaction. The seller sells a widget to a customer and the customer pays the seller money for it. There can of course be intermediate sellers in between and forms of financing provided by another firm. But the essential one-to-one relationship is there in some form.

In the case of a charity, they may be helping vulnerable individuals such as the homeless, drug users, those in food poverty or those in debt. They are unlikely to have such a simple customer/supplier relationship. They are likely to be funded by a third party, donations or a grant, for example, and so are acting as a kind of go-between. They will make efforts to locate these individuals but the nature and style of their marketing activities are different to those of commercial firms. The relationship is different and this has a direct impact on a charity's marketing methods.

Another difference is that a business is about *growing* its market. They either want to sell more stuff, or increase market share, or a mixture of both. A charity on the other hand hardly wants to see an increase in the number of homeless people, or see more people go without food. The ultimate success of a charity is to work itself out of business: a cure for cancer is found or there are no more homeless people. This is not the objective of any commercial business. These, and other differences, mean that a straightforward use of commercial marketing skills is not always justified or successful.

Similarly to marketing, the idea of getting people with business experience onto boards is frequently desired. Both these assumptions seem to be based on the notion that those with private sector experience are in some way superior to those who work in a not-for-profit or public sector environment. This derives in part from the political climate. Of course it is often the case that someone who has worked in the business world has useful and relevant experience to offer. If you have grown a small firm, and seen it become a major enterprise, then it can safely be assumed you have a high degree of skill. Likewise, if you have been a senior manager in a major enterprise it is likely you have acquired a lot of experience. But the question is how well that skill and the experience behind it is relevant to the needs of the charity. The difficulty might be in the adaption or application of those skills to the different world in which the not-for-profit organisation operates. I have known a number of people with impressive credentials and first-rate experience gained in the private sector who have volunteered to be on the board of a charity or not-for-profit organisation, and have not stayed long.

In addition to the different relationship between customer and supplier I have mentioned above, there is a different moral universe.

The public expects a charity to be whiter than white. While they may disapprove of the goings-on within some of our corporations – the grotesque salaries and bonuses, the sometimes shady employment practices, and tax avoidance – this does not on the whole prevent them from being customers of such firms. They are cross at the salaries paid to chief executives of some of the larger charities, however. These salaries are tiny compared to the sort of multimillion packages paid to FTSE directors, yet there is a belief that someone working for a charity should not be so highly paid. When people give money to a charity they want it to go to the 'front line' and are angry at the thought of money going – or being wasted, in their view – on 'administration'.

The climate for charities changed with the Bristol case in 2015. The story was that a woman, Olive Cooke, received around 3,000 mailings from charities and there was a media storm when she committed suicide. It was suggested that the huge number of mailings may well have contributed to her depression and her feelings of being overwhelmed by the requests. The individual charities would not have known of the mailings from other charities, the problem being the circulation and sale of details between them, which contributed to the large number of requests she received.

One thing which is immediately obvious when talking to someone who is involved with a charity or not-for-profit organisation is the pride they have in what they do. It is seldom, if ever, just a job to them. They will usually take any opportunity to describe the difference they make or to talk about a particular individual they have been able to help. I have noticed, however, that this pride and the sense of achievement they get from helping others does not always translate into pride for the sector. There is often a sense of being somewhat apologetic. There is almost a matter of pride in *what* they do but not such a pride in having to do it. This applies mostly to smaller organisations – less so, if at all, with the bigger charities.

Charities are often working in the cracks of our society. Many charities have stepped in after the budget cuts, the austerity measures and other failures by governments, national or local, to help those unable to help themselves. Without their collective efforts, many millions of our fellow citizens would suffer more severely than they do now. Just think of the food banks for example or the work of the Salvation Army. Those at the bottom of society would suffer much more without the help of thousands of volunteers who regularly turn out to seek funds or help those in need. It would not be fair to argue that all charities exist because of failures of government. Government cannot do everything or cure every ill.

Yet somehow this massive and vital contribution does not really register with the world at large. Jesse Norman, in his book *Adam Smith: What He Thought, and Why it Matters*,[2] argues that:

> *The focus on market exchange also meant that for a long time mainstream economics tended to ignore much one way human activity such as personal giving and philanthropy and the work of non-governmental organisations. These subjects were viewed as 'soft' – a telling word – or as mere 'sociology in disguise'.*

I argue in this book that some charities do not always help themselves. A regular feature of a local paper is a photo of the local MP stood with a collection of charity workers at some event or other. They are all smiling. The MP looks as though he or she is in support of the charity and the charity people look as though they are happy to have the MP there. He or she gets their photo in the local paper and the impression is created that they are in support of the charity's efforts. Often the MP is invited because it increases the likelihood that they will get into the local paper. But what if the MP has voted through all the measures which have negatively impacted on the work of the charity? All the austerity measures, budget cuts, cuts to local authorities, the so-called 'bedroom tax',* and legislative changes which have led to disadvantage being made worse? What is the message being conveyed by everyone stood about smiling? Did they hammer the MP on their voting record? Did they explain in graphic detail the effects of what the MP voted for? Did they insist on the MP asking a question in Parliament or voting differently? Or was it all smiles and comforting words? My experience of people when they get to meet someone like an MP in person is they become deferential.

Another curious aspect is the lack of real coverage of the sector in our media. Newspapers and other media are full of sections or supplements on sport, fashion, holidays, business and money, films, theatre – the list is endless. Yet with the possible sole exception of the *Guardian* newspaper, the charity and not-for-profit sector rarely feature. No supplements or special features for them. If a charity steps out of line, for example Oxfam, Kids Company or the abuse scandal in Haiti in 2019, they can burst onto the front pages, but otherwise, the positive work they do is largely carried out unnoticed and unreported.

A factor in this partial invisibility has been the Lobbying Act of 2014. The Sheila McKechnie Foundation published a report titled *The Chilling Reality* (June 2018)[3] following a series of interviews with ninety-two voluntary and charitable organisations. As the title implies, the act has had a chilling effect on the ability and willingness of charitable organisations to lobby and make their voices heard on behalf of their beneficiaries. There are a variety of reasons listed in the

* Properly called the 'social sector size criteria'.

report but they include being fearful of the rules, an unwillingness to engage in what the report terms 'coalition activity' – that is, joining with other charities and organisations – and a desire to avoid issues which are politically 'live'. Respondents also report that the effects of the act are to divert effort away from core work and this can make it harder to pursue their mission. The act has been described as a 'gagging law'. Ironically, a past prime minister, David Cameron, became embroiled in a scandal concerning lobbying on behalf of Greensill Capital but did not fall foul of the act.[4]

This chilling effect is a great shame because these organisations are on the front line and are acutely aware of the problems faced by those they are seeking to help. It means the airwaves are full of opinions from people who often have little contact with or knowledge of what life is like for those at the margins of society, or for those who have been unable to access help in whatever form. The five-week wait to receive Universal Credit is an example of politicians being unaware of the hand-to-mouth existence of people at the bottom of the social ladder. Meanwhile, lobbying in one form or another by commercial entities seems to continue unabated.

The main theme I explore in this book is that small charities and not-for-profit organisations operate in a different way and in a different environment to other organisations. Understanding these differences is, in my view, key to being a successful trustee. Although people with experience from outside and from different environments (commercial, local authority, professional and so forth) can and do contribute significantly, it is not always straightforward. There are similarities – the need to stay solvent is true across all organisational types – but the relationship with clients and with the public is subtly different.

This impacts on being a trustee of a not-for-profit organisation. It can be bewildering to begin with. I have already mentioned one of the key themes of this book, namely information. What information you receive, in what form and how often is one of the key factors, in my view, to being a successful trustee. This is information about the organisation itself, how it operates and its staff, but also client information and what is going on in the outside world. I shall introduce what I shall term the SCAPS model in connection with information: Selection, Collection, Analysis, Presentation and Storage. These will form the basis of an information plan. Despite its importance, few charities actually have one of these.

Information is key to the subject you will often hear about as a trustee, namely governance. Good governance is, or at least should be, a central part of a trustee's duties. Governance has its own problems, as is seen in the increasing concern with safeguarding. Many charities are now almost drowning in policies. Whereas, once upon a time, there were a handful, now there are scores of them. Some are introduced for defensive reasons. No charity wants to be sued because it does not have the appropriate policy in place if something goes wrong. Nor is it just about the policy – it has to be promulgated and training offered to ensure staff are aware of what is required. They have to be managed. The danger is that governance, risk assessments, safeguarding and other procedural matters begin to consume significant amounts of time and mental energy. Negative duties can also assume great importance. The policies have to be updated regularly and staff brought up to date. The worry is that it leads to a kind of risk aversion, with staff and volunteers working to what 'the policy' is rather than the needs of whomever the charity is trying to help. It is a kind of 'work to rule'.

One of the particular difficulties of being a trustee results from being detached from the day-to-day workings of the organisation. On the one hand, it is vital to maintain a detached, strategic view and not to get involved in the everyday affairs of the organisation.

On the other, you do need to know what is happening in the organisation, since even quite small errors or omissions can have serious consequences – IT failings are a case in point. If you have come from any kind of job environment where you work with others, you will know that for every story there are two versions: the version the managers want you to know, and the actual version which emerges through gossip. Someone suddenly leaves and the official version is they 'left by mutual consent'. The real story is that there was a terrible row and the individual was fired or stormed out. You know this because someone heard the almighty row taking place and gossip in the kitchenette or in the pub did the rest. Now the problem for you and your fellow trustees is that you only get to hear the official version. The issue might have been that the individual had a grievance or a difference of view which was in fact legitimate. As a trustee, you may not know the reason for their leaving or whether the problem resided with them or the manager who is still in place.

I discuss some of the things you can do to remedy this while maintaining a detached view. Exit interviews are vital and trustees need to be involved in disciplinary matters and appeals. Both of these will provide useful insights into the organisation and a 'worm's eye view'. Another process is staff surveys, which if properly conducted by an outside contractor will sometimes reveal problems.

I also discuss the issue of who should be a trustee and the skills that are needed. There are some who think trustees should be people with experience in what the charity does. I am not so sure that this is necessarily a good strategy. It is useful of course to have some on the board with direct knowledge of the sector. But a trustee's role is wider than that and sometimes too much knowledge can get in the way. So it is a question of balance and having people who are able to ask those difficult questions about, for example, the focus of the organisation, its image and brand, or its direction of travel. I have already mentioned the belief that private sector skills are in some way superior to those of the public sector. Sometimes of course it can be true, but not always.

This links to a similar problem: how close in fact should you be to the workings of the charity? It is difficult to be both a trustee with a focus on the long-term strategy of the charity and governance issues, and, in addition, to be involved in the day-to-day management of the charity itself. You cannot run with the hare and hunt with the hounds. This is a problem with smaller charities, where it is quite common for trustees to be involved in aspects of the daily running of the organisation. Maintaining detachment is difficult, especially if there is a mistake or problem with something with which *you* were involved. As far as possible, I suggest staying away from day-to-day involvement, although you could be involved in particular things like manning a stall at a show or events in the street.

This book is written for someone thinking of becoming a trustee or who has just become one. I try to illustrate some of the key issues likely to confront a new trustee and to offer some guidance on how to approach them.

My final point is that the world in which not-for-profit organisations operate has changed in the last few decades. They have had to become more professional, or some would say 'businesslike', in their manner of working. I have mentioned the issue of the increasing numbers of policies, but regulatory issues and fundraising have imposed disciplines on these organisations and to some extent changed their character. Managing the need for professionalism and a businesslike approach with the ethos of a charity can be difficult. Businesslike does not mean being like a business. Retaining this balance is perhaps one of the more difficult parts of being a trustee.

I hope this book will encourage you to become a trustee or to be of help if you are already in such a role. I sincerely hope it will be of help to you. The sector needs people to act in these roles.

So these are some of the issues I want to explore in this book. I should say straight away that my experience has been with smaller charities and not-for-profits. Bigger charities are unlikely to experience all the issues I discuss here – but not having been there, I cannot really say.

CHAPTER 1
Fundamentals

In this chapter I want to set the scene and set out the basic principles to help you become a successful trustee. It would not be possible to list everything, such is the diversity of the not-for-profit sector and the range of factors which need to be taken into account. The Charity Commission and the National Council for Voluntary Organisations (NCVO) both provide copious amounts of excellent information, guidance and advice.[5] NCVO also runs courses.

Such is the extent of the advice, many would-be trustees might be put off. Don't be. The need to be vigilant, operate legally and operate within the charity's objects are all vitally important. But the plain fact is that most trustees take part in sensibly run charities and make a worthwhile contribution to their communities. I do not propose to list all the legalities since websites already do this. I want, instead, to focus on some of the key issues which will help you to be a successful trustee.

Information is key to your performance as a trustee. I devote Chapters 6, 7 and 8 to this important topic, so I don't propose saying much here. I will refer to the 'official' versus the 'actual' description of something that happens in the office, typical of so many organisations of whatever type. The 'actual' is frequently revealed by gossip. The problem for you as a trustee is that you are unlikely to hear any gossip, so you only have the 'official' version to go on. One way to overcome this potential problem is getting good information. I will devote a sizeable part of this book to the topic of information, so important is it for a trustee.

In the first of those chapters, I will introduce what I call the SCAPS model:

- *Selecting* what information you need;
- *Collecting* it;
- *Analysing* it;
- *Presenting* the information in a digestible form and finally;
- *Storing* or saving it.

I will discuss the need for an **information plan**. Although your charity is likely to have a strategy and/or a work plan of some kind, having an information plan is something of a rarity.

KEY POINT

Make sure you are getting the information you need in a digestible form. Ensure your charity has an information plan.

Communication is another key element. The essence is simple to express: what are you seeking to communicate, and to whom? What do you *need* to communicate, and to whom? These are questions that get tangled up with marketing and can lead to confusion. I devote Chapter 9 to this topic because it raises a number of fundamental questions which impact on information collection, social media and the design of the website.

Closely linked to communications is the topic of marketing, which I develop in Chapter 10. It is a skill that charities often agonise over. I will argue that simply grafting commercial marketing principles and ideas onto a charity is unlikely to work. There are key differences of purpose, organisation and relationships which mean these techniques should be used carefully and sparingly. One key marketing concept from the business world is known as the '7 Ps', and I argue that 'price' (one of the Ps) is unlikely to be of concern for a typical charity. I suggest however that 'presence' is an important consideration and is linked to the brand. To be effective, you need to be recognised as the relevant charity that acts as a repository of information and the place to go to if something of interest in your bailiwick emerges in the local community. You need to develop these links with appropriate press releases, events, breakfast meetings or lunchtime seminars and perhaps preparing an information video to discuss a report or some statistics you have collected.

It is important to include *all* staff in the marketing of the charity and not to leave it solely in the lap of someone with 'marketing' in their job title. This really is an important point because all your staff and volunteers – and you and your fellow trustees – are effectively ambassadors for the charity. They should be your eyes and ears. Staff and volunteers should be encouraged to be on the lookout for potential success stories, examples (appropriately anonymised as need be) or anecdotes which can be used to supply input for the website, social media platforms or the annual report.

As a trustee then, you need to watch out for blanket suggestions or proposals to hire someone with a commercial marketing background. They can be good and give good advice. But equally, they can simply try to apply commercial marketing ideas which may not be appropriate, as I have argued. Trustees need to enquire of any such consultant or adviser at interview, what their understanding of the differences are and whether they can justify the procedures they propose using.

KEY POINT

Ensure your charity is clear about what it wants or needs to communicate, to whom it wants or needs to communicate, and that it has a plan for doing so.

Staying solvent is crucial and since, as a trustee, you are conceivably at risk if the charity becomes insolvent, it is vital that you pay close attention to it. In essence it is being able to pay bills as they fall due. Having good financial help is crucial to avoiding the situation of insolvency. You need to ensure that the person handling your financial affairs is on top of the situation and is competent. Remember, anyone can call themselves an 'accountant' and need not be qualified.

Fortunately, I have little experience of this, but one thing that can trigger the problem is a legal action of some kind, for example a successful claim against the charity by a member of staff. You need to ensure that the event is not consuming everyone's attention and the issue of insolvency does not get forgotten. Legal claims are, by their nature, independent of the size of the charity so the impact on a small one is likely to be more severe.

On the question of finance, reserves are another factor that needs to be kept in mind. For a long time, I believed that the rule was a requirement to have three months' reserves and I still occasionally hear this said. I have not been able to find this rule and I am not even sure it exists. What needs to happen is a careful consideration of what outgoings you will have if you are unable to continue to function as a going concern. What liabilities will you have, not forgetting that you may well have to continue paying rent for any premises until a new tenant can be found? Is there a clause in the lease requiring you to carry out repairs? There will be savings – the photocopier can go back for example. Staff expenses are likely to be lower. These considerations will enable you to derive a figure for what reserves you need. This figure needs to be regularly monitored.

KEY POINT

Play very close attention to solvency and the level of reserves.

Still on the subject of finance is the tricky subject of fraud, theft or other things going wrong and leading to losses. It can happen to any organisation and the effects can be extremely damaging, going beyond the actual loss of money or property. Your reputation can be damaged and staff morale can be hit when they learn that one of their number has been cheating or stealing. It is important therefore to be on the alert for this activity and to look for signs of it happening. I devote a short chapter (13) to this topic.

KEY POINT

Be on the alert for fraud and dishonesty, and ensure that procedures are adequate to reveal instances quickly.

Your prime purpose as a trustee is to ensure the charity is abiding by its mission and following a clear path as set out in a strategic plan. The governing document is important, indeed the most important document the charity has. How up to date is it? All too often, it is filed away and forgotten, sometime for years. It does need to be looked at, and I would suggest once every three years or more frequently if you have made major changes to your operations.

Another of the documents you should receive on joining is the strategy. First note how up to date it is. If it is older than three, and certainly five years, then it is likely to have become out of date. Not everything in the strategy needs changing or updating all the time. Some elements will simply get carried forward, sometimes for years. Other aspects do need amending in the light of external changes, as I discuss in Chapter 4.

In relation to the strategy, it is not uncommon for considerable time to be spent on preparing one, only for it to get forgotten. So does it get referred to in meetings? Is there in fact a work plan which sets out what the charity is going to do to carry out the strategy? A useful acronym to remember in the preparation of a work plan is SMART. It stands for Specific, Measurable, Achievable, Realistic and Timebound. Not every element of a business plan can be all of these things, but the absence of them can mean the plan has little force. Words like 'increase' or 'improve' mean very little unless you can say increase by how much, improve in what way and by when.

KEY POINT

Pay close attention to the strategy. How up to date is it? Is it SMART? Is it being reported on? How up to date is the governing document? Is it still relevant to what you do?

It won't be long as a trustee before the word 'governance' will appear. It has become an increasingly important issue for charities especially following various scandals. There is considerable guidance on the subject on the Charity Commission and NCVO sites, so I will not be repeating the detail here.

The rise and rise of governance has in my view created a problem. Governance is important and it is vital that it is attended to. You do need policies, if only to ensure that 'What do we mean by …?' is clearly spelt out. Having protocols and procedures in place for things like lone working are crucial. Potential risks need to be identified and a routine plan or risk assessment put in place to monitor them. But just because all the boxes are ticked and all the policies put in place, it does not mean the charity will be a success. One of the reasons for all the concern about governance is a fear that if something goes wrong the charity will be put under threat of legal action. Not having policies in place leaves you vulnerable. Having them, by contrast, gives the sense of a 'wall' around the organisation, ready to repel boarders when and if something does go wrong.

This can act to distract attention away from other aspects important for a successful charity. Not being alive to changes in society, a failure to be outgoing, not looking after staff and volunteers sufficiently are just some of the factors which can lead to your charity getting into trouble. The attitude to change itself can be crucial. These do not appear under 'governance' so risk being overlooked. So it is important you do not get drowned under the weight of compliance and governance issues, nor see them as a kind of insurance against failure. They aren't. The important thing is balance. It is also to be regretted if governance acts as a disincentive to new ideas or innovation.

The need for compliance can be irritating, especially I think with volunteers. They are giving their time to a cause they believe in and they often find the increasing amount of time they have to spend on these issues an irritant. The need in some charities to require their staff to fill out Disclosure and Barring Service (DBS) applications can feel intrusive. DBS helps organisations make safe recruitment decisions, which is especially important where charities are involved in helping children or vulnerable adults. The problem of course is that, as far as the law is concerned, it does not matter if the person is a volunteer or a paid member of staff if and when something goes wrong. This means it has to be managed. Management cannot duck their responsibilities to ensure there is good governance, as I have said. But they can ensure that the reasons and justifications are explained. 'We need to do this *because* ...' and a reason given has to be best practice. Simply sending out a form or instruction (or a form and instruction) does not cut the mustard. As a trustee you need to be aware that the management are sensitive to these tensions. How will staff be briefed and will the reasoning be provided?

I might add – while discussing the issue of policies which have proliferated in recent years – that you do need to ensure staff and volunteers are aware of them and understand them. It is one thing to have a stack of policies all neatly stored away on a computer; it's quite another to ensure that your people are aware of them and are acting on them. It is all very well for the CEO or management to say 'it is our policy that …' or 'our guidance is clear that …', referring to a particular policy document when something has happened. It may be so, but has it been properly disseminated? Have the essential points been explained? Are they reinforced from time to time? Failure to do so increases the risk that someone overlooks it or, in the heat of the moment, forgets what the policy is. It might put your charity in hot water and possibly lead to a financial or legal claim. It is something you need to check on with the management.

KEY POINT

Don't drown under the weight of governance issues. Try and maintain a sense of proportion. Ensure that staff and volunteers are briefed and reminded of them from time to time.

Meetings. The very word can strike a chill in some, and everyone has a ready curse to hand about meetings and what a waste of time they are. I devote a chapter to the subject since as a trustee, much of your contact with the charity, your fellow trustees and the CEO will be at meetings, board or otherwise.

They should be enjoyable and you should try to enjoy them. Yes, 'meetings' and 'enjoy' in the same sentence. There are issues of management and how they are run, which I discuss in Chapter 11. In that chapter, I set out eight key points concerning meetings and how they are organised.

KEY POINT

Try to enjoy the meetings you go to and be prepared for them. Play a part in trying to ensure they are well run.

Change is ever present and many think the pace of change is increasing. It affects everything from technology (the arrival of

Zoom and Microsoft Teams during the pandemic, for example, dramatically altered how meetings were conducted and people's work patterns), changes in the law, prices and significantly, people's attitudes and beliefs. It is impossible for a charity (or any organisation for that matter) to ignore change without risking acute problems as time goes on. It is important therefore that the charity is aware of change and actively keeps an eye on matters which could affect its operations. I started writing this book when the Brexit saga was in full swing and this alone will bring a number of changes in our society. I shall be taking these matters forward in Chapter 11.

KEY POINT

Accept that change is a normal part of the life of the charity, and embrace it. Ensure the charity is actively considering change with periodic reviews of its likely effects.

On the question of staff and volunteers – and related to the above discussion – it is vital that their interests and expectations are catered for. People volunteer or work for charitable organisations for a mix of reasons. Often though, a sense of wanting to help people, animals, the environment or a cause is uppermost in their thinking. Money or the opportunity to advance a career is not usually a primary motivation. 'Giving something back' is an oft-quoted comment used by volunteers. Altruism is a genuine motivation for many. Thus motivated, they want to see their efforts devoted to the cause itself and do not take kindly to being distracted by bureaucracy or red tape in some form. The need for charities to act within the law and to follow good governance can lead to a tension in some staff who feel that way. 'Form filling', 'box ticking', 'red tape' and similar epithets can be used if management, in their attempt to meet governance or contract conditions, demand copious (as it may be perceived) information from their staff and volunteers. The need for training can be a disincentive for some.

Another key need is to inform the staff of the value of their efforts. They have been asked to fill in forms, write a report or generally provide information, either as part of governance or for everyday management reasons. Are they thanked for this? If the information was instrumental in the charity gaining recognition or winning a contract, were the staff who contributed it thanked or, even better, told how what they provided was a key element of the success? Were they thanked in front of colleagues? Sometimes they are; sometimes they get forgotten and they aren't. Often the problem can be the passage of time. Months may pass from the time when the information was provided to when the result was achieved, and the contributors simply get overlooked. Nor do I think the slightly ritual thanks at an annual general meeting or conference is good enough, especially when they come after the phrase '… and finally, not forgetting our staff and volunteers'. People need to be thanked or recognised individually during the year.

So recognition and keeping in mind the motivations of the charity's staff and volunteers are important factors which can just get forgotten in the hurly-burly of a busy office. Neglecting it, however, can result in feelings of management forever demanding and never giving. Staff in any organisation, charity or otherwise, want to feel valued. This is achieved by ensuring a two-way conversation. People reading this who have worked for a number of years know the phrase 'my door is always open' is often more than literally untrue.

Although altruism or the desire to 'give something back' are oft-quoted reasons for people volunteering, some may wish to progress in their chosen charity. This means there has to be a system of staff appraisals linked to the possibility of real development taking place. It can pose problems for a small charity where the range of development possibilities are likely to be small or even non-existent. In a smaller organisation it can result in people being overlooked when opportunities do arise. This can be quite wasteful since the process of sorting out an advertisement, the cost of the advertisement, the selection and interview process and then waiting for the notice period to play out, is extremely time consuming. A job may also be offered but then not taken up because the existing employer suddenly realises they will lose someone they had undervalued and offers a pay rise to keep them. As a trustee it is important to interest yourself in the people aspect of your charity and ensure that there are policies and processes in place to achieve the best for the charity and its people. I have worked in a civil service environment where it is usual for people to be moved around every two years or so as part of the process of staff development.

Many will recognise Herzberg's hygiene theory,[6] which built on Maslow's hierarchy of needs. This suggested a two-factor model leading to individual satisfaction or dissatisfaction in the workplace. People gain satisfaction from what they *do* in the charity, although Herzberg does argue that the absence of gratification by these means does not lead to dissatisfaction (which I have disagreed with above). This might be because his research was carried out with engineers and accountants working in the commercial world, not in a charity setting.

Dissatisfaction comes instead from the absence of 'hygiene' factors, which are the salary, the benefits and the work environment. There are therefore two dimensions to employee satisfaction, according to this theory. There has been both support and criticism of Herzberg's ideas and they need to be treated with some caution. As I have argued, the majority of people working in a not-for-profit environment do not do it for reasons of salary or the prospect of financial reward. They want fairness and for their contribution to be recognised. They also gain satisfaction from the work the charity does. Nevertheless, managers should not trade on the motives of their staff as an excuse to neglect their legitimate hygiene factors.

In one of the information chapters, I suggest keeping an eye on staff turnover. People leave for all kinds of legitimate reasons: they have got a better job, their partner moves away, changed family circumstances and so on. But if there is a problem with the CEO or someone else in the team, then this can show itself in higher than expected levels of staff leaving. As a trustee, you are unlikely to know what is happening (since the conduit for most of your information is through the CEO) so another key activity is leaving interviews. People will sometimes be revealing once they have left. If no one wants to give an interview, then there could be something badly wrong. Staff surveys should also be undertaken, certainly no less than biennially.

KEY POINT

Keep a close eye on staff issues. Are they being looked after properly? Are there staff appraisals? Are they being offered training? Are their pay levels appropriate? What is the rate of staff turnover like?

The difference between the public and private sectors is a topic I devote a short chapter to because it suffuses much of our society and how we think about things. It was behind the privatisation policies of the 1980s. In simple terms it was the belief that private firms were innately more efficient than the public sector. The latter was bloated and inefficient. This is a political and economic argument which has no place here, except to say that it has led to a belief that the private sector is the go-to place for expertise and help in how to run a charity. These arguments came to the fore during the early part of the Covid-19 pandemic in 2020 when the government consistently favoured private companies over public sector organisations.

This assumption can of course be true, and there are people from industry or commerce who do make useful contributions to the functioning of a charity. In Chapter 3 I explain that there are many differences in how the for-profit sector and the not-for-profit sector are run. These have many implications for a charity. It is not the case that private sector techniques can simply be grafted onto a charity for it to run successfully. Such ideas have to be looked at carefully and not swallowed whole. Use them appropriately. (I am excluding commercial activities such as charity shops, which many charities have established.)

KEY POINT

Don't assume that private is always superior to public, or that private sector techniques can be easily or straightforwardly grafted onto a charity.

When things go wrong, it is usually because of a series of failings, not just a single cause. As you track back, it is not unusual to find you are rising up the organisation's seniority in terms of whose decisions – or lack of decisions – led to the mistake or accident. So it is incumbent on trustees, when listening to explanations after something has gone wrong, to ensure that the true cause has been identified. Explanations which focus the blame on a sole individual – especially if they are quite junior – should always be treated with some scepticism. Each circumstance is different of course, and I suppose there are examples of an employee being entirely responsible for something going wrong, but in my experience they are rare. Always be prepared to ask: Why did that happen? Were the rules clear? Was he or she supervised properly? Were they properly trained? And so on depending on the incident.

Another trope we hear regularly from all kinds of organisation these days after some disaster is the statement 'lessons have been learned'. You will have heard it often in the news and on TV following an investigation after a disaster of some kind. It has almost become a go-to phrase to act as a kind of comfort: there was a disaster but not to worry, we have 'learned the lessons [and it won't happen again]'. It is often combined with the 'moving on' phrase. The problem is that they haven't learned, and so often it does happen again. So if you are told that 'lessons have been learned' you do need to ask 'what lessons' and, depending on the seriousness of the incident, how thorough was the examination into the causes? Were those who may well have been responsible involved in the 'lesson learning'? You just need to probe more deeply. It is natural for staff to play down such incidents and to assure trustees that (the dread phrase) 'lessons have been learned', and to say they have adjusted such and such a policy to ensure it doesn't happen again.

The '5 Whys' from the Toyota Motor Company is a useful technique.[7] It is a process of tracking back from the actual incident, by asking 'why' five times, to what is likely to be its root cause. What is often revealed in this process is that the cause of the incident is quite unrelated to what finally happened. It can show up a lack of induction or training in members of staff, weak management or poor systems.

KEY POINT

When something goes wrong, ensure that the root or real cause has been identified. If it is claimed that 'lessons have been learned', ask 'what lessons?' and how they have been learned.

Looking after the brand. The very word 'brand' can be a difficult one for those in the charitable sector to take to. Its link to commercial marketing can strike some as inappropriate. It must be remembered that brand is more than the logo and a snappy strapline, and it is vital to look after it. This is the sum of a range of factors large and small which I go into in Chapter 9. There I discuss various methods to establish what your brand is, how you are perceived by the public and people of influence in your area, and how to go about creating a brand. The brand is something which you and your fellow trustees should discuss and review from time to time. If it doesn't crop up in meetings then it may be necessary to introduce it. I mention the supermarket test, for example, and the placing by customers of tokens in one of three bins on the way out. How does your charity compare to the two others?

Beware, if you are a small charity, of appointing expensive consultants to advise you on this. You risk spending a lot of money on what can be expensive or impractical solutions. If you do employ a consultant or consultancy firm, ensure that they will actually come up with practical strategies. Check that they have done equivalent work for another not-for-profit organisation and discuss the results with them. Beware the hundred-page glossy report which tells you nothing.

Do simple things well. Remember that attitudes are formed by quite simple things like how the phone is answered or how quickly an email is responded to. Spending thousands on expensive makeovers is wasted if the basics aren't done well. Just think of your own experience of dealing with companies that have sophisticated marketing campaigns with celebrity endorsements, etc., but who can be frustratingly difficult when you try and buy something from them.

KEY POINT

Look after the brand.

***

Up to now I have been discussing fairly tangible aspects which I think are important for a trustee to be aware of. I now want to move on to some less tangible – but no less significant – issues.

The first and most important thing to say is that you must enjoy being a trustee. As it is a voluntary position which involves giving up your time and some evenings, if you don't enjoy it, you will quickly give it up. Enjoyment comes in many forms, but might include the company of others, the pleasure in helping people, the environment or animals, or simply altruism. Some get satisfaction from using the skills acquired in their working or professional lives to help a charity to manage their affairs well. One of the dangers of offering advice in any form to someone thinking of taking on such a duty, is that the list of things you have to be aware of can be quite formidable. I have already mentioned the Charity Commission, which has a dedicated part of its website called the 'Essential Trustee' – a comprehensive analysis of all you need to know. It is an excellent resource and essential reading. The density and complexity can however be a little off-putting. The pages aren't numbered but there must be around fifty, with links to yet more advice. Much of it is common sense. But I would say to someone thinking of becoming a trustee, try not to be put off by the pages of stern warnings and, of necessity, their legal tone.

KEY POINT

Enjoy being a trustee!

Your approach and attitudes towards the charity you have volunteered for (or are thinking of volunteering for) are going to be extremely important and will determine to a high degree how successful you are in the role. You might be tempted to think, 'Surely, relevant knowledge of the work of the charity and the area it works in are what's important?' Or you might think that a specific skill such as finance or human resources is what is most crucial. They are of course valuable skills and people with them who volunteer are nearly always welcomed with open arms. I want to start, however, with a brief discussion on attitude and motivation. They are crucial both for you as a trustee but also for others in the organisation.

There is considerable literature on the psychology of both these aspects, reflecting their importance in a variety of ways. There is also a lot of material on what leads people to volunteer and to continue volunteering.

A lot of people who volunteer do so for a mix of reasons. Some common themes emerge among people asked, and a desire 'to give something back' is the most common. Others included supporting a cause they believe in and exercising a fundamental belief. The University of Winchester carried out a sizeable survey in June 2020: *Volunteering during Covid-19: Understanding Volunteer Motivations and Experiences.*[8] They showed that motivations changed over the course of the lockdown. For example, 61% gave 'helping people' as a motivating factor before lockdown, and this increased to 89% after lockdown. It seems clear that the issue of the cause or fundamental purpose of the charity is a key component in their reasons for volunteering. What is also clear, here and elsewhere, is that people volunteer to be practically involved in the cause. They seek direct contact with the people (or animals or the environment) who (which) are the purpose of the charity.

For a trustee, the reasons are likely to be different since in a large charity, the trustees will not be involved in the day-to-day business of helping people. Although by their actions as trustees, they will be helping the charity to survive and prosper, they are unlikely to receive the 'buzz' of direct contact. Their motivations are likely to be more about team working or contributing to the strategy and direction of the organisation. This distinction is not always clear in studies on the voluntary sector, which are nearly all about working on the front line. In smaller charities, trustees are more likely to be involved in some day-to-day matters.

One comprehensive study of volunteering noted that managements did not always involve their junior staff or volunteers sufficiently in the development of new projects or in the management of the organisation generally. This is an issue that goes beyond charities, since many commercial firms do not involve their staff sufficiently in these matters either. Volunteers are likely to have a range of skills acquired during their working lives (assuming, that is, that they are of a certain age).

Another key aspect is attitudes, which are one of social science's most central concepts. There are three components: cognitive, affective and behavioural. Simply put, they are our knowledge, perceptions and beliefs about something (the cognitive element), our feelings towards that something (affective) and our inclination or otherwise to do something towards it (behavioural). I shall return to this issue in a later chapter, since something similar is at play with the reasons why people donate or not to a cause or charity.

There are other ideas such as expectancy theory with notions of 'instrumentality' (our attitudes towards charitable organisations) and 'valency' (our attitudes towards helping others). The crucial point I want to put across here is that the motivations and attitudes that we have play a key part in our decision to volunteer. They are of course important in why people choose *not* to volunteer, so they can have negative impacts.

The key points therefore are:

1. Recognise that attitudes and motivations are a key factor in why people volunteer.
2. Recognise also that these are very individual. Some people want direct contact with those being helped; others want to use their skills to best help the charity survive.
3. It is important to involve volunteers in the development of projects and other management issues.

It is said that pessimists are usually proved right, or as Daniel L. Reardon said: 'In the long run, the pessimist may be proved right, but the optimist has a better time on the trip.' It is important to be optimistic. Without it, there would be no desire to explore new opportunities or to consider a change of direction. It becomes important in times of stress. If a major shock hits a charity – either internal (a member of staff caught stealing, for example) or external (such as the Covid-19 pandemic), then a reserve of optimism is essential. If it is not present, the desire to give up can be quite strong.

KEY POINT

Be optimistic. If you and your fellow trustees – and the CEO – lose this, then the future is likely to be bleak. You have to believe you can make a difference. You have to project confidence.

In that vein, *thinking* of the future is an important quality. In the 'Meetings' chapter I will talk about looking at the agenda and assessing how future-oriented it is. If meetings are consumed with the present and the immediate past, not only do opportunities not get taken up, they may not even get noticed. Be alert for some sign that staff are looking for potential opportunities. Many might come to naught, but there should be a process of looking.

Sometimes ideas just pop up without anybody really noticing. So your staff need to be alert to a request (from the public for example) for something you may not be able to do but which might be an opportunity for your charity to consider in the future. In this regard, it might be useful to keep a log of requests with which you are not currently equipped to deal. This will serve two purposes: firstly, to suggest possible ideas as above; and secondly, it will give you a statistic for potential unmet demand. If you then decide to submit a bid for a project, you will have a log of the requests which match your proposal, and you will also have a ready-made set of statistics to support your application.

There is nothing wrong with looking at past events, but an important element of this is learning from them. I will discuss the Japanese practice of *Kaizen* and how, if some project is undertaken, it is important to review it afterwards and ask the question, 'If we were to do this again, what would we do differently; what could we do better?'

KEY POINT

Be future-oriented. It is linked to being optimistic. Learn from the past but don't live there.

There are people who sit through meetings nervous of making a contribution. Constantly interjecting is not recommended but neither is silence. If you find speaking up and making yourself heard difficult, let the chair know at the beginning of the meeting (or before) that you would like to say something about a particular agenda item, and a good chair should respond to that.

KEY POINT

Don't be shy!

Be proud of the work you are doing. Charities make a significant contribution to our society and you will be part of that.

And that is the subject of the next chapter.

CHAPTER 2

The role of the charity sector

A new trustee to a charity will be contributing to a sector which plays a significant part in our society. There are several hundred thousand not-for-profit organisations which help millions of people, animals, the environment and other causes. They raise funds for causes such as cancer research or Alzheimer's. Yet despite their ubiquity and importance, they do not receive the attention they deserve. There has been only limited research into the contribution they make[9]. They operate below the radar in many communities and are often all but invisible. Unlike commercial firms, they do not usually advertise or adopt a conspicuous presence. The smaller ones rarely advertise and could not afford the sort of TV adverts the major charities engage in.

Despite their significance, not everyone is a fan of the sector as a whole or of some particular charities[10]. This may be because of the bad publicity which the sector has attracted recently or because some believe that the people being helped are undeserving in some way. Salaries paid to senior staff of the larger charities – which after all are multimillion pound organisations – is resented by some.

Being aware of these views is important, since it affects how your charity is perceived and may also affect fundraising efforts. Your charity may not pay your chief executive anything like what a major charity's CEO is paid, but does the public recognise that? There has always been a degree of ambivalence here. Going back to Charles Dickens, for example – in his novel *Bleak House* he gently mocks Mrs Jellyby, a philanthropist, who was forever raising funds to establish settlements in Africa yet neglected her own children at home.

One immediate problem is agreeing on what to call the sector. There are charities large and small, not-for-profit organisations, community interest companies, social enterprises and groups that formed to help their neighbours (as happened in the Covid-19 crisis), and companies limited by guarantee. They are sometimes referred to as the 'third sector'. A further confusion is the fact that public schools are charities despite many misgivings about their lack of charitable purpose, discussed in Robert Verkaik's book *Posh Boys: How English Public Schools Ruin Britain*, published in 2018.

The dictionary definition of 'charity' is 'an organisation to which you give money so that it can give money and help to people who are poor or ill, or who need advice and support'. This definition is all about people, you will notice, and there are more charities now dealing with animals and the environment. 'Charity' as a word also has a meaning of benevolence and a feeling of generosity towards others. On the other hand, there is an almost resentful meaning, as in 'I don't want your charity'. So there are a variety of meanings and a range of organisational types. Not all not-for-profit organisations become charities, many because they are too small.

There seems little doubt that the public's view of the sector has undergone a change in recent years. High-profile scandals have left their mark. These have included Oxfam, where allegations of hiring sex workers for orgies in Haiti following the 2010 earthquake were enormously damaging.[11] The inquiry also examined Oxfam's wider approach to safeguarding and concluded that the charity's own commitments and promises in the past had not always been matched by its resources. Another high-profile case was that of the lady in Bristol, Olive Cooke, who at peak, received 466 requests for funds in one year.[12] The inquiry, established after her suicide, concluded that, although no individual charity was to blame, the problem was the practice of selling details between hundreds of different charities, which contributed to the huge influx of requests for money she received. Another high-profile case which gained considerable publicity at the time was the collapse of Kids Company. This concerned the mismanagement of funds, a large chunk of which came from a government department, and had done so for some years. When they called a halt to these practices, the charity failed. Bernard Jenkin, who chairs the Public Accounts Committee, said they had heard 'an extraordinary catalogue of failures of governance and control at every level: trustees, auditors, inspectors, regulators and government. However, in 2021, a judge exonerated the charity from blame, saying it had organised a plan to ensure its survival – which unfortunately came to naught because unsubstantiated allegations of sexual abuse were made.[13] All these scandals provoked considerable media coverage and an enormous amount of negative publicity.

These scandals provoked an inevitable response in people's attitudes to the not-for-profit sector. A Populus poll in 2018[14] showed that trust levels were similar to those in 2016, at the time of the major scandals. The proportion of people who felt uncomfortable with the fundraising methods used by charities also rose. A total 45% of respondents said their trust and confidence in charities had decreased. The overall level of trust had suffered a 'significant decrease'. This puts charities in something of a bind: on the one hand they need to campaign hard to secure funding and on the other, keep their administration costs low to appease public opinion. On the positive side, respondents trusted charities more than banks, private companies or politicians. Interestingly, when asked what they had in mind, they did not think of small local charities, the sort this book is aimed at.

A Civil Society report in 2018[15] concluded that 'the public do not, at this time, give charities as institutions the benefit of the doubt. The public values voluntary effort, generosity and care for others. But they are not, currently, convinced that charities as organisations are delivering those values'.

A common feature of these and other scandals within the sector was the issue of management and governance. Charities and NFP organisations generally handle considerable sums of money and sometimes employ large numbers of people. Both need managing and the organisations need systems of control. The pressure on them however is to devote as many resources as possible to the cause itself and not to 'waste' money on what is seen as 'admin' or 'red tape'. Yet another feature of the Populus poll was a complaint that people did not know where the money goes. Clearly, providing this information requires administration and management. After a number of scandals and problems involving the sector, in 2016 the Fundraising Regulator was established, which examines complaints and publishes advice on governance and fundraising issues.

We saw an example of this during the Covid-19 pandemic. A 99-year-old war veteran, the late Sir Captain Tom, raised nearly £33m by walking round his garden.[16] He originally hoped to raise £1,000. The funds were raised using the online service JustGiving, who originally took a 5% fee but changed this to an invitation to contribute 10% voluntarily. This prompted a Labour Party MP to ask JustGiving to reveal how much they were taking. His Tweet said 'This is amazing, now we need to make sure @JustGiving do not make a profit off the money raised by this international emergency.

Public donations should reach the intended beneficiary'. We can debate how much the fee should be and there are ethical questions to ask about how much is reasonable, but the concept of a cost to fundraising seems alien to many even supposedly informed people.

In the 'You're the expert' column of the *Guardian* newspaper (18 April 2020), also during the Covid-19 pandemic, people were asking how they could donate to help others and one anonymous respondent said:

> *I suggest that before you donate, you check your chosen charity on the Charity Commission's website. Just put in the charity name or number in the box. Then see how much it spent on admin and so on. A charity claiming to be 'local' set up a stall in our town centre alongside their shiny new vehicle. I found they spent a tiny percentage on charitable work and the bulk on 'fundraising'.* partridge636

There is obviously a dilemma here. If there is to be greater efficiency in the use of funds, then money has to be spent on administration. There have to be controls on how the money is spent. Charities will have to recruit suitably skilled managers to ensure compliance and good governance. They will need to invest in IT to manage the collection and storage of data as well as train their staff.

Recent legislation has increased the need for better administration, and in particular the introduction of data protection rules with the General Data Protection Regulation (GDPR). Most charities are small: around 75% have income of less than £100,000 per year and only 1% are large organisations with an income over £5m per year.[17] A total 97% have incomes below £1m. For them, increasing controls and legislation come at proportionately a greater cost.

It is not perhaps fully realised (by some of the public, that is) that charities and NFP organisations are subject to the same laws that apply to commercial entities. They have to operate safely; they have a duty of care to their staff and volunteers; they are subject to employment laws and they can be sued by a member of the public for any of their actions which cause harm. These risks and responsibilities cannot be wished away. They involve training staff, setting up control systems and managing the risks exactly like other organisations. Yet there is a feeling when a member of the public puts a pound into a collection box that that pound, all hundred pennies of it, will – and should – go to the cause. It needs to be said that if you are new to this world then do not think that because the charity is doing good work and your motives are impeccable, that this somehow puts you in a special place as far as the law is concerned. You can still be sued, fined and conceivably, imprisoned – although I suspect this latter penalty is exceedingly rare. An example is the founder of Little Heroes Cancer Trust, who was sentenced to twenty months in prison for stealing £87,000 from the charity.

Salaries paid to senior staff – particularly for the larger organisations – induce particular ire among many in the general public. There is a feeling that someone working for a charity should do it for fulfilment in the task and as a vocation, not seek a salary comparable to the private sector. There may also be a feeling among many of 'I don't earn that much, so why should I give my money to your organisation knowing that a chunk of it goes into your pocket?' This links closely to the desire for all the money donated to go to the cause.

From the charity's point of view, they would no doubt like to recruit staff and high-quality managers for less than the going rate or for very low pay. In all the recruitment exercises I have been involved in, however, we have sought outside advice and offered a salary which we thought attractive. We have yet to find someone – with private means perhaps – who is willing to work for very low pay. It is not unusual to advertise and get no responses at all.

The charity sector occupies a significant part of the economy yet rarely gets the attention it deserves. According to nfpSynergy there are 880,000 paid employees in the UK charity sector (2018 figures).[18] The total income for all charities is around £48bn, which is larger than the higher education sector. The value of formal volunteering is estimated to be £22.6bn. It is clearly a big part of our economy and the sector funds almost half of all medical research in the UK.

Despite its size and significance in society, it is in many respects invisible. It does not, for example, merit a special supplement in our newspapers. As I said in the introduction, there are supplements on all sorts of things nowadays but there is no regular supplement on this sizeable and important part of our political and economic life. The only possible exception used to be the weekly 'Society' section in the *Guardian* newspaper.

Relationships with government are also poor. A Civil Society report from 2019[19] notes that engagement between government and civil society has 'not lived up to its potential'. Many organisations in the sector are left frustrated and excluded from the decision-making process. The department responsible for the sector is the Department for Culture, Media and Sport and the current Minister for Civil Society (March 2020) is Baroness Barran who does not, of course, sit in the House of Commons. The report argues for consultations with the sector to be 'meaningful, inclusive and deliberative'. There has, it claims, been 'a rapid decline in engagement'. Despite the contribution by the voluntary sector of approximately £15.3bn to UK Gross Value Added – which is more than the arts or agriculture – it does not receive the recognition it deserves from government. This is arguably a failure of organisations like NCVO who claim to 'champion' the sector.

We saw this lack of concern in the Covid-19 pandemic in the spring of 2020. Once the government began to realise the full seriousness of the outbreak in early April and started the 'lockdown' process, the Chancellor announced a comprehensive scheme to aid businesses which had to shut down. Called the 'Coronavirus Large Business Interruption Loan Scheme' (CLBILS), it promised loans and other financial aid to the business sector. Help was first announced in the Budget speech on 11 March 2020. Yet help for the charity sector did not emerge until over a month later at the No 10 briefing on 8 May. This after warnings from the National Council for Voluntary Organisations and some other large charities about the loss of donations. With people confined to their homes, things like street collections and charitable events generally were impossible to hold, leading to a big loss of income. A joint letter by a number of charities to the prime minister Mr Boris Johnson asked for emergency support due to a £10bn shortfall as a result of the pandemic.[20]

No doubt MPs lobbied ministers as well, but it is nevertheless revealing that ministers' minds were focused on the business sector (which was going to suffer immensely) but by contrast, the charitable sector was not considered until later. In his briefing at No 10 Downing Street on 8 April, the Chancellor Rishi Sunak said, 'We are all taking part in a collective national effort to protect the vulnerable and each other, to secure our public services, and to save lives. This endeavour is underpinned by an important, simple idea – that we depend on each other.'[21] He went on to praise the importance of the sector, said that there were 170,000 charities in the UK, and announced aid amounting to £750,000 which he acknowledged would not replace funds lost to the sector.

One issue of concern is the increasing tendency to see charities as *suppliers* not stakeholders, hence the lack of meaningful consultation. This is a problem with wider significance, as local authorities have had their funding reduced during the decade of austerity. This has led to many charities becoming suppliers in some form, and can pose issues of independence and vulnerability. If we also consider the new lobbying rules which make charities feel inhibited from putting their case to local and national government, we can see a further weakening of the voice of the sector. Charities can still lobby and can express their views, particularly concerning their field of work, but the legislation has, I suspect, made many nervous of doing so.

A major distraction, of course, has been the three years (2016–2019) spent on Brexit negotiations. This has led to civil servants being moved from ministries to staff the departments set up to handle the issue.

The Big Society idea, introduced in a speech in 2009 by the prime minister David Cameron, was an attempt to offer support for co-ops, mutuals, charities and social enterprise. They were to have much greater involvement in the running of public services. However well intentioned, little happened as a result of austerity policies introduced following the banking failures. Similar sentiments are evident in the report produced by Danny Kruger MP in September 2020: *Levelling up our Communities: Proposals for a New Social Contract*[22]. Kruger was part of the Big Society team. Whether anything of value materialises remains to be seen. Ministers seem to like the sector and promise big things for it, including better recognition. Little happens, however, partly because of weaknesses of lobbying combined with a lack of vigour by those who represent the sector, and because the bulk of charities are small scale and their voices diffused.

Although this is part of the story, the attempts by David Cameron to establish the 'Big Society' were tarnished by the programme of austerity launched following the financial crisis. This austerity programme removed approximately 40% from local authority budgets, forcing them to reduce or remove the discretionary funds they would have passed on or given to charities in their areas.[23] It is important to note that Cameron, and those who advised him, seemed not to realise that the big society they wanted already existed. It needed support, not reinvention.

There has been little recognition of the fact that it has been the charitable and not-for-profit sector which has in large measure picked up the pieces of austerity. As funds were cut by central and local governments, it was they who stepped in to deal with the resulting hardships. Most notably, it has been the food banks which have expanded their operations and who have received a degree of publicity. Indeed, their expansion has almost become a bellwether for the state of the poor in the country. That some recipients receiving food parcels are nevertheless in work, has also been a shock. But the effects were felt not just by the food banks but by other charities as well, as problems like homelessness and drug taking rose, partly as a result of the cuts. Domestic violence also increased. Child poverty has increased alarmingly, with some estimates suggesting a near half million increase since 2010[24]

Professor Guy Standing in his book *A Precariat Charter* says:

> *The neo-liberal state has reduced public provision of services, so as to facilitate tax cuts and subsidies for selected interests, and has been helped by drawing on people's goodwill to fill the gaps with charity. It is vital to re-marginalize the role of charity in society. It is being used to cover up regressive policies, imposing unfair pressures on donors and on supplicants*

He argues that without the charity sector, the neoliberal state would not have been able to get away with it.[25] He goes on to argue that despite this dependence, the state has treated the sector poorly, with no regard for the knock-on effects of their policies and cuts on their level of activity. This raises the thought that the health of the charity sector is a measure of stress in society. After all, if there were no homeless people, a cure had been found for cancer, child poverty had been eliminated and everyone had enough to eat, what need of charities? He develops this theme in *The Corruption of Capitalism*.[26]

There is also the problem of where charities are based. A paper by New Philanthropy Capital shows that those 'left behind' areas most in need of charity support and increased social capital are precisely the areas where they are the fewest in number.[27] Charity density (number of registered local general* charities per 1,000 population) varies between 2.61 in the south-west of England and 1.43 in the north-east.

Civil Society – using research by Pro Bono Economics, the Institute of Fundraising and the Charity Finance Group – revealed that 19% of charities have already made redundancies and more are expected to do so. This has been as a result of the pandemic. It also noted a mismatch between demand and the ability to deliver, with 59% of respondents saying they expected demand to increase.[28]

Austerity also had an effect on individuals' ability and motivation to volunteer. In *Hard Times* by Tom Clark with Anthony Heath, the authors explain that 'the number of volunteers and the level of their commitment slid with the economy'.[29] In one way this is surprising since there were more people with time on their hands and thus better able to volunteer. However, there was a disincentive because of the cost of volunteering which although small and unnoticed in more prosperous times, became a real hurdle when times were hard and money short. Another factor is the gig economy, with many people not knowing when or if they will get employment. The knock-on effect was not being able to promise time to volunteer.

---

* Excludes sacramental religious bodies, places of worship, independent schools, government-controlled bodies and housing associations.

There seems little doubt that charities were put under great financial pressure during the Covid crisis, for the same reasons that many businesses, restaurants and shops were. Charity shops could not open and street collections ended.

Another factor of interest to trustees is the motives which lead people to donate to a particular charity or cause. This matters when street collections or donations from the public are a significant part of their fundraising. Research has shown a variety of factors which incline people to give (or not). Firstly, there are the broader factors which lead someone to give to a good cause; and secondly, there is the question of *which* cause they choose to give to. Educational level is perhaps a surprising factor, the assumption being that the more educated are more socially connected and thus more likely to receive solicitations. The second argument is that the more highly educated someone is, the better they are enabled to understand the complex factors behind a particular cause, especially if it is a distant one. As one would expect, people with higher education levels tend to earn more so have higher levels of disposable income.

A second factor, empathetic concern – the ability to place oneself in someone else's shoes – is also important, although it does not affect the amount such people give.

As expected, income is a determinant although it is not always clear cut.

Not all charities and NFPs are dependent on the public for their funding – indeed, many do no fundraising with the public at all. I shall return to the issue of stakeholders in a later chapter. The essential point for trustees arising from the above discussion is that you may care deeply about the problem the charity was set up to tackle, but not all of the public will necessarily agree with you. For whatever reason, they may have little sympathy for, say, the homeless – perhaps thinking that they have brought it upon themselves.

They may disbelieve the figures for child poverty, claiming that children are not really poor if they can afford video games. They will question the very definition of poverty, essentially not agreeing that they are truly poor as in some kind of Dickensian sense. They may just be indifferent or untouched by the problem of women who have been battered by their partners. They may feel that drug addicts have brought their problems upon themselves and so may be reluctant to contribute. Or they may just feel overwhelmed by the sheer number of causes and problems in the world.

The attitudes, beliefs and emotional responses that people have around particular causes are of importance, however. They mean that seeking to appeal to them from the point of view of facts and statistics is unlikely to be successful. As I have said, if someone has little sympathy for the homeless, data telling them how many homeless people there are will not have an impact. They are unconcerned about them, however many there are. If you want to persuade, you have to concentrate on developing arguments and approaches that address the problem at the emotional or human level.

The public's attitude to charities as a whole and particular charitable causes has implications for how charities go about fundraising, and for their branding strategy. These are matters of concern for trustees and the management of the organisation. The most obvious point is not to assume that there is goodwill or understanding for your cause or charity.[30] Often there is – especially for those organisations helping children or seeking funds for a cure to cancer – but other causes may be more problematic. Not everyone is sympathetic to the poor, the homeless or the jobless, for example.

You may need to distinguish your charity from how the people view the sector as a whole. By concentrating on the cause itself, you may be able to focus people's concerns and attention on the problems and what you are doing to help.[31] If people can be engaged with the issues and can be guided to empathise with those in need of help, that is likely to be more successful. The interesting point from surveys is that when people are asked questions about charities in general, the criticisms arising from the problems and scandals noted earlier often emerge[32]. They are still however well disposed to particular causes.

In a later chapter I shall be talking about communication in more detail, because it is a crucially important topic. But for now I just want to say that how you communicate and the messages you give out need to be targeted at your various interest groups and stakeholders. A 'one size fits all' approach is unlikely to be successful. That may be a statement of the obvious but a glance at some charity literature and websites often reveals a lack of such focus. It is not at all clear who is being addressed.

On the question of communications – facts, data and statistics have little appeal for many people. They might be of interest to potential or actual funders, for example, but are unlikely to persuade or convince clients, the public or potential volunteers. Most of the survey results demonstrate that one of the things people want to know is what you have achieved[33]. In simple terms, if I give you a pound, what will you do with it? What proportion of that pound goes to the cause you are supporting? One of the ways to communicate this is through narrative and telling a story. This can be actual words but increasingly, video is being used to this effect. There seems to be a real hunger for knowing how effective an organisation is.

A final point is to explain the value of the charity and not just in terms of the recipients of help. It is tempting, and to a degree understandable, to focus on just this. After all, it might be reasoned, people give money because they want to help a cause, to right a wrong, or to help generally. But a charity does more than this. Those who volunteer for charities (and about 20 million of us do so for clubs, groups and various organisations including charities) are likely to see an improvement in their wellbeing. As well as helping a particular cause or campaigning on a particular issue, the function of volunteering is to be part of a movement which is of great benefit to society. There is a value to the givers as well. They are likely to feel a sense of gratification from doing something – however small the widow's mite is – to help their fellow man or woman.

The overall point, though, is that the great majority of charitable organisations are small.[34] It is easy and natural to think that what you are doing, and the help you are providing, is accordingly small and relatively insignificant in the scheme of things – valuable and appreciated by those helped, but of no massive consequence. This is a pity; I suggest it is better to think in terms of being a small cog in a very large network of vital organisations. As was discussed above, the government would never have been able to carry out the range of austerity measures and the large-scale cuts to local government, the NHS and social provision generally if it did not have the charity sector to step forward and fill the gaps. The thousands of charities, the millions of volunteers and the thousands of fundraising activities have enabled some of the rough edges of austerity to be smoothed over. Millions are raised for medical research or to buy vital equipment for hospitals. Being a trustee therefore is to be part of a vital network of organisations. It is only to be deprecated that their vital contribution so often goes unsung (and this paragraph should not be read as an endorsement for the policy of austerity).

Looking to the future, there are those who argue for a greater role for the volunteers as AI, robotics and the fourth industrial revolution gets underway.[35] Charities and NFP organisations will have a major contribution to make if and when this takes place.

The principal messages to draw from this chapter are threefold. Firstly, those involved in the not-for-profit sector should do so with **pride**. Not just pride in their achievements and the help they offer, but the contribution they are making to society and the improvement in the wellbeing of their volunteers.

Secondly, it is important to have **confidence** in what you do and the difference your organisation is making, however small it might seem. Also, be aware of how essential you are to society and how – as I have said – much of the austerity agenda would not have been possible without the backstop of charities there to pick up the pieces.

Thirdly, and most importantly, it is crucial to be **outgoing**. The value of your contribution should be told with confidence.

Perhaps it is something to do with the British character and our gift for understatement. But many not-for-profit organisations and charities 'quietly beaver away' and seem to accept their low profile as a matter of course. Sending in press releases to the local paper which seldom see the light of day is accepted as a fact of life.

In the rest of the book, I shall be discussing some of the ways your charity or NFP can make a contribution to correcting this.

Some key facts (mostly from NCVO):

- There are 880,000 paid employees in the charity sector.
- There are nearly 200,000 registered charities in the UK.
- The total income of all charities combined is about £48bn. This is higher than the higher education sector, and about £10bn less than Tesco.
- The value of formal volunteering in the UK is around £22.6bn.
- Individuals account for almost half of the sector's total income.
- The median for the 100 highest-paid positions is £185k per annum.
- Charities have over ten regulators.
- Charities fund almost half of all medical research in the UK.
- 35% of the total voluntary sector workforce work in the social care subsector.

CHAPTER 3

Private and public sectors

It may seem odd to devote an entire chapter to discussing the differences between private sector organisations and the charitable and not-for-profit sector. I do so because in many meetings I have attended – both in charities and in local authorities – the prevailing belief is that the skills of former are superior to, and are readily transferrable into, the latter. Of course sometimes they are. Equally, they are often not, so I feel it important to examine the differing types of organisation, their outlooks and skills, to see if there can be a crossover.

The notion that the private sector is superior to the public sector is part of a belief system that has been around for about four decades. This is a component of the neoliberal philosophy which, in summary, said that small government, low taxes, limited regulation and the market economy were superior to the post-war policies of collective and public sector provision of many services. This resulted in many aspects of public provision being privatised, including organisations like the railways, parts of the NHS, and many schools being turned into academies free of local authority control.

The Labour Party in government hugely increased the Private Finance Initiative (PFI) in which hospitals were built using private funds and then leased back to the NHS. They kicked off the policy which became the Academy movement.

Following the financial crash in 2008, doubts began to emerge about the wisdom of these policies. The banks had massively expanded their risks and had to be bailed out to the tune of around £1 trillion. The railway system had, in effect, to be renationalised after years of mismanagement and a timetable fiasco. Doubts were raised about the whole concept of capitalism and its assumed benefits.[36]

There have also been spectacular private company failures. These include Carillion, BHS, Debenhams, Patisserie Valerie, Arcadia and Thomas Cook. These took place before Covid-19 struck. There have been many others since the pandemic. Despite the misgivings and a sizeable number of corporate failures, there still remains a belief by some that people coming from a private sector background are, by virtue of that background, superior to those working in the not-for-profit sector. I am devoting some space to this topic because the differences between the two sectors are significant in many important respects. These differences manifest themselves in several ways but most particularly when the question of marketing arises. There is a belief that private firms know about marketing and hence are well placed to advise or help a charity on how to do it better. This belief is not always true in ways I think it important to explore.

I should say straight away that marketing in a commercial setting is now a highly developed discipline. A glance at any decent bookshop will reveal a number of titles devoted to various aspects of the subject. Having studied the subject and acquired a postgraduate diploma in marketing myself, I can attest to the wide range of techniques, ideas and theories which underpin the subject. Much of it was developed to help the sale of what are termed 'fast-moving consumer goods' or FMCG. Considerable research has been undertaken into people, their buying behaviours and how firms can adapt to the changing marketplace. Marketing thought and practice have ancient roots, with ideas for example of branding, differentiation and segmentation being found in Middle Eastern cultures and in China. So it is not some modern invention.

The key aspect is that it is about commercial activity. The Chartered Institute of Marketing's definition sets the scene well: 'Marketing is the management process responsible for identifying, anticipating and satisfying customer requirements profitably.' This embodies the elements of marketing and in turn, the commercial nature of the transaction. It is about developing a relationship with customers and doing so at a profit. Having identified a customer need or want, a firm supplies a good or service for which the customer pays the firm. Although there may be intermediaries such as retailers, wholesalers or factors of some kind, that does not alter the nature of the relationship. It is ultimately about exchange between supplier and customer.

A charity operates in a different way. It does identify the needs of the group being helped and in that respect there are some similarities – however, it raises money from elsewhere, either from the public or from grants. It uses those monies to offer assistance to those whom it wishes to help. Those receiving the help do not usually pay the charity. Unlike a firm therefore, there is no direct relationship between the recipient and those providing the money. Indeed, it is unlikely that the funders will have any notion of who exactly is being helped, nor will the recipients know who is providing the funds for the help they are receiving. There is, in short, no direct one-to-one customer/supplier relationship. Profit is not a factor either; although charities do seek to achieve a surplus and to maintain their reserves, there is no dividend or payment to stockholders.

This poses a series of problems for both the charity and the providers of funds. The direct relationship a firm has with its customers means that, if a customer is dissatisfied with the product or service, they can ultimately go elsewhere. This provides a powerful signal to a firm that it is not performing as it should, or that the quality of its product is not satisfactory. If a firm's product is too expensive, a fall in sales is a valuable signal to them that something is wrong. Because the provider of funds to a charity is disassociated with the 'customer', there is no relationship between them. Funders have to rely almost entirely on what the charity says it is doing to help those in need. There is no 'price signal' to speak of and the absence of a direct relationship also means there is no mechanism for quality control by this method.

Firms do not, for the most part, have to concern themselves with moral issues. As long as they act within the law, they are free to sell alcohol, tobacco and to provide services such as gambling. There are legal restrictions – for example minimum ages at which people can buy these products or services – and controls over the display of tobacco products, but firms are still free to supply a range of goods which consumed excessively can cause harm. Currently, there are worries about problem gambling and the effects this has on the wellbeing of addicts.

There is an important distinction between *wants* and *needs* which needs to be considered. Of course, some wants become needs over time. Mobile phones are an example: where once they were desirable but not essential, life now without one is all but inconceivable for many, especially teenagers I suspect. A commercial firm will wish to supply wants. If my customers want yellow trousers, then I shall do my best to source and supply them with yellow trousers. Having quantities of blue trousers is unlikely to be a recipe for commercial success. Moreover, a firm will not concern itself too much with those few customers who want blue trousers. For a charity on the other hand, there could be a difference – indeed it could be a significant difference – between what someone wants and what they need.

So a charity involved in alcohol abuse and helping those to overcome such an addiction, will be directing their efforts towards what people *need*, not what they want. They cannot readily ignore inconvenient 'segments' of their clientele.

Companies are typically concerned about growth expressed in one of several forms. It can be return on capital employed (ROCE), shareholder return or simply rising profits for a smaller enterprise. Larger firms will also be concerned about market share. In one form or another it is about growth and increasing in size. A successful firm has to exhibit growth or it will find itself vulnerable to its competitors and too small to invest in innovation and developing new products. Marketing is the key management process involved in this activity, as the definition above reveals.

Firms are engaged essentially in exchange.

A charity will have a different mindset. Although most charities wish to see their services offered to the widest extent, the ultimate test of success is their own extinction. No charity involved in helping the homeless or drug addicts, for example, wishes to see *more* such individuals. It does want to get to as many as possible, but it does not want to grow the market in the same way a commercial firm does. So its activities are about reach not about growth per se.

Good charities also have a strong moral interest in their clients and their relations with them. Indeed, many meetings are spent discussing various aspects of these moral or ethical relations. Just as importantly, they are concerned with welfare issues as well. Whereas a firm will not adopt a moral stance when selling a car say, as long as the person is of age and has the necessary documents to drive it away, charities often adopt a more directive approach to their clients. The services a charity offers are seldom purely demand led. It is an aspect of the difference between needs and wants discussed above. Their approach is more akin to that of a medical practitioner and will involve an element of judgement about what is best for the patient. They are not therefore simply responding to pure client demand or want. Often, they are seeking to influence the behaviour of those they seek to help. The exception to this observation is advocacy, which is a service enabling vulnerable people to have their voices heard. There are many individuals who, for one reason or another, can find expressing their views and wishes difficult and who need the help from an advocate especially in their dealings with people in authority.

The problem here is patently the 'we know best' criticism which can be levelled at charities, and the accusation of paternalism.

More widely, cultural issues are at play. Since the neoliberal policies which became established in the 1960s, there has been a certain set of beliefs which has underpinned much government policy and been influential with the public as well. There was firstly the idea of small government. Governments were seen to be poor managers and inefficient at allocating resources. The private sector, driven by the unforgiving marketplace and competition, was superior at providing what people wanted. Markets were superior to planning. Importantly, as far as the charitable sector is concerned, attempts at creating a more equal society were regarded as counterproductive. Those who were less equal should be more enterprising, so in a sense, they were at least partly to blame for their circumstance. Those who were more enterprising created wealth which would trickle down through society. There was more than a hint of the old notion of the 'undeserving poor'.

In many respects, the charity sector is largely forgotten in UK cultural and political life. Its activities do not directly feature for example in the nation's GDP figures. The third sector often feels neglected, as the minister in the Department for Civil Society – which includes sport, heritage and tourism – is often the last appointment to be made in a reshuffle and is very low in the 'pecking order' in Whitehall.[37]

These beliefs percolated into society as well as being influential in government policy. The idea that competition forces firms to be efficient because, if they are not, competitors will take their place, although sometimes true, forgets the role of market power and the availability of finance. Following the collapse of many firms, chronic inefficiency, mismanagement and a failure to adapt to changing circumstances often come to light. A fairly recent example is the outsourcing firm of Carillion, which collapsed in 2018.[38] What was revealed was inadequate financial management, poor controls and weak auditing. There were also allegations of corporate greed. The firm grew in size partly because of the very belief in the superiority of the private sector and government's desire to outsource as much work as possible to private sector firms such as these. This belief was dramatically disabused. There have been many other corporate collapses: Debenhams, Jamie Oliver's restaurant chain, Thomas Cook, and Mothercare are all examples from the recent past. One recurring theme was a failure to adapt to a changing marketplace with more and more goods and services being purchased online. These failures took place before Covid-19.

Despite the revelations which followed some of the more high-profile corporate collapses, the belief in the superiority of the private sector over the public and charitable sectors still lives on. It is for the latter to learn lessons from the former. The banking collapse in 2008 provided only a temporary pause in these beliefs.

Looking at the two universes, we have to conclude that neither sector has any kind of monopoly of skills and management expertise. There are excellent and well-run companies but there are also some poorly run ones as well. If we also take in the different objectives: growth, profitability and market share for companies in comparison to charities where these objectives do not figure so strongly, and we also consider the moral considerations, we have to conclude that the cross-fertilisation of skills is not straightforward. The assumption that someone with a private sector background is *automatically* in a position to help a charity is questionable. These observations do not imply that *no* crossover can be achieved or that the private sector cannot teach a charity how to be more efficient, more that it is not automatic or straightforward.

As a trustee therefore, I suggest that you are on your guard for the idea that someone with a private sector pedigree will automatically be able to make a valuable contribution to the future of the charity.

I must emphasise that people with a private sector background can and do make significant and beneficial contributions to the sector. It can be thanks to a 'can do' attitude. They can bring energy and a fresh way of looking at things. They may have relevant skills to offer in the running of the organisation. If you have a private sector background and are at the stage of considering becoming a trustee (or similar role) in a charity, the purpose of this chapter is to suggest that some rethinking may be needed and that the 'transfer' is not altogether straightforward – but not to dissuade you from doing so.

CHAPTER 4

Developing your strategy

One of the key roles for a trustee is to help your charity develop a strategy. It is not a precise science and requires judgement and careful assessment of differing options to get right. In this chapter I want to set out some guidance which I hope will help you with the task. If you come from a business or commercial background and have experience of this activity, you will recognise some similarities but it is not completely the same. As you will recall from the previous chapter, I said that the role of a profit-seeking business is to increase profits and to achieve that it is likely to grow in size and to increase its market share. That will drive its strategic plan. A charity, by contrast, is ultimately seeking its own extinction since it hardly wants to see, for example, more homeless people or more people needing food parcels. This does inevitably lead to a different approach.

We start by looking at the factors which will set the scene for this work. The underlying principles are a confident and positive approach. There has to be some kind of driving force which the trustees and staff all believe in and which motivates them. Without this, however good and well-crafted the strategy is, it is unlikely to achieve much.

There are five key questions you and your fellow trustees need to ask yourselves:

1. **Purpose**. Is our purpose still relevant? Is it clearly expressed in our strategy?
2. **Effectiveness**. Are we being effective in what we set out to do? Are we achieving positive outcomes as a result of our activities?
3. **Branding**. Does our brand convey what we are trying to do and what we stand for? Do our audiences easily recognise us and our cause?
4. **Fit for purpose**? Are our organisation, systems and management fit for purpose? Could we grow or diversify with confidence?
5. **Environment**. What is going on in the world around us?

PURPOSE

The first task is to ask if the issue your charity was set up to help with still exists. Has it changed in some material way? You may answer that quite quickly by saying the phone doesn't stop ringing and everyone is very busy. That may be so, but are the staff effective and are they achieving anything? Have the needs changed in any way? For example, food banks were set up to provide emergency supplies for those in dire need. They have grown massively and, at the time of writing, over a million and a half people avail themselves of this service. They seem to have become a fixture in the lives of many people. Clearly there is a need. Clearly they are extremely busy. Clearly they are providing a valuable service. But is this what the charities should be doing? Have they become a kind of de facto social service? By existing, do they absolve government from ensuring that people don't need such a service, certainly not on the scale at which it now operates? These are difficult questions and raise profound philosophical and ethical arguments. Trustees may need to consider the issue of 'need' quite carefully, and being very busy may not be enough.

It is really vital that you address the fundamental essence of the organisation and what it does. One essential consideration is that as a charity, what you do must be for the public benefit. As far as you can, set aside issues of how things are done, difficulties, problems and potential restrictions and try and get to the heart of what you are attempting to do. If you are involved in a group exercise – which is a good way to tackle this kind of activity – ask yourselves, 'If we could look back on our work in a year's time, what would we like to see?' You might try a flip chart exercise and ask people, 'What three things would you like us to have achieved twelve months from now?' Some of what is suggested is likely to be fanciful or simply unachievable. It doesn't matter. It gets people thinking a tad more ambitiously than perhaps they are used to doing. One suggestion, whatever it is, may well inspire someone else to think of something valuable.

Those charities that are engaged in doing work for local authorities, or that receive funds from various organisations, can get sucked into doing what is required by the funder, not what they want to do or what they think they should be doing. It can become a kind of treadmill and can certainly act to limit thinking or ambitions. In thinking about your purpose and about the future, therefore, it is important not to get fixated on funder pressures or expectations.

One final consideration. Try and address what the *fundamental* issue(s) is (are) and not just the results. This can be difficult for a small local charity (the type of organisation I have in mind in this book). The risk is that you are engaged in just picking up the pieces of wider policy failure rather than making a real and lasting difference. If, for example, you are tackling homelessness, what are the causes which lead people you are helping to become homeless? The reasons are many and include losing a job, mental health issues, coming out of prison, drug addiction or for women, escaping a violent relationship. Your charity may wish to explore 'going upstream' and trying to focus more work on the causes. This can change the focus of what you do quite significantly.

EFFECTIVENESS

I must start with a cautionary note: there is no single or simple method to assess the effectiveness of a charity. I cannot suggest a set of measures, or a list of procedures which will give you the answer to the question 'How effective are we?' If it were a business, we could look at sales and growth of sales, profits, some ratios, the return on capital and do some comparisons (benchmarking) with other like businesses, and this would give us a good picture of how the business was performing. These measures are not readily applicable to a charity, which makes answering this question especially difficult. Yet it is a key one to address because – and it hardly needs saying – if you are not effective then the charity is unlikely to exist for long. I would also add another cautionary note: there is a danger to measuring *activity* and *outputs* which can confuse rather than enlighten. These are not the same as effectiveness. As was noted in the introduction, people are anxious to know what you are actually achieving rather than what you are just doing.

The first question to ask is: What does effectiveness look like for our charity? What does effectiveness actually mean? Following the homelessness example above, it can mean several things. Shelter is a well-run charity and has gone to a great deal of trouble to set out in some detail what its impacts are.[39] Such a charity might be involved in helping those in poor accommodation; giving advice on money matters; sourcing furniture; finding accommodation for those without it and so forth. Established in 1966, it aimed to be 'one organisation that would speak for the millions of "hidden homeless"'. They may also engage in lobbying politicians both local and national. In terms of effectiveness therefore, there will be a range of measures but, at the end of the day, a degree of judgement will still be needed.

One part of Shelter's work is carrying out decorating assignments for those living in poor accommodation. This involves 'hands-on help to enable people to turn unfit accommodation into a safe, comfortable home'. The impact is explained elsewhere in their report and can be monitored and reported on easily. Other aspects of their work involve before and after feedback surveys from users (as they call them). Another technique is to use a scoring assessment tool where children are scored by their support worker using observations, feedback from the school, self-assessment by the young person and feedback from parents. Details can be found in Shelter's report in their appendix (ibid).

It is clear that a lot of planning has gone into their system, and this point is crucial. The diverse nature of a lot of charity work means careful thought needs to be given to the setting up of reporting systems, a subject I shall return to in a later chapter. The system needs to be established at the *start* of projects to enable outcomes and impacts to be reported on. What else can be done?

- To repeat: ask yourselves what success would look like. A homeless charity would answer along the lines of helping those in housing stress via a programme of refurbishment, advocacy, advice and active support. Each of these can be described and some kind of measure attached to them. I argue elsewhere to avoid targets which have a variety of largely adverse effects.
- Look at other charities in the same line of work, something relatively easy to do these days with the internet. Visiting one

in another area is a good idea – an offer to buy lunch will help oil the wheels.

- Listen to your staff and volunteers. They are the people on the front line and my experience has been that they are all too willing to question why something is being done a particular way and to offer suggestions for change or improvement. The suggestions may not all be practical or even desirable, but some might be. They will appreciate being asked.
- Look at your current performance. Reporting on trends is something I shall discuss in Chapter 6. But for now, how you are performing currently is a useful input to the exercise. Assessing this performance against the existing strategy may also trigger questions: if you hoped last time to achieve X, why have you only managed half X? This should not come as a surprise or a bolt from the blue if the strategy is being regularly reviewed, but it is surprising what you notice when you stand back from something.
- If your charity is dealing with people, then feedback from them is vital. Similarly, seek feedback from other stakeholders or partners. These are potentially important insights and will tell you what the outside world thinks of you.
- And don't forget research. There are more journals and support organisations these days – as well as academic research – which often contain useful advice and background material. There have been criticisms that charities do not use research results sufficiently, perhaps regarding them as too academic and detached from reality.[40] While that may be true in some cases, the insight gained by researchers into the performance and effectiveness of charity work can be useful. It should certainly be reviewed. Conferences and other forms of gathering are also valuable. It is a commonplace to say that the benefit of a

conference comes not from the speeches or presentations but the social contacts and chance conversations in the intervals.

Reviewing the effectiveness of your charity is an activity where the experience and detachment of trustees can make a significant input. There is a danger that staff, being close to what is happening and involved in the day-to-day, can overlook strategic issues and lose sight of the big picture. The elements of assessing effectiveness and helping you answer the question 'How effective are we?' are partly answered as follows:

- Do you know what effectiveness looks like? Could you recognise it if you saw it?
- How are other charities performing? How well do you compare?
- How have you measured up in terms of the strategy and work plan?
- What is the information you are receiving at board meetings telling you?
- What do your staff and volunteers say? Do you get the impression they think they work for a charity which is doing something worthwhile?
- What do clients or stakeholders think? If you have contracts with funders, are they likely to tell you what they think?
- What did you glean from research?

A lot of questions – and although there will be some solid numbers among the answers, there is still a need for judgement. In my notes for this book, I wrote 'intuition' and I was nervous about writing it down here. But I do think there is room for it. It is about seeing through the mass of information and trying to discern the truth, the essence of how you are performing. It is a major role for trustees and it is where experience does count.

BRANDING

Another subject you need to consider when thinking about your strategy is your brand. It is closely linked to your reputation. I discuss this in more detail in Chapter 9 where I note that there is sometimes resistance to the idea of branding when it comes to charities. It is seen by some as unseemly, flirting too closely with the commercial world and not really relevant. Some feel that what the charity does should sell itself. Many people think it is not that important and overrated. However, how you are seen and perceived is central to your success. Whether you are collecting in the street or otherwise raising funds, or when you are seeking volunteers to help you, the beliefs that people have about you and their knowledge of you and your cause are vital considerations.

FITNESS FOR PURPOSE

Having a superbly thought-out strategy, a first-rate brand and carefully defined purpose is of little value if your charity is not in a position to carry out that purpose. Assessing fitness for purpose is not a straightforward exercise and there is a risk of entering into a jungle of questions and data leading to, well ... what? The key issues for a small charity are, I suggest, as follows:

- **Staff and volunteers**. Do you have confidence in the staff to manage change, especially if that change involves growth? I honestly think that, for a small charity, this is a lot about impressions. You can conduct all kinds of investigations, but ask yourself: at meetings, does the chief executive come across as competent and in command of his or her brief? Do they have that hard to define skill of leadership? Is the board provided with information and reports which are accurate and on time? What is the level of staff turnover and what have you learned from exit interviews? The opinion of the chair is important since they have the most contact with the CEO.

- **Systems**. This covers IT but also office systems generally. IT is central to all organisations these days and weaknesses can pose a real risk. Inadequacies can make operating efficiently difficult. There is the risk of hacking and viruses. The system can simply collapse. I have sometimes experienced programs and software being installed by 'someone who somebody knows'. There is also the risk of over-sophistication, resulting in nobody being able to make routine changes without seeking professional advice. Altogether, it is a potential minefield. Even quite small charities need a reliable supplier, who is properly briefed, able to install a system of adequate sophistication and on hand to sort out problems.
- **IT and the future**. IT and in particular AI (artificial intelligence) are going to change the environment for a host of organisations in the future. Jamie Susskind, in his book *Future Politics*,[41] discusses the factors which will change the landscape for all of us – the ever increasing power of computers and devices able to do more and more. He admits that predicting where it will all lead to is next to impossible. Charities will not be immune to these changes and it would be wise to be mindful of their effects and, it has to be said, their potential. Machines that lip-read or translate are already in an advanced state.
- **Trustees**. The board should have a mix of skills and experience. I discuss in Chapter 12 some of the attributes of trustees – experience, judgement, energy and enthusiasm, an ability to see the big picture and so on. To have a few trustees with knowledge of the sector is obviously desirable, together with some offering technical skills such as finance and HR. There is

often a debate about whether boards should be representative of the area or sector in some way, versus boards which are more 'technical', shall I say. My vote is for the latter. I strongly believe that boards are about strategy and direction and making sure the charity is run well. They should not be there representing some other organisation's brief.

- **Financial matters**. The finances and financial controls must be in good shape, as discussed in Chapter 8.
- **Information**. Are you getting good information, presented properly, as discussed in Chapters 6 and 7
- **Governance**. Having good governance arrangements in place is important. This is discussed more fully in Chapter 5 with a warning not to become so dominated by it that the charity becomes risk averse. Much of governance is good management practice anyway.
- **Getting things done**. How good is the charity at actually achieving things? Does it get things done, whether internally or for those it is trying to help? Are plans made and yet nothing actually happens? This links to a recurring theme of this book: that organisations can have all kinds of strategies, governance, policies and procedures and yet, and yet, nothing seems to actually happen.

ENVIRONMENT

Your charity operates in an environment which is ever changing. There are a range of factors to consider and a useful acronym is STEEPLE, which stands for Social, Technological, Economic, Environmental, Political, Legal and Ethical. Each one of these areas needs to be looked at carefully in terms of how any changes might affect how your charity operates in the future.

For example, safeguarding issues and the Care Act in 2014 brought in legislation which has had a significant effect on how vulnerable people are treated. Greater environmental awareness is increasingly influencing behaviour and attitudes in a wide range of organisations.

Some changes are easily identified – new laws for example. They are announced, contain specific provisions and receive publicity, especially in specialist publications and websites. It is essential that you comply. GDPR* is one recent example of regulations introduced to protect people's information. Other changes can be subtle and not so easily identified. Social attitudes evolve gradually over a period of time. Attitudes towards women, race and children have changed significantly and are continuing to change. We have seen dramatic examples of this with the Black Lives Matter protests in 2020, and the anger which followed the murder of Sarah Everard in March 2021. Fierce arguments arose around footballers 'taking the knee' before matches. People with disabilities are regarded and treated quite differently these days, although there are still examples of less than perfect equality. It is therefore important to be aware of these less obvious and more gradual changes, any one of which can affect the operations of your charity.

A useful source of information and analysis of changing attitudes in Britain is the Social Attitudes Survey (Scotland has its own separate version).[42] These surveys have been running since 1983 and are a valuable and respected source of how attitudes are changing towards various topics in our society. It is possible to fund your own survey but this may be out of the reach of a small charity. Analyses are published at a more affordable £142. YouGov is another useful source on a wide variety of attitudes held by the public.

---

* General Data Protection Regulation

It is worthwhile spending some time on this activity, and doing it reasonably methodically, since changes in the environment can have significant and 'game-changing' effects on the future of a charity. A suggested rubric is set out in Appendix B. Do try and keep it within bounds. There is a danger – especially if there is a group exercise set up to look at this (which I recommend) – of more and more factors being suggested, walls covered in Post-it notes, and a mammoth set of potential changes being put forward. Select two or three, four at maximum, of the most important. And remember, since no one can foresee the future, always be prepared for the unexpected – which can either be a potential problem or a potential opportunity.

If the organisation is basically in good shape – it will never be perfect of course – then you can proceed to look at the future. But if you, and some or all of your fellow trustees, feel that everything is not as it should be and that there are major weaknesses, then it might be advisable to bring in someone from outside to help you explore the issues in more depth. They can help guide you through various exercises and prompt more questions. They will be independent and an experienced person who has been involved in this kind of work for some time, will bring a fresh perspective to your charity and challenge some of the thinking. If you can get a recommendation from another charity in the area, so much the better. They will also form an impression of how you work and fit together as a team.

Should you start by looking at the previous strategy or the work plan derived from it? The danger here is that there can be a temptation to carry on doing more of the same. Certainly, an examination of the previous plans is a useful place to start as long as it does not inhibit critical thinking and some fundamental questions being asked. This really is an important role for you and your fellow trustees.

EXPANSION

One question to emerge from any kind of strategic analysis is: should we expand or stay roughly the same? There are often divergent views surrounding this tricky issue. It can arouse considerable passions. There are those who like the smallness and intimacy of the charity as it is now. They may be frightened of the risks involved with expansion. They may worry that their role in the charity will be diminished in some way. There are many who do not like change, seeing it as some kind of threat, which to be honest, it sometimes is. Never forget that many people – especially those of more mature years – may well have experienced reorganisations or restructures of some kind during their work careers. They will know that there are often casualties and that these are usually to be found at the bottom of the organisation. There will, consequently, be a degree of (probably justified) suspicion or cynicism among some of your staff. It is therefore a topic which has to be approached with care.

A commercial, profit-seeking enterprise more or less has to expand. The threat of competition, the need to seek extra profits, rises in costs of various kinds including compliance costs, more or less force growth on such businesses.

The situation for a charity is not quite so clear cut. As I said above, the ultimate objective of a charity is to extinguish itself. In an ideal vision there are no more homeless people; the environment is sorted and global warming stabilised; nobody is taking illegal drugs anymore and a cure for cancer has been found. Well, I know that these are all very unlikely and utopia a long way off, but the fact remains that no charity wants to see an *increase* in the social, medical or environmental problem it is trying to tackle. Growth is not some kind of given or a state of nature. There will of course be costs. Whereas with a commercial firm, the driver will be increasing profits (or return to shareholders, or some kind of financial imperative), a charity will be driven by the needs of those it is trying to help. There is likely to be an element of emotional capital involved. Elsewhere I have said that many who work or volunteer for a charity do so for reasons of altruism, or to 'give something back'. A natural and laudable desire to help more (of whatever the charity is engaged in) needs to be set against the risks, additional costs, management issues, and the availability or ease of securing additional funds.

What are the advantages of growing the charity? There are several. There are economies of scale. Several costs are fixed and do not depend too much on size or level of activity. Compliance costs, IT and accountancy are examples that are largely fixed for a range of activity. It is likely to increase your credibility: becoming larger makes you just that bit more noticeable. A growing charity is likely to find recruiting – especially to senior positions – a little easier because applicants can see that there is a future for them in career terms. Since costs are inexorably rising, then growing enables you to cope with this, although it is by no means a direct connection.

The disadvantages? Management is one. Expansion may well involve moving into new geographical areas which brings with it greater risk. A very small charity, like a small firm, is a fairly intimate affair. A lot of 'management' can be done informally and visually. I used to visit small firms, and a glass wall between the owner's office and his or her workforce was a not uncommon sight, enabling the proprietor to maintain visual control over what was happening. Grow and this becomes progressively more difficult. There is a need for improved systems and controls. HR becomes that bit more difficult. Delegation becomes more important, essential in fact. Indeed a range of management skills are needed and there is likely to be a need for training. Things like cashflow become important – not because a small charity doesn't need to monitor this, but because more is going on and the very act of growing can lead to liquidity problems.

Another aspect is that the character or the culture of the organisation can change. This is quite hard to explain. A small organisation, as I said in the last paragraph, is an intimate affair. Everyone knows everyone else. The founder may still be in evidence. There is a high degree of informality. Meetings can be quickly arranged. When growth happens, these things begin to change, especially if the charity expands geographically. Gradually rules start to appear. Things become more formal and structured. Everyone may no longer know everyone else. There is a need to become more organised and formalised. There is nothing inherently wrong in this but these changes can be unsettling for some staff and volunteers. Instead of 'popping in' to see someone, for example, they have to make an appointment or 'book some time'. Rivalries can appear. In short, in sometimes imperceptible ways, the character or culture of the charity is different. This is *not* a reason *not* to expand the charity but it is a factor that has to be recognised. I think for a small charity the effects can be quite marked. Consider this: a small charity of say five staff takes on someone extra, which means they have grown by 20%. A large charity employing a hundred staff employs one more, which means they grow by 1% – hardly noticeable. The issue of character – another word is culture – is in my view extremely important. In summary, this is all about managing change. Change is a permanent feature in life today and adapting to it is crucial to success.

Finally, the issue of timing. 'Pain before gain' is a useful phrase to bear in mind. The changes needed, the pain, will happen before the gains materialise. If not everyone was convinced about the desire to expand, then the changes and disruption can lead to attitudes of 'I told you so' occurring. All this is rather gloomy I realise, and reading the last few paragraphs might lead you to give up on any idea of expanding your own charity. I hope not! My intention is to point out the issues that need to be addressed and to say – forewarned is forearmed.

A key point to consider in this section, by the way, are your memorandum and articles of association. These need to be checked to see whether you can do what you propose. For example, your M&A may say you carry out your activities in 'the county of Midshire'. If you propose operating in Southshire, then you will need to amend them.

WHAT EXPANSION?

A useful diagram from the business world when considering expansion or diversification is something called the 'Ansoff matrix'. First developed by H. Igor Ansoff in an article in the *Harvard Business Review* in 1957 entitled 'Strategies for Diversification', it neatly sets out the two main options and compares the results. The two options are diversifying into a new area or offering a new service. I have adapted the language slightly to make it relevant for a charity:

Area	*New*	Increase activity in a new area (medium risk)	New activity in a new area (high risk)
	Existing	Increase activity in your existing area (low risk)	Existing activity in a new area (medium risk)
		Existing	*New*
		Activity	

Fig 1 Ansoff matrix

The four boxes show the main options and the attendant risks. Expanding or diversifying into a new area with a new service is, as you might expect, the riskiest strategy. It is quite a useful starting point in any discussion about strategy and how the charity might develop.

A useful way of addressing this problem is to try and imagine where you see the charity in say, three years' time. This is often the basis of a workshop session with staff and trustees and lends itself to group exercises with Post-it notes, flip charts and so on. This needs to be held away from the offices to avoid interruptions or distractions. It can be a fun exercise and so much the better for it. You may wish to frame it in terms of the matrix discussed above. The idea is not to think in terms of where you are now and just adding a bit more, but to invite people to think more adventurously and imaginatively. I have been involved in this kind of exercise over the years and it is surprising how it is often the junior staff who come up with the ideas. Well, it shouldn't be surprising since they are the people out on the ground and seeing the problems first-hand. Once some ideas have crystallised, then it is a matter of working back to the present and saying 'This is where are now – what have we got to do to get there?'

I mentioned Post-it notes in the last paragraph and the development and history of this useful office tool is instructive.[43] The brief was to develop a more powerful adhesive and Dr Spencer Silver, who worked for 3M, came across an adhesive during his research which was really quite weak. He could have discarded results then and there, and higher up the management tree, someone might have said, 'interesting, but it's not what the brief asked for'. He persisted and the rest is history – it is quite possible you have a pack in your office drawer. It is an example of 'thinking outside the box'. Many organisations would have rejected the adhesive as it did not match the brief, and then we would not have had Post-it notes.

Having considered the various options in the Ansoff matrix, the next step is to analyse the outside forces which are going to be important over the coming years. The use of the STEEPLE process can help with managing this thinking. In passing, you will see

PESTLE which is nearly the same thing, the difference being the additional 'E' for Ethical, especially important in the charity and not-for-profit context. Earlier, I mentioned the change in attitudes towards charities as a result of some well-publicised scandals. Other issues might emerge and these need to be monitored. The implications might mean policy changes or a tightening in management practice, around safety for example. Each charity will have a different set of circumstances. The important point is to analyse as best you can what the changes are and to consider carefully how you will accommodate them or mitigate their effects on your organisation. It is important to look at the forces and change dynamically, and to consider carefully the implication for the charity of those identified. It might be useful to approach it with the following rubric in mind:

Current situation	*Forces identified*	*Implications for us*
Social		
Technological		
Economic		
Environmental		
Political		
Legal		
Ethical		

The idea is to look, under each heading, at what changes there have been or are likely to happen, which will have an impact on your charity. Under technology, for example, a major change has been the increase in social media and, following Covid-19, an increase in home working and online meetings. Environmental includes the increasing concerns about climate change and the need for policy responses to that. Legal might be new legislation or regulations.

Economic may include the effects of austerity. Having identified the forces, you need to consider the impact they will have. Increased homeworking means team working is that bit harder to accomplish. Some people will find working at home difficult, especially with distractions such as small children or home education of older ones. Some, on the other hand, will find the freedom from commuting an enormous relief. There are possible mental health issues. As time goes on, the lack of social contact will reduce the pleasure of working in isolation. Despite the normal complaints that people make about having to go to work, many enjoy the contact and like being able to get away from home.

STEEPLE and Ansoff analyses will generate several issues, and it is easy to get a bit lost with the increasing list of forces – potential or actual – which have been identified. In this diagram, I offer a means to analyse the options and forces and to look at the implications of dealing with them. I cannot of course provide a complete list since every charity is different, but I have offered some examples to illustrate the points.

Step	Process	Notes
1	STEEPLE	
2	Is one of the threats existential?	*This can arise if for example new legislation or government action removes the* raison d'être *of the charity. Assuming the answer is 'no' …*
3	Set priorities	*It is not unusual to have five or more threats identified under each heading. You cannot deal with them all, so you need to agree the top three, or at most four.*
4	Options: A: Reduce the size of the charity B: Consolidate and maintain your current size C: Expand the charity (how based on the Ansoff matrix above)	

Each of these options will, as you would expect, have different implications which have to be thought through. A key point in STEEPLE analyses is that they are looking at *external* forces. This is similar to Porter's Five Forces discussed later. A point to bear in mind is that these forces are changing all the time. An annual away day where everyone discusses and lists them is a good thing to do but is largely static in character: it captures things at a particular moment. Change is happening all the time: new laws are passed; political changes happen with elections local or national; the economy changes, so it goes on. How these forces are responded to will depend significantly on the abilities of the charity to identify, if necessary adapt to, and then manage them – in short, largely *internal* capabilities. The key aspects to be considered are: management, financial, communications and marketing, information and IT, risks. Under management will be issues of competences, staffing and training needs. I have populated some of the matrix to give examples.

	A: Reduce in size	**B: Consolidate**	**C: Expand**
Management	• Handling morale • Amending job descriptions and roles • Retaining key staff who may want to leave	• Lack of growth may mean fewer opportunities for staff – implications?	• Assess the competencies of staff and management • Consider training needs • Management at a distance issues • Maintaining the 'culture' of the charity
Financial	• Redundancy issues • Will we still be able to cover our overhead costs?	• Will income continue to exceed rising costs over time?	• Closely monitor cash flow and finances generally • Need for funding to be assessed

(Continued)

	A: Reduce in size	B: Consolidate	C: Expand
Communications	• Being able to explain reasons	• Managing expectations	• What new messages will be needed? • New audiences?
Marketing	• Altering marketing materials, the website and social media		• Carry out market research • New marketing materials, revised social media • Promotional strategy may be needed
Information and IT			• Are our systems and IT adequate? • Modifying/improving information to the board
Risks	• Being able to cover core costs • Handling staff issues	• Being able to cover core costs	• Maintaining quality with management spread more thinly • Being able to recruit suitable staff • Cash flow
Other	*Depending on particular factors in your charity*		• Do you need to change your legal details?

NEXT STEPS

Let us assume you have looked at the needs, reflected on the performance of your charity, and considered the environment and how that will affect its future. You have considered whether to expand or diversify and after some kind of workshop session with your staff, volunteers and fellow trustees, you have settled on a course of action. You may even have rethought your mission. What next?

I have already mentioned the issue of management and staff skills. Whether it is change or diversification, there is likely to be a need for training. Outside observers of the charity sector often remark that too little attention is paid to this aspect. Since many small charities struggle to find adequate funding, the cost of sending someone off for management training of some kind is too easily shelved. I confessed above to being a little gloomy about expansion but the risks multiply if the management of the charity is not up to the task. The fact that everyone is committed to the future of the organisation does not mean they will perform well without adequate training. Commitment is not the same as competence. In all sorts of ways, you will need people to be capable, efficient and confident. The chief executive in particular needs a range of management skills and competencies and these need to be regularly discussed and assessed with the chair of trustees. It may cost hundreds of pounds to send them on a suitable course, but what is it going to cost if they become stressed, need time off, or leave and you have to find a replacement? More junior staff struggling with databases or trying to update the website will hamper your operations.

Later on in the book I will be discussing the issue of information and the need for performance to be monitored. This becomes ever more important if there is a change of direction. There will be a need for measures – KPIs* if you like – to keep track of performance.

It is not unusual for a great deal of time and emotional energy to be spent on thinking about strategic matters, for it then to quietly drift away. The process is only halfway through with discussing the strategy and a way forward. This has then to be turned into a plan, a

* Key Performance Indicators

work plan, which as far as possible is SMART: specific, measurable, achievable, realistic and time bound. I think the best approach is for the plan to be ambitious, such that achieving everything may not be possible. This may seem to contradict the 'achievable' element of SMART but perhaps 'stretching' best describes the point. It does need to inject some energy into the organisation and it does not really serve any purpose if it's all done and dusted after six months or so.

Then, trustees need to review progress at their meetings. That does not mean a full-scale review of progress, but one good idea is a chart summarising the key elements with either 'traffic lights' to indicate progress or some short phrases.

I once headed up a strategy document I was preparing with John Lennon's quote 'Life is what happens to you while you're busy making other plans.' One of the problems with strategies is that essentially, you cannot predict the future. Stuff happens. Plans drawn up in December 2019, for example, were so much trash when Covid struck. An idea which looked good when it was proposed may turn out to be completely impractical on closer examination. An opportunity may arise out of the blue. I will discuss the notion of 'presence' in the marketing chapter and if you do have a good presence in the community, you may be approached by someone, or an organisation, with a project for your charity to consider.

Strategies should not therefore become straightjackets. They should not inhibit looking at unthought-of or unplanned opportunities. If a strategy leads people to say 'we cannot do that because it's not in our strategy' then in my view, something might be wrong. There is a military quote (that seems to be attributed to several authors) which says 'no plan survives contact with the enemy'. On the other hand, President Eisenhower said, 'plans are useless but planning is indispensable'. This emphasises that although the plan itself may change or be abandoned because of new opportunities or changed circumstances, the process of looking at your charity, assessing its competencies, systems and training are useful things in their own right. It is a bit like making sure your car is roadworthy: it doesn't really matter whether you decide then to drive to Cardiff or Carlisle, the preparations were essential.

Following on from the strategy is the work plan, which sets out in more detail how things are to be done, when and by whom.

FOUNDER SYNDROME

Another issue here is 'founder syndrome'. This arises with a charity where the person who established it is still in evidence and maybe the chief executive or chair.[44] It is probably more prevalent with smaller charities. They are proud of their creation which is almost like a child to them. To set a charity up requires a considerable degree of determination and founders often exhibit a kind of entrepreneurial trait. Part of this characteristic is 'not taking no for an answer'. As the charity expands, change in all sorts of ways begins to happen and this can have the effect of diminishing their control. Once the charity is established, however, there is the need for team working, delegation, seeking advice and being open to change and improvement. This can prove exceedingly difficult for such people. The combination of the personality type needed to get things going and the emotional attachment to 'their baby' can make this difficult. At the start, trustees may be friends or acquaintances of the founder, forming a kind of 'shield' around them. Board meetings may be perfunctory since no one wants to rock the boat or display disloyalty. If you are a trustee in such an instance, it can be a difficult position to be in. Essentially, unless the founder changes their ways – equivalent sometimes to a leopard changing its spots – there are only problems ahead. You are unlikely to get support from fellow trustees and any suggestions you make are quietly forgotten. You may have to consider your position. That is a polite way of saying 'leave'. In any event, it is unlikely to be a fruitful time for you.

This has been quite a long chapter and I am conscious that it has twisted and turned in places. The process of forming a strategy is not scientific. The *process* itself, however, is valuable and essential. It underpins a lot of other activity and is a key role for you as a trustee. It is where your contribution is likely to be most effective.

I now want to discuss the vexed question of governance, which has risen up the political agenda in the past decade or so.

CHAPTER 5

Governance

One of the key areas that trustees and management have to pay close attention to is governance. In recent years the issue has assumed great salience for charities and not-for-profit organisations. It is a subject which does have considerable potential to distort how a charity behaves and how it is managed. There is a real risk that it becomes the tail that wags the dog.

I am not going to write much about governance itself: considerable advice is already freely available on the Charity Commission's website and also from NCVO. I see little point in reproducing it here, and providing summaries risks doing more harm than good. I would suggest aspiring trustees to read the material available. Much of the advice is what you would expect. At the start of the Commission's advice document CC3, *The Essential Trustee* (2018 version) it sets out the legal duties:

- Act in the best interests of the charity
- Manage the resources of the charity responsibly
- Act with reasonable care and skill

There is little that is surprising here. If someone – acting as a trustee of a charity – was not acting in its best interests, was careless with its resources and did not act with reasonable care and skill, you would not be surprised if, when caught, they suffered some kind of penalty. My fear though is that the issue of governance has assumed in the minds of some trustees and managers an almost paranoid level of fear. I know, anecdotally, that some who would like to become trustees are put off by the fear that the slightest mistake will land them in court with the clanking of keys close behind. I argue, therefore, for a degree of balance and a sense of proportion.

There are a number of potential issues connected with governance:

- It can make charities risk-averse.[45] If, before crossing the road, you drew up a risk profile of what might befall you in doing so, it might lead you to stay where you are. If risk and governance become the prime concern, then considering a new venture for the charity may well get squashed before it ever gets going.
- In like manner, it can dominate thinking. A significant chunk of management time, and time in meetings, can be consumed by discussions about governance. Risk analyses can run to pages and pages with likelihoods attached to each and lists of mitigating factors set out in copious detail. Keeping a sense of proportion can be made more difficult.
- It can lead to 'leading from behind', by which I mean an idea or venture can die at birth because the issue of risk is quick to emerge almost from the moment the idea is first explained. You may care to notice in meetings you attend how soon it is that the question of risk first emerges if a new idea is put forward. Once upon a time, a new idea or proposal would find its feet some time before the question of risk was first mentioned. Now, I notice, it emerges very soon and can cast a pall over the discussions. This makes being opportunity-led all the harder.
- Another major danger is that it drags trustees more and more into the area of managing the charity. Ploughing through the detail of governance or a risk analysis means trustees inescapably becoming managers of the charity and moving away from

their strategic focus. In some small charities, a subcommittee is formed to examine and manage governance issues and risk. This is almost unavoidable in some cases and it is true that some trustees are well equipped to offer good advice on such matters. In a sense, there is a perfect circle. More and more emphasis by the Charity Commission on good governance forces this kind of activity since trustees, naturally enough, worry that an infringement will put them at risk. They feel they have to 'delve into the weeds' to minimise that risk. This drift into becoming almost quasi-managers is a serious issue.

- A further problem is staff and volunteer motivation. People who work and volunteer for charities do so – almost to a man and woman – for reasons of altruism. Yet more and more of their time is spent on aspects of governance. Forms to be filled in, DBS* checks to be carried out, declarations to be submitted each year, training to be undertaken, on and on the process of checking and monitoring to ensure the charity is 'legal' and not at risk if something untoward happens. This can for some seem oppressive, particularly so if people are only volunteering for an hour or so a week. I was recently involved in setting up a money advice project which required – as you might expect – a fair degree of checking and training for the volunteers. Several pulled out, finding this too onerous. It generates a feeling that they are not to be trusted and that there needs to be a kind of 'Big Brother' effort to ensure they are acting on the straight and narrow. As I have said elsewhere, people work or volunteer for a charity to help the cause, not to spend time on bureaucracy.
- Not to be forgotten is the time involved in discussing, reviewing and monitoring governance. It is not inconsiderable.

---

* Disclosure and Barring Service

Governance should not, on the other hand, be seen totally in negative terms. It should be looked at as codifying common sense and good practice. You do need to think about the lone working of your staff as part of your duty of care. You do need to know information about performance, much of which is coincident with governance information. You do need to look after the resources of the charity, its money, buildings and equipment, as well as information and data. A lot of the information you are collecting and the systems you are putting into place, you are going to need anyway. Another important aspect – especially if your charity is involved with helping people – are the potential risks to those you seek to help.

These points – both negative and positive – need to be considered by trustees, to enable them to ensure that governance doesn't take over the charity and dominate the mindset of its staff and volunteers.

MANAGING GOVERNANCE

The first point is to instil the belief that most governance is about common sense and good management. If it is seen in purely negative terms it risks assuming a bogeyman status and not being addressed properly. If trustees become paranoid about the risk they are running and become more and more involved in the minutiae of their charity, then they can overlook their strategic duties.

It is important to maintain a sense of proportion. The Charity Commission publishes its investigations and it is worth perusing these to see the kind of misdemeanours and mismanagement that will result in such an inquiry.[46] Thirty-seven were published in 2020 and the small number – as a proportion of the 166,000 charities in the UK – is itself worth noting, representing about 0.02% of the total. These are the most serious of course and not the equivalent of 'police warnings'. The reports reveal not minor infringements or falling foul of some petty rule, but quite serious wrongdoing with considerable sums of money unaccounted for or going into the pockets of trustees.

Just looking at two of them at random reveals some fairly extreme behaviour. A trustee received a substantial payment from the charity, further substantial sums the trustees claimed not to be aware of, and acting while inquorate. Another involved loans of £1m from the charity to a subsidiary of which a trustee was sole director, and private medical care of £250,000 to a person connected to an original trustee. Also, the accounts failed to describe the activities of the charity properly. Others describe similar behaviour of unauthorised payments, failure to account for payments properly and failure to provide proper accounts. They all involve quite substantial mismanagement and egregious failings, not minor slips or technical rule-breaking. Some of them could be described as 'jaw dropping'.

I do not imply that since these are serious examples of wrongdoing, then one need not concern oneself with the small details of governance. But I do argue that a sense of proportion should be maintained.

How should a trustee behave in relation to governance? I suggest the following rules are important:

- As a trustee you need to read the Charity Commission's guidance on governance and note those matters which are particularly relevant for your charity. You will be relieved that the guidance is written in a clear and digestible style and is not at all difficult to follow. There is also government guidance in *The Essential Trustee: What You Need to Know, What You Need to Do*.[47]
- You need to check that the suggestions are incorporated in the management of the charity.

- Ensure the charity does manage its risks, meetings are quorate and accounts are prepared according to the SORP** guidelines.
- As trustees, you need as far as possible to ensure the work is done while not actually doing it yourself.[48] That is what the staff are paid to do.
- You need to check that there are a suitable range of policies and procedures in place which reflect the work of the charity. These need to be clearly written and reviewed every three or so years. Check that they are in fact dated and have a review date incorporated.
- Importantly, you do need to ensure that these policies are promulgated to all those staff and volunteers involved. The growth in number of these policies in recent years has itself become a problem. It is not unusual for there to be thirty or more – certainly twenty at least – and there can be a tendency for managers to think that once they have the policies in place, the job is done. Policies have little value if staff and volunteers are not aware of them, which means effort expended in briefing and training. Refresher sessions are also essential. Having reminders about key points dotted around the office may also be a good idea, especially concerning things of a security nature (lone working for example).
- In a similar vein, you need to be alert for attitudes based on the idea that once all the policies are in place, the charity is somehow safe and secure from 'attack'. They should not be seen as a kind of defensive wall, like living in some medieval castle with a 'moat' of policies surrounding it. If you'll forgive me mixing my metaphors, you can be driving a car which is mechanically perfect in every way, yet still make a mistake and have an

** Statement of Recommended Practice

accident. People and policies still need managing. However good the policies are, they don't manage the organisation. You may notice this if something goes wrong and during the discussion afterwards about how it all happened, you hear 'we have a policy about this' or 'our policy on this is clear' or 'so and so didn't follow the correct protocol'. This may be a hint that policies have become a kind of surrogate management tool, a substitute for actually managing people. Policies are *not* a substitute for good management. They are not some kind of comfort blanket. The essential question for you as a trustee is 'Is someone in charge?' The Arabic proverb is apposite: *If I am a prince and you are a prince, who shall steer the donkey?'*

- Finally, and to repeat myself, it is important to maintain a sense of proportion about governance, and not to become obsessed with it to the extent that the charity shrinks from new ideas.

Reporting on governance is almost always done in the form of a chart, usually with colour coding to help the reader. Risks are usually graded in some way. A governance report can accordingly run to a number of pages and leave the reader a little confused. I suggest separating those aspects which are going to plan from those issues where may be some unresolved problems. Using the exception principle, trustees only need to be kept informed of progress with problem issues and to reassured that other matters are all in hand.

Governance and strategy are two issues which trustees need to keep an eye on, which need to be reported to the board in some form but which do not lend themselves to a handful of measures without the risk of distortion. However, separating those matters which are going to plan from those where there may be delays or problems can help focus trustees' minds on things which might need their attention. Do not be beguiled by pages of colourful charts!

Key to this whole issue of governance is trust: that is, you trust your staff to be honest with you and your fellow trustees to tell you if there are mistakes and if (non-trivial) things have gone wrong. As a trustee of a small charity, you are unlikely to experience the sort of scandals we have seen in the national news such as those surrounding the NHS and BBC concerning Jimmy Savile, or the shocking stories in the children's homes in Lambeth which emerged in 2021. There have also been major issues with the terrible treatment of women by some powerful men in the entertainment world. Even so, all these, and other scandals, illustrate one point: these organisations had policies and procedures in place to prevent what went wrong. All the various governors/directors/councillors/trustees would undoubtedly have sat in meetings with risk analyses and governance reports, all carefully marked out as 'high', 'medium' or 'low'. Some may have taken part in governance subcommittees where risks were examined in more detail.

In the book *Catastrophic Failures* by Victor Bignell, Geoff Peters and Christopher Pym,[49] the reasons for the failures they describe are examined in some detail. The ones they examined were of a physical kind, e.g. plane crashes, a railway crossing disaster, Aberfan and such like. Nevertheless, a common feature include human factors, what they term 'message overload', and attitudes. These attitudes include 'fobbing off' complaints from members of the public and outsiders. The message overload is partly behind the emphasis I have placed on the proper and succinct presentation of information in Chapter 6.

What's to be done? What can you do to ensure that, unknown to you and your fellow trustees, there isn't some horror story taking place right under your noses? In Chapter 13 which discusses fraud and similar matters, I have provided several suggestions which are relevant. A particular technique relevant to this problem – if technique be the right word – is what is termed 'management by walking around' (MBWA), although when I checked it is 'wandering' not 'walking'. I just wonder – referring to the various disasters we have seen on the news – whether any of the directors, governors, councillors *et al.* had ever walked (or wandered) around their domains?

I strongly suggest that you devote some time to this activity. In a small local charity, it should not be such a problem. Slightly larger charities may mean more effort. Simply nothing beats going and seeing for yourself. Being visible also helps lower the mystique that can exist between trustees, staff and volunteers. There can be difficulties with charities involved with people – issues to do with confidentiality and sensitivity – which may be tricky to overcome.

In summary, the questions to keep in mind are: is there a system in place, and is it being monitored and reported on? Maintaining a balanced approach and refraining from becoming obsessed with risk avoidance, to the extent of overlooking opportunities and new initiatives, is important. Much of good governance is really good management under a different name. Risks should be managed, not always avoided. Trust is important and you have to trust that you are, or would be, informed of significant breaches. And don't forget MBWA.

DELEGATION

Delegation crops up in several areas of a charity's activities and except for the smallest of organisations, is an essential matter to consider. Some trustees are nervous around this topic since it depends crucially on trust. The board is in essence saying that we the trustees, trust you the CEO and managers of the charity, to carry out a range of activities without seeking our permission each time. The managers will accordingly spend money, recruit staff to a certain level and engage in various other activities without the trustees being aware until after the event if indeed they get to know at all.

The first thing is to develop what is termed a 'scheme of delegation'. Usefully, there are many examples readily available on the internet which will form the basis of your own. You have to decide *what* to delegate and the *level* of delegation especially where money is involved. The more you delegate, the greater the risk of course especially if staff make a bad decision or worse, engage in some kind of fraud. The bad news is that you can never eliminate the risk of bad behaviour or dishonesty and I discuss this further in Chapter 13. This argues for good feedback and information as argued elsewhere in this book.

The scheme of delegation will mean the approach is methodical setting clear limits on what the management can do and what decisions are reserved for the board to take. In practice, if there is good rapport between the chair and the CEO, then spending and recruitment decisions will be regularly discussed and if something comes up that the chair feels the board should know about, it can be arranged accordingly. As so often in life, having a scheme of delegation is a good and prudent thing to do, but maintaining common sense is also important. Sometimes, even quite small expenditures or decisions can have profound effects and despite the scheme of delegation allowing such a decision, informing the board and keeping them in the picture might still be advisable.

A key element both of governance and delegation is information, how it is collected and dealt with. That is the subject of the next chapter.

CHAPTER 6

What's going on?

There you are, at a charity meeting, gazing at the agenda. The question that lurks at the back of your mind is 'What is going on in this charity?' How do I know that it is being run well? What in fact, is actually happening? What are they all doing? Are we still fulfilling a need? The answer to these and other questions is to be found in information. Without appropriate information, provided in a digestible form, you will struggle to understand what is going on and as a result, to make a meaningful contribution as a trustee.

In this chapter I want to explore the role of information in the performance of a charity or not-for-profit organisation and how you, as a trustee, can gain an understanding of what is happening[50]. There will be few people who will not agree that information is a key factor in being able to manage any organisation effectively.[51] Yet getting this information can pose particular difficulties in a small charitable organisation. Unless we, as trustees, get adequate information about what is happening in the organisation, we will not be capable of performing our duties. Despite this, it is surprising that the actual business of acquiring that information rarely gets the attention it requires. Information management is seldom discussed. Information has to be obtained, organised and presented in a way that is timely and makes sense to the recipient. Like other aspects of management, it needs to be thought about and some kind of a plan prepared. If you are already a trustee, think back to your last meeting and ask yourself, how much do you really know about what is taking place in that organisation? Do you know how many staff you have and what the staff turnover is? If the charity is trying to help people, how many recipients are there currently and what are the changes in the numbers over time? On the financial side, is it solvent? In fact, was that actually stated at the meeting? Do you know what the management costs are as a proportion of the income and how that has changed over time? What funding activities have there been and how successful were they? Where are you in progressing the strategy? I suggest that if you think of the organisation you are involved in, it is likely there is a lot you don't know and there may well be many gaps in your knowledge.

As trustees, you will be divorced from the day-to-day running of the charity. Indeed, you may only have contact with it at the trustee meetings which means that the information you receive at those meetings is crucially important. It is vital therefore that what information you should receive, how often, and in what form must be carefully planned. Although a great deal of time is spent on strategic matters, marketing and governance, next to no time is devoted to this topic.

It is likely, however, that some significant changes need to be made to institute an information plan. Systems may need to be set up, staff and volunteers may have to make changes to their methods, and there may need to be an IT upgrade. None of this may be universally popular. If expenditure is needed, there is likely to be a feeling that funds should go to front-line activities rather than being spent on collecting more data. The charity will also have managed for some time – maybe many years – without any need for an 'information plan'. There may be an issue of culture and a feeling that it is not necessary, that the charity is not a business and that it represents a distraction from the 'real' work. A genuine concern is that it is not for trustees to manage the business but to focus on strategic and long-term matters. Increasing the flow of information will invite trustees to become involved in too much detail and to become distracted. This has more than a grain of truth in it. The counter-argument is that if trustees receive good-quality information, in a digestible form, it will provide them with greater confidence that the charity is running well and should *lessen* their propensity to try and 'out-manage' the managers.

Commitment will be crucial, therefore. If there is a reluctance by management or staff – or even both – to develop new methods, then it is unlikely to happen. Or it may happen for a few meetings and then be quietly forgotten. One of the features of people who work or volunteer for charities and NFP organisations is that they want to contribute directly to the fundamental purpose of the organisation.[52] They often wish to help people or the cause in some direct way. They derive satisfaction from personal contact, especially if they have been able to ameliorate someone's problems. Some may have spent a working life subject to targets and performance measures and want to leave all that behind. They do not volunteer to fill in forms. Statements about being very busy or short-staffed often appear to justify resistance to setting up new methods.

So if the trustees seek to introduce systems which take people away from front-line activity and also remind them of what they left behind in their previous occupations, there can be reluctance or even resistance to take part. What is important, therefore – vitally important in fact – is that the purpose of and need for this information is explained. It is likely to involve team sessions where the benefits and purposes can be spelled out and queries answered. In other words, it has to be sold. In these days of IT, the issue of compiling and analysing data should not be a problem. Programs like Excel can perform an enormous amount and take the drudge out of analysis.

It is worth considering the other purposes of assembling good clear information about the charity. Up to now I have concentrated on the need for you, as a trustee, to know what is going on. But the management themselves need to know what is going on, almost certainly in more detail. It is sometimes troubling at a trustee meeting to find that quite simple questions cannot be answered by the managers. There is an important point here: the need for you and your fellow trustees to access information should not be seen as something *you* need divorced from what the *managers* need for themselves. There can be an attitude that it is only the *trustees* who need this information, with the subtext that it is all a bit of a nuisance to put together. 'We are busy doing the real front-line work and we don't have time to spend on assembling all this information *you* want.' But they should be aware of this stuff and acting on it. You might hear the CEO or a manager asking 'What is it *you* [i.e. the trustees] want to know?' The process should be that they are in possession of adequate data and should be sorting, analysing, organising, summarising and sharing it with the trustees as a matter of course.

Although in this chapter, I will talking about what information is needed and how it is presented, in Chapter 7 I will sound a cautionary note about the risks of 'management by numbers'. You cannot manage by numbers any more than you can paint by numbers. Data has a horrible tendency to give people a false sense of certainty, and it can drown out narrative arguments which cannot always be reduced to a set of figures. This is a potential risk of the 'balanced score card' approach which I will discuss in the next chapter. Numbers are important and often essential, but they do not give the whole picture.

What are the benefits? Firstly, the formation of a plan will mean thought has to be given to what information you actually need. It may indeed lead to less than is collected now. Secondly, it will mean managers and trustees having a much better grasp of the essentials of the charity and how it is performing. This may result in a reduction in tension between them, since it is often the case that trustees have a feeling they are not getting the whole picture from the managers or chief executive, a situation which arises because no dedicated thought has been given to the subject. Nobody has specified what they want, leaving a feeling of dissatisfaction. Worse, they may be burdened with masses of information about things they don't really want to know about. This tension where the trustees feel they aren't getting the information they want and the CEO and senior staff wonder what it is you think you want, has often rumbled on in meetings I have attended. Thirdly, it will almost certainly improve the image of the charity with funders and other stakeholders. As an ex-funder myself, it always gives a good impression – in meetings with organisations seeking support – if the representatives have a grasp of the essentials of their organisation.

Another aspect is training. Pressures on charity budgets have been significant in recent years. Austerity has led to reductions in funding by local authorities. Covid-19 meant street collections and public charity events had to be cancelled. One of the things which has suffered is training and this often means that staff may not have the skills to do the necessary legwork in assembling and analysing the data using software. This will clearly be a drag on implementing a new system.

On this subject, and moving forward a bit, once systems are set up it is essential to provide feedback. There is nothing more soul-destroying for staff and volunteers than slogging away providing a sheaf of information and statistics and not hearing anything back about how it was used or what value it had. It adds to the sense of 'I'm wasting my time' and 'I came here to help people, not tot up reams of statistics.' It can also engender a feeling in staff that all anyone wants is numbers and the higher-ups (the management and trustees) are not interested in what the staff do, just how much of it they have done. I will explore these issues in greater depth in the next chapter.

BASIC PRINCIPLES

My car is doing 29 miles to the gallon. This is quite an interesting fact but as a one-off piece of data, it doesn't mean much. If my car had been doing 35mpg, then a drop to 29mpg suggests something to look into. In other words data by itself is of only limited value. It gains value by being set in context, either by reference to a plan or strategy, or by showing trends over time. The key principle is the difference between *data*, *information* and *understanding*. From data, we derive information, which leads to understanding:

Data → Information → Understanding

This is the key objective of the information plan. You may want to refer to reports you have been provided with at or prior to a recent meeting and see how much information was in the form of data. The essentials of an information plan are about securing data, turning it into information, and providing managers and trustees with an understanding of what is happening.

There is often no shortage of data in any organisation, particularly so in these days of computers, laptops and other devices. The problem of course is seeing the wood for the trees. It is an interesting historical point that it was Florence Nightingale who was the first to start presenting statistics in a way that told a story.[53] She invented the 'polar diagram' – which we would today call a pie chart – to show visually the rates of death month by month in the Crimean War and their causes. Her work was written up by Harriet Martineau in a book called *England and Her Soldiers*, published in 1859, and is likely to have influenced some of the social changes that were subsequently introduced. The Army already had the information but it was not presented in a way that told a story or made sense.

A useful analogy to bear in mind is the car dashboard. Typically, the instrument panel provides some basic information about the car and what is going on under the bonnet. This includes the speed the car is going, whether the lights are on, a rev counter and how much fuel there is. If something goes wrong – the oil pressure falls for example – then a warning light comes on. Different cars have different instruments but the principle of simple information about the basics, with warning lights if there is a problem, is a good analogy for what you should be receiving as a trustee of your charity. Good, simple information about the basics, with a report from the management if there are notable departures from normal.

In short, I would argue that many NFP organisations collect too much information, of the wrong kind, and with an absence of information about trends. This is combined with almost no information in some other areas. So in this chapter I want set out some ideas about how a NFP might put together an 'information plan' to help trustees and managers keep on top of the organisation's affairs. The next chapter will add some words of caution concerning some of the difficulties about this process, since it can represent a significant change. This change needs to be managed carefully. But for the moment, I just want to focus on the information gathering and presentation. There will be subsequent chapters on communications and marketing which will follow on logically from this.

Good information has other purposes. It can be reassuring for funders and grant givers if it is obvious that the managers of the charity have a good command of the data. Although most funding decisions are made by electronic application with little if any face-to-face contact, such meetings do sometimes still occur. Questions may be asked about aspects of the bid and, if the representatives are able to give good back-up to support or answer such queries, that can be reassuring.

The information can also be used for publicity and similar purposes. Simple statistics can help give focus to a press release – for example, 'we had our 1000th client this week', 'we raised 20% more this year than last', 'we had record enquiries for our help last month' and so on.

> *We are drowning in information, while starving for wisdom. The world henceforth will be run by synthesizers, people able to put together the right information at the right time, think critically about it, and make important choices wisely.*
> – E.O. Wilson

It is worth spelling out the purpose of the plan:

> The purpose of an information plan is to assemble and present a range of relevant information, providing the management and trustees with a fair view of how the charity is performing, how it is fulfilling its strategic and charitable purpose, and reassuring them of its continued relevance as a charity.

THE SCAPS MODEL

I start with a simple question: what information do we need? A simple enough question, but quite hard to answer and harder still to enact. I want to introduce here the SCAPS model, which will discuss the process involved in the information plan. SCAPS stands for:

1. **S**election
2. **C**ollection
3. **A**nalysis
4. **P**resentation and
5. **S**torage.

These are the elements of an information plan vital for the functioning of your charity.

1. Selection

We start with selection, and these are the basic questions to address:

- What information do you need?
- How often do you need it?
- How accurate should it be?

What information do you need?

Another list, I'm afraid – and the things you need to know as a trustee are:

- Progress with the strategy and work plan
- Staff and volunteer issues
- Client or customer information (if relevant)
- The finances of the charity and its solvency and reserves; also funding
- Some management accounts
- Governance and safe working
- Other (because your particular charity may have special issues).

	Information need	Comment
Strategy	Progress with key issues in the work plan	This is usually – and probably best – done with a chart and using colour to show progress. With a work plan of any length, it is best to group those parts of the plan which have been achieved (green), those which are likely to be achieved (amber), and those which are on course not to be achieved (red) together.
People	• How many staff and volunteers employed • Staff turnover • Sickness levels • Training activities • Vacancies	Staff are a key to almost every organisation and trustees need to keep a close eye on the issue. Staff turnover needs monitoring with exit interviews carried out. Training is not just that which is obligatory, but staff development training as well. This is an area where trustees may need supplementary information and background in addition to the raw data.
Client or customer	• How many are there? • Of what type • Location • Throughput	This is information concerning who or what it is the NFP is trying to help. The questions are examples only. 'Throughput' recognises that for some charities, the amount of time devoted to an individual problem or case can be an important factor.

Fig 2 Information needs (Continued)

	Information need	Comment
Funding and finances	• Sources of funding • Solvency • Reserves • Funding applications and/or fundraising	Funding is one of the key issues and one which gives most charities the greatest headaches. Raising funds is a constant problem. More charities are bidding for a declining amount of cash. Years of austerity have reduced people's propensity and ability to donate. There is also 'fashion' to consider: the public can suddenly get seized by a particular issue and that's where their money goes.
Management accounts	• Ratio of staff costs to income • Cost per day	This will depend on your charity and what some of the critical cost issues are. It is most likely to be staff, but it may be travel or some other factor.
Governance		Similar to the strategy, this will be in chart form and sometimes with colour to help trustees navigate through it. The exception principle is key here – your attention needs to be drawn to those areas which pose particular risk.
Other		Because some charities may have particular issues which they need to monitor closely.

Fig 2 Information needs

Such is the variety of work undertaken by charities that it is impossible to list all the factors that need monitoring. The main issues of management, performance, finance and strategy provide a rubric which will differ in detail terms for each charity.

It is an important part of the charity's management to have a plan which is monitored at least once a year in the light of experience. Any new activities may need to be incorporated. Most charities nowadays have a range of policies which are – or should be – regularly monitored. An information plan should be part of that process.

Equally important in the list above is what is *not* included. You do not need month-by-month figures for stationery expenditure, electricity consumption, detailed wage breakdowns, how much is spent on postage and the like, which can clutter up reports to the board.

How often do you need it?

There is little point in having information if it is not presented and made use of. At the very least, it should be presented to trustees at their regular trustee meetings. This will be the 'high-level' material showing the main areas of activity. Later on I shall give some suggestions of how this might be done. But some information will also likely be needed by the management on a more regular basis, and almost certainly in more detail.

There may be an argument for a regular monthly bulletin with some headline figures for the main areas of interest. This can be important for those trustees whose only contact with the charity is at the quarterly trustee meeting where the full suite of information is presented. To receive a monthly set of perhaps four, five or six pieces of key information keeps them in the picture and maintains the link in a positive way. If the system of collecting is being done regularly in any event, then this will not be a burden on the management team. I cannot provide definite answers to this question because every charity is different – what might be crucial for one is less so for another. I suggest though that the issue of frequency is thought about and built into the plan.

How accurate should it be?

Accuracy is an issue worth devoting some thought to. Anyone reading this with an engineering, technical or similar background will be familiar with tolerances, which specify how accurate one needs to be. Some information needs to be accurate – for example, financial details, wages and tax calculations. Errors here can be important because although they may be small, they might hide much bigger problems and there may even be potential fraud. Getting it wrong can also have repercussions.

Ideally, the information you are getting is perfectly accurate. Unfortunately, this is usually unachievable except at enormous cost in terms of time and effort. Even something as simple as 'How many clients do we have?' can be difficult if a client is dormant for a long time and does not respond to phone or email requests. Volunteers can dip in and out depending on their circumstances and they don't always think to tell you. If they have to go to hospital suddenly, letting your charity know might be the last thing on their mind. So there is inaccuracy inherent in the data.

Some of these errors can be corrected at a subsequent meeting once a fact becomes known. One aspect to bear in mind is that what you are interested in is *change*: the absolute fact may be less important than how much it is changing over time. Some errors can matter less in these cases. Think of your bathroom scales for example. If you are trying to lose weight, then even if the scales are less than accurate, if you weigh five pounds less this week compared to last (hopefully), this tells you what you want to know because the error cancels out.

When figures are presented, they are sometimes given to a needless level of accuracy, especially if percentages or ratios are used. I said above that this is rarely if ever necessary: it is quite spurious and does not help. Other information need not be accurate to the last decimal point. Getting that accuracy can be costly and may not reveal much in any event. It can also take a lot of time, and as Jack L. Warner is quoted as saying, 'I don't want it good, I want it Tuesday.' I myself once heard it said (with a strong New York accent): 'I don't want it perfect, I want it Thursday.' So timeliness is a factor and you do not want to be in a position of not having any information because someone is agonising over a fine detail. We could learn from engineering and other disciplines where they incorporate tolerances into their work, as I said. You do want it to be reliable in the sense that actions may well be taken on the basis of the information presented.

2. Collection

How the information is collected is an important matter. It really is for the management to decide and arrange this and not trustees. However, you do need to be reassured it is being done efficiently. At the beginning of this chapter I said deciding on *what* information you needed was the starting point. The selection process should set out what it is you need to collect and how often. The basis for this is the strategic purpose of the charity. This will be stated in general terms in the memorandum and articles of association and should be fleshed out into a strategy or mission statement of some kind. If your charity is about helping people or animals or the environment, say, then this will dictate the top-line information you will need to collect. You then need operational, managerial and financial information to keep track of how the charity is performing.

For effective functioning, what information is needed and how it is to be collected and processed needs to be thought about at an early stage. There is little point in trying to collect data weeks or months later. That is why having a plan for information is crucial to the success of your charity. Information requirements need to be built into the system as early as possible.

The simplest and most efficient way is using IT. If all staff enter data into a database then the hard work of storage and analysis is largely done for you. Not all charities can afford a specialist or bespoke database, however, so are likely to be using an off-the-peg system or standard packages such as Microsoft Access or similar. That still leaves the question of what information to collect and the actual process of obtaining the data in the first place. The old adage 'garbage in, garbage out' still applies.

For a small charity, not having up-to-date IT or a sophisticated database need not be too much of a problem. There may not in fact be that considerable an amount of data being collected, and doing it manually and transferring it to an Excel spreadsheet may be perfectly adequate if slightly tedious. This program has got more sophisticated over the years and it is relatively simple to create charts, graphs and statistical calculations using it. The Mac equivalent can be used likewise. A quick word here concerning training and the ability of someone to do this work. I have emphasised the importance of information – so, if it is not being produced, you do need to explore the reason. The answer typically is that there is no one familiar with Apple Numbers or Excel, or the person who was has left. I think it essential that you insist that someone is trained to do this and that one day familiarisation courses are readily available. In passing, one of the curiosities of our society is that admitting you cannot read is regarded as shameful: admitting you know nothing of numbers or statistics is often a badge almost of pride.

I also want to stress the importance of simple systems that work, rather than some highly sophisticated one with bells and whistles that works for a while and then doesn't – and nobody knows how to fix it. Many years ago, someone crashed into my car so I went to Winchester hospital to have myself checked out. I needed an X-ray so I was told to follow a painted line on the floor down some corridors from A & E to the imaging department – then follow it back with the film when it was done. Simple, cheap and effective.

With the strategic purpose in mind, you need to work out how the information is to be collected and how frequently. Which will work on a paper-based system and which will be electronic? An issue here is that front-line staff may not be comfortable using a laptop or other electronic device in the presence of a client. It can act as a barrier and people are worried at their information being logged in this way, even though it would be anyway once the member of staff got back to the office. Despite GDPR, people are still nervous.

An additional consideration is volunteers. Many charities have a number of volunteers who are involved in various aspects of the charity and they are going to be involved in the collection of information as well. If you have an IT system with a cost attached to allowing access, giving such access to all your volunteers may be too much especially if the volunteer is only occasionally involved. It may be therefore that they will stick to paper systems or perhaps they will be asked to come to the office periodically to input their data. This might have the advantage of having people around who can help with this task.

In one way or another, you are likely to need forms of some kind. I remember the first time being involved in designing a form and discovering that it is a lot more difficult than I first thought. The arrogance of youth, obviously. The issue which comes up most frequently is definitions and 'What do we mean by … ?' What does 'address' mean when people are moving around a lot or are actually homeless? Even simple words like 'date' can cause great confusion: Date of the meeting? Date when the form was filled in? Today's date? Depending on the activities of your charity, designing a form and making sure you are in a position to collect all the information you need can be quite demanding and, as I have found, a lot more difficult than it first seems. It will need a small team to work through it and to define the questions to ask. Once the form is designed, it needs to be tested in real life. And how many forms have you had to fill in where the address space is tiny and there is half an acre of space for the postcode?

One additional point to keep in mind is data about those people or activities you *cannot* help or have to turn away. This can be important if, for example, an opportunity arises to seek additional funding. Knowing how many people you *weren't* able to help can be a really useful statistic. It can just be from phone calls and/or people calling in at the office if you have that kind of set-up. It can provide you with an estimate of the size of the problem you are not currently able to tackle.

Periodically, there is a need to audit the system. There are two main aspects to focus on. The first are system issues. Are the questions still relevant in view of changed circumstances? Do we need to add some additional questions in view of those changes, or abandon some which are no longer necessary? The second thing to look at is the accuracy of what is being collected. In my experience, there is no simple answer to this. You need to look for gaps, inconsistencies or things just not looking right. If one member of staff is reporting x for example, and another member of staff – doing essentially the same piece of work – is reporting 5 times x, then it would be worth exploring why. Generally, asking questions together with some gentle probing usually brings up a range of issues great and small. It is also worth looking at the database and any files.

In the next chapter I shall discuss the human aspects of this together with the issue of qualitative information as well.

Security also needs to be borne in mind, particularly GDPR. Homeworking also increasingly needs to be thought about. If the information is at all sensitive, then it's essential to ensure staff and volunteers working from home do not leave their PCs, laptops, etc. accessible to prying eyes – not forgetting that teenagers are both curious and very tech-savvy these days!

So although trustees should not be involved in the mechanics of the collection process, you do need to be sure the process has been thought about and things like security, IT and training have been considered by the management.

3. Analysis

The main theme at the start of this chapter was the principle of data leading to information and hence to understanding. There are many definitions for analysis but for our purposes, I suggest the following four are relevant:

- Combining information to help with understanding
- Showing trends and changes over time
- Linking information to what was planned in the work plan and strategy
- Generally, trying to make sense of the information collected

There are two basic aims involved. The first is to achieve as much simplicity as possible. It should not be necessary, in most instances, to provide huge amounts of information to achieve understanding. Secondly, adhering to the exception principle. If things are going to plan then all that may be needed is a note to that effect. Sometimes there is a kind of habit, or a belief that the 'board needs to know this', leading to a great sheaf of data when all that is required is to say 'things are going to plan' and a brief summary. There is also a human desire – of which many of us are guilty, I suspect – to produce as much information as possible for our bosses to show how busy we are.

Trends and changes

One aspect of the analysis is the need to show *trends*. If the core purpose of your charity is helping people in some way, telling the trustees that X were helped in the last quarter or month is not, by itself, conveying much information. In most meetings of such organisations which I have attended or seen minutes for, the information is often descriptive – that is, reports from the chief executive and possibly another manager – and then there are minutes of the previous meeting and reports from subcommittees which again, are mostly descriptive. Financial information is often presented in a spreadsheet form with columns showing months and a list of expenditure items down the side. There are usually columns showing the budget figures and an adjacent column showing the current situation. Rarely are there any percentages. There is usually a lot of extraneous information such as how much is being spent on the electricity month by month or on office supplies likewise. Whilst this information is of value, the missing element is often how things are *changing* over time. All through the Covid pandemic, we were given graphs of death and infection rates and latterly, the number of people who were being inoculated. The daily numbers – apart from being shocking in themselves – did not mean much; what mattered was the trend in death rates and so on which were displayed in the form of graphs. It was this trend information which enabled us to see how things were changing: getting worse at the start and getting better as time went on.

A useful thing to include is the *same* month/quarter in the previous year. This can help iron out seasonal factors which can affect numbers in all sorts of ways (weather, holidays, Christmas and so on). It also provides a year-on-year insight as to what is happening.

By providing a series of figures over several months or quarters, changes can be seen. Using graphs is also a good idea – easily done with modern IT. Another useful tool is the humble percentage. It is surprising that percentages are not more often used, especially with financial information.

Exception principle

In a similar vein, the exception principle is worth bearing in mind. The idea is that if things are going to plan, then only matters which represent a serious deviation from the strategy need to be reported in any depth to the trustees. This helps remove a lot of clutter from reports and data. If we planned to do X and we have done X (plus or minus a small variation), then it is not necessary to spend much if any time on it.

Change

Before looking in more detail at the information plan, it needs to be recognised that it may in all likelihood involve change in some form or other. This is not just the actual information that is collected, but a change in attitudes and even in culture. Staff may have been presenting information in a certain way for a long time. Agendas tend to get repeated ad infinitum without anyone really thinking about what is needed. Habits have been formed and can be deeply ingrained. There will be people who have come from other organisations who have also done it that way and they may be reluctant to change. Some of the ideas I have put forward here can seem, at first glance, to be radical and likely to involve a lot of time and effort – time the charity does not have. I am not going to deny time is needed, but unless your charity is almost bereft of information, it will involve adjustments rather than major upheaval.

The information also has to be collected and organised. Where organisations have good systems – whether IT or paper-based – this may not be a problem. But many do not and may require changes to systems or the introduction of new ones. This can be difficult and time consuming. If it involves altering or buying new IT software, it can be expensive as well. So there has to be commitment from the trustees and senior management to make it happen. There is likely to be need of budgetary provision. This commitment will come if the trustees are convinced that they need this information and are perhaps nervous that they are not on top of what is going on. People buy things because of the benefits they will gain. They buy a washing machine because it will do the washing and save time. So it is with the system I propose: it will give them the information they need to feel confident as a trustee that they are on top of things.

Ownership

It is important that the information presented is 'owned' by the chief executive. I go back to the point I made earlier: the managers need the information to manage the charity effectively. You are being provided with a summary focusing on the key issues as discussed above. Now clearly, a senior manager or chief executive cannot be expected to know everything or to anticipate every question a trustee might ask them. But there should be good evidence that they are aware of the information presented, know something of the background and can answer most of the questions asked.

4. Presentation

How information is presented is truly important and is worth spending time on. The use of charts and graphs is to be encouraged to give a visual feel of what the data is telling you. Under 'presentation' I want to mention ensuring you have the information for a board meeting around a week before the actual meeting. There can be reasons why a report has to be tabled at the meeting – something last minute, illness or some other event – but this should be the exception.

With computer programs such as Microsoft Excel or Apple Numbers, producing charts in various forms is relatively easy nowadays. However, I have sometimes been given reports filled with numerous charts spreading rather like a rash. Not all sets of numbers can usefully be turned into a chart. The important point is what is the author trying to convey by using a chart? What are they trying to make you understand? By providing a chart, what is the point that is being put across? As the Cambridge University statistician Professor David Spiegelhalter has explained, 'numbers don't speak for themselves' – you have to tell a story about them. Just turning numbers into a chart does not by itself convey any extra information or indeed, any information at all.

Underlying the presentation of information to the board is the principle of trying to inform them on the state of the charity and what is going on. You are trying to increase your understanding of what is happening and the progress made in delivering the strategy.

Rather than spend a huge amount of time on this topic I think it best to produce examples, and these can be found in Appendix C.

5. Storage

Storage of information is something that doesn't often receive the attention it deserves. What's at stake? Firstly there are likely to be some legal requirements concerning how long some information has to be archived. Secondly, you need to be able, from time to time, to access historical information. This means a filing system – electronic or otherwise – which is logical and understood by all.

A not unusual problem is information stored on someone's machine that only he or she knows how to access. They leave and a whole mass of material suddenly becomes effectively inaccessible. I have had experience of this recently when an accountant left and gaining access to the system to find out what was happening took his successor quite some time. It is becoming less of a problem now with cloud systems but it still needs thinking about.

A similar problem is someone who decides to set up a kind of maverick filing system with a private system of file names and folders. Not only is this bad practice – preventing colleagues in a networked system from gaining access (which might in fact be the reason) – but if and when they leave, there is a major headache in finding out what has been done and locating things like meeting notes and so forth.

I have mentioned elsewhere the importance of learning from events and things you have done as a charity. I have lost count of the number of times in work situations where it is decided to run a similar event a year or two years later only to find the papers are nowhere to be found. The person who ran it has left and the experience gained from last time is no more.

Security is clearly an issue, especially concerning client files and GDPR. But it also matters because of hacking and the introduction of malware and the like. Your system is only as strong as its weakest link and it only needs one member of staff to violate the protocols for serious damage to be done. In one local authority position I had, a member of staff wrought havoc that resulted in a bill of around £30,000 of a consultant's time to put right. So mistakes can be costly. You need also to alert to the recent and dramatic rise in Ransomware where hackers lock computers and the victims have to pay large sums to gain access to them.

I do not suggest, once again, that trustees get involved in the minutiae of storage. You do need to be satisfied that there is a system in place, as part of the information plan, that there are file protocols being followed by all staff, and that there is a policy in place to ensure that security is being followed by all staff and volunteers. Not forgetting, of course, back-up in case of emergency.

Files may need to be weeded from time to time. An office can quickly fill up with paper files even in these days of electronic storage. It is worthwhile setting aside some time, early in the New Year perhaps if things are quiet then, to spend time going through files and getting rid of things like drafts, inconsequential emails and routine correspondence. Client files may need to be kept for a specific period of time and then securely destroyed. Tax and financial information needs to be kept for several years. It needs a protocol and some time set aside for routine housekeeping.

One final point. From time to time, a charity might want historical information – at a significant anniversary for example. This can be a time for celebration and an opportunity for some PR in the local media: 'Local charity celebrates twenty years of helping …' and such like. It can be surprisingly difficult finding this historical information, especially as the decades slip by. The 'memory' of the charity can disappear with the staff over time. I suggest therefore setting up a 'history file' either physically or online. This need only be a one-page summary of the year showing various pieces of information at the start and at the finish. For example, for each year you note: income, staff and volunteer numbers, where you operate from, any significant events, how many people (if it is people) you helped, income for the year, who the CEO was and who the trustees were. If, as you hope, the charity survives, then this file can become a useful source of what went before and a basis for articles and stories.

In this chapter I have tried to set out the importance of information and that as a trustee, it will be difficult to see what is happening unless you have the right sort of information presented in a clear and digestible way. You need to have a plan for what information is vital for your charity, and this will have four main components: management, regulatory, performance and external factors. In this chapter I have focused on management and performance. In addition to the information plan itself, attention needs to be paid to the collection and storage of the data, how accurate it needs to be, and how often and in what form it is presented.

In the next chapter I want to look at the more qualitative aspects of information.

CHAPTER 7

Information problems

The previous chapters discussed the importance of information and discussed methods of obtaining, handling and presenting it to the trustees among others. In this chapter I am going to discuss some of the problems and issues which can arise.

The first point to repeat is that you can no more manage by numbers than you can paint by numbers. One can count the notes, measure the length and weigh the score of a Mozart symphony (No. 40 in G Minor is my favourite by the way) but it will never convey to you the ineffable beauty of the music. There are many things such as the enjoyment of fine art, music, a splendid view or a poem, where the pleasure cannot be measured or counted. Although information is vital as I have discussed, it is not the be-all and end-all of managing an organisation, and relying just on numbers is likely to lead to significant problems.

Problems come in two forms. Firstly, *qualitative* information is of great importance as well as *quantitative*. Secondly, in the context of a charitable organisation in particular, there can be problems with staff attitudes. Simply put, people join a charity to help people or to be of use, not to collect and sort statistics. They can regard that activity as largely useless and burdensome (sometimes with good reason) and it takes them away from what they see as the main purpose of the charity, which is helping. So one way or another, staff attitudes need recognising as a potential problem and managing.

Numbers can acquire an importance beyond their actual merit. They can seem exact when they are not. They can be based on assumptions which are erroneous thus making the whole edifice shaky or just plain wrong. Scientists writing academic papers learn to be very careful over the presentation of statistics. They quote sample sizes, give confidence levels and are concerned about matters such as consistency and validity. This is not common in numerical information presented at organisational meetings. Beyond the occasional 'average' it is unusual to see reference to other statistical techniques. This leads to data being presented with a level of accuracy it does not merit. On the question of averages, the average number of legs that people have is 1.97. This is because most have two legs, some have one and a few none at all. It just goes to show the perils of averages.

Quantitative information has to be viewed with caution, therefore, and care taken to ensure it does not crowd out or overshadow qualitative material and reports. Some writers giving advice mention the 'balanced score card' approach and this will enable a proper balance of information – numeric or otherwise – to be presented. There is a growing literature online about this technique. In simple terms it is presenting a range of information in an organised way to give managers a holistic view of the state of the charity. It is built around the elements of finance, process, learning and development, and the client group. The success of the technique will depend on selecting the right elements to measure and report on. Its origins are in the commercial world and its advocates suggest it is a means to show how efficient a charity is. Doubts have been expressed about this view.[54]

Staff attitudes have to be carefully considered and as with any change to organisational procedures, explanation or training may be required. As I have said above, there can be some reluctance to spend time garnering data as it can be seen as a distraction from what is perceived as the main purpose of the charity, which is to help those in need or to pursue a cause.

One immediate problem is that presenting information is often vital for the charity as a whole if it is to secure funds. Funders of more or less any kind – whether it be the public or a funding organisation such as a local authority or the Lottery – want to see some evidence of what has been achieved. This can be expressed as 'outcomes' or 'outputs' and both will involve collecting and assembling data. As far as trustees and the management are concerned, this is a vital and important task. Worries of a shortfall in what was promised can involve anxious discussion at meetings. The staff on the ground on the other hand, those actually engaged in the front-line activities, are likely to be far removed from these discussions and may not see them as so important. For them, the task in hand is the key issue, not assembling data and information on what they do.

If the current system is inadequate or deficient then radical change is likely to be necessary. Those charities which have been in existence some while are likely to have slipped into a way of doing things which can be difficult to change. Meetings of trustees can follow a familiar routine with only minor changes to the agenda from one to the next. Much of the reporting can be in narrative form, especially by managers and the chief executive. Where numbers appear, they can refer only to the immediate past – i.e. the last quarter if it's a quarterly meeting – without any comparative analysis to see how things are changing. Ratios and percentages may be completely absent, which can make trying to understand the numbers difficult. Financial information can contain a lot of extraneous detail. Changing this will be a challenge.

Not only will staff and trustee attitudes have to change, but there are likely to be procedural, administrative and IT changes as well.

IT skills in small charities are patchy and with shortages of funds, training staff is often seen as an unaffordable luxury. So all told, establishing a new system will take a lot of effort and persuasion.

Where to start? A good place is to explain the *benefits* of the proposed changes. If it is just seen as an exercise in rather pointless number collection, then progress is unlikely to be achieved. It might be worth pausing here and describing why people buy goods and services. It is fairly well established that people buy things because of a perceived or actual benefit to them and the life they lead. A washing machine is purchased because it does the washing and saves a lot of time. I am old enough to remember washday, which was a major exercise involving boiling water, tongs and a mangle which I used to help my mother turn. My grandmother spent all day Monday in the washhouse at the back of their cottage in Cheshire. Younger people don't know what they're missing (I suspect they may not know what a 'mangle' is!).

We buy clothes to look good in and perhaps impress others or even to attract the opposite sex. We buy a car for a range of reasons including speed, reliability, colour and so on. Possibly to impress others as well.

So it is with introducing a better system of reporting. How will the charity, its staff and its management benefit from the changes? And you do have to convince both. This is vital. If the staff aren't convinced, then resistance or foot-dragging will take place and it might happen for a while before the excuses pile in and the scheme is abandoned. If your fellow trustees aren't convinced, it won't get off the ground: likewise the senior management. So explaining the benefits is the clear first step. What are the benefits? There are several:

- It will provide better confidence in the progress and performance of the charity. Reports will be better grounded – that is, instead of just being a narrative account – and they will be supported by actual data or numerical information.

- Trustees will have greater confidence in the management of the organisation and will have a greater understanding of what is going on.
- Funders will have more confidence.
- You will have a source of useful data for annual reports, press releases and publicity.

Information is not only of significance to the internal management of the organisation but for the outside world as well. The Charity Commission has commented on a need for a:

> *step change in trustees' attitudes to public benefit reporting. It is disappointing that nearly half of charities fail to explain the activities they undertake and the impact they have. We want to see charities thrive, so charities need to be clearer about who they help and what difference they are making.*

This is significant for the charity's marketing, its 'presence' which I will be discussing later on, its brand and the impact it makes generally.

***

What then are the key issues you as a trustee should pay attention to in connection with information? I suggest the following ten points as a summary of this and the previous chapter:

1. The fundamental importance of information should be accepted and understood by your fellow trustees and the management of the charity.
2. There should be an *information plan* built around the SCAPS model: Selection, Collection, Analysis, Presentation and Storage.

3. The plan should, in part, reflect and report on the strategy.
4. The *benefits* and *value* of good information should be explained to all concerned, especially to staff and volunteers.
5. Staff involved in the information plan should have the necessary tools (IT principally) and training to enable them to do the work easily.
6. The information the board of trustees receives should be much the same as the information the management itself needs to manage the organisation. It should not be seen as something extra.
7. The information should show *trends* over time, not just a snapshot.
8. Although numbers are an important part of any plan, *qualitative* information should be part of the plan where necessary.
9. Those contributing the information should be recognised and thanked for their contributions. There has to be feedback and staff need to be told if their information was acted upon – and if not, why not?
10. Not to forget the exceptions principle: if things are going to plan, they may not need that much reporting on.

WHAT INFORMATION?

Before we discuss the 'how', we need to consider 'what' information we are going to need. There is a lot of literature about 'balanced score cards' as a means to present information to a board in a coherent way. This idea was promoted in the *Harvard Business Review* in 1992 by Kaplan and Norton,[55] and although others discussed similar ideas, they are usually credited with the concept in its present form. A business might consider financial stewardship; customer and stakeholder matters; internal processes and organisational capacity; and the encouragement of a learning culture. It is easy to see the similarities with the first paragraph of this chapter. The idea is to see, in one place, a kind of map or summary of the performance of the organisation and to link this to its strategy. As you might expect, since 1992, the idea has been refined, developed and altered and there are now a host of different models. The idea, however, that there is going to be a model that will comprehensively and completely demonstrate to trustees how the charity is performing is almost certainly chimerical. Looking at the various iterations of the basic idea is to see increasing complexity in attempts to cover all the angles.

I think there are several problems with the BSC method and its application to a charity organisation:

- Firstly, the problem of defining or articulating quite what 'success' means. This is more easily defined in a business environment where a range of measures such as profitability, return on capital employed and market share all give a sound view of the progress of the business. True, Kaplan and Norton's *Harvard Business Review* article added other measures, namely internal factors, innovation and learning, and customer perspectives, but the core is financial performance. None of these measures has significance for a charity and since, as has been said, the ultimate success of a charity is to work itself out of existence, growth and similar ideas have limited salience.

  I was discussing homelessness with a senior officer in a local authority. They had a programme of monitoring the homeless in their area and were confident they knew who most of them were and where they spent the night. They liaised with various charities to ensure they were looked after reasonably well and secured other funding as well. They felt they were doing as best they could with the funds and resources at their disposal. In terms of efficiency and morality, they would probably regard their programme as a 'success'. The word got round, however, that if you came to their area you would be looked after reasonably well and the number of homeless people began to grow. How does one regard this in success terms, therefore? A commercial firm would be delighted if word got round and more customers appeared to buy its product or service. A local authority, on the other hand, will see increasing demand as pressure on its budget. 'Success' in this example is a double-edged sword. Success was making the problem worse.

- Measuring results is also a problem. A perennial criticism of charities is that they are weak at explaining what they have achieved or what outcomes they have. This may in part just be due to poor management or record-keeping, but it may also be because what you can measure is not wholly relevant to the problem the charity is dealing with. For example, a food bank charity can say how many clients it has, how much food was given out and how many centres it operates. But what effect is it having on food poverty? In other words it can measure 'outputs' easily enough, but outcomes? A related problem is that it is often the case that those being helped by various charities live chaotic lives. Filling in forms and returning documents is not always their forte.
- Another danger is focusing on the quantitative over the qualitative. Having a set of numbers might seem like the Holy Grail for the trustees, enabling them to cast their eyes over a table of information – a bit like looking at a set of dials and flashing lights on a machine's control panel. This is sometimes called the 'McNamara fallacy' or the 'quantitative fallacy' after the American Secretary of Defense during the Vietnam War. The fallacy was in believing that a collection of metrics told

you whether you were winning the war (or not, in the case of Vietnam). Success or otherwise for a charity is a lot more ephemeral and nuanced and accordingly, harder to define. I would go further and say there is a risk of being misled by quantitative measures alone.

- I have discussed at length in Chapter 6 that things like trends are important, more so than single data points. Some of the examples I have seen suggested for a charity BSC are strong on a selection of single measures. Sometimes, a single measure is all you need – the level of reserves for example – but in other cases you need to see what is happening over time.
- The diversity of charities poses problems. There are essentially two basic types: those who campaign and those who provide services. One could argue a third type: those who do both. There are large charities with resources of millions of pounds and a national or international scope, down to the great majority of small local organisations (for whom this book is intended). As was said in the introduction, not all organisations are actual 'charities' or even registered at all. This makes putting together a single BSC to fit all this diversity difficult.
- Perhaps the biggest danger is giving a sense of completeness. Assembling a score card of data – resembling, as I said above, a set of dials on a machine control panel – can lull trustees into thinking that they are in control and seeing the whole picture. The problem is that so many aspects of a charity's success (however it is defined and being careful not to fall into my own trap) are matters of judgement. How is it perceived, what is its image, how strong is its brand, how flexible is it to changing circumstances, is it still fulfilling a need? These are some of the matters that can determine a charity's success or continued existence, and they are not easily reduced to a single metric.

That is not to say however that we need to abandon the exercise altogether. We just need to keep in mind that understanding how your charity is performing is a complex matter and the 'What do we mean by … ?' factor is a significant one.

The value of a reporting process is threefold. Firstly, it does provide trustees with the fundamental information concerning the performance of the charity. It is not the whole story but it will certainly be a good start. Secondly, it helps managers organise their information in a systematic and holistic way. This links of course to the information plan I discussed in an earlier chapter. Thirdly, it will help the charity in negotiations with funders by adding credibility. They will always ask themselves, 'If we fund this charity, will they do what they say they'll do and will they be able to evidence that to us?' As an ex-funder myself, I know this is one of the questions you have in the back of your mind in discussions with someone seeking funding for a project. If they are able to answer reasonable performance questions at interview, this does add to their credibility and does give you greater confidence.

STRATEGY

The chief concern here is how the charity is performing against the strategic objectives as set out in the strategic plan. This is likely to have been refined into a work plan and typically these are structured over a year (sometimes they are for longer periods but updated annually). You are actually looking at the progress with the work plan itself. It is not unusual for work plans to slip quietly out of view as the year progresses and no mention of them to be made at board meetings. This is partly due to pressing concerns of the moment. Board meetings focus on the here and now and strategic matters can just get pushed aside.

A key role for the board is to maintain a focus on strategic matters, so it is important to keep the strategy under review and to receive regular updates on progress. The work plan is likely to be a reasonably lengthy document and run to several pages. A 'traffic light' or other colour-coded system is quite usual, showing item by item what progress has been made. The problem though is that if the work plan is six pages long, say, then the board is presented with a kaleidoscope of words and colour which ends up being difficult to take in. These are some suggestions to make the process a little easier:

- Ensure that as far as possible, the work plan is SMART,* – that is, the tasks are well defined; if possible, measurable; and have milestones. Also avoid vagueness such as 'improve' or 'increase'. These end up being meaningless since it only takes one of something to claim an increase.
- The tendency is to report against the work plan *as it was written*. This means as progress is made in certain parts and not in others, it becomes difficult to absorb with red, amber and green squares all over the place. Far better is to bring those elements not being achieved (those in red if you are using the traffic light system) to the top followed by the amber projects and finally, the green ones which have been achieved. This will effectively bring the chart down to one or two pages and focus attention on those matters where progress is not being made. Chief executives might wish to reverse this order on the understandable reasoning that what *has* been achieved risks being overlooked! Fine, but grouping them does still make sense.

---

* Specific, Measurable, Achievable, Realistic, Timebound

- It might be tempting to suggest selecting a handful of tasks to focus attention on, thus reducing the work plan to manageable proportions. I do not recommend this. Too often have I seen selected targets (or objectives or whatever they might be called) receiving the attention and others being neglected. Remember Goodhart's law: when a measure becomes a target, it ceases to become a good measure. It is an example of where the BSC method can come adrift.

In this chapter I have emphasised that not everything can be reduced to numbers and that qualitative information is just as important. Keeping it simple, or KISS – Keep It Simple Stupid – is key. If you get information overload you end up not noticing what is important. You should encourage staff to give you the basics and to explain, either at the meeting or in a narrative note, reasons for significant differences or departures from what was planned. As far as possible, link it to the work plan or strategy.

SWOT

Sharp-eyed readers will have noticed that I have got some way into the book without discussing SWOT which, for those unfamiliar with this acronym, stands for Strengths, Weaknesses, Opportunities and Threats. It is a widely used technique and appears in just about every management textbook. I have to say straight away that I am not a huge fan of this, particularly its use with charitable and not-for-profit organisations.

It appears to have emerged in America in the 1950s, although quite who first developed the idea is uncertain. Some say it was in the Lockheed Corporation, others Harvard University. It is part of the strategic planning process and its use in commercial organisations is widespread. There are problems, however, and its use in not-for-profits serves, I would argue, as an example of a technique useful in the commercial world being transferred to the not-for-profit environment without any real thought being given to its relevance. My doubts are based around the following issues:

- It depends a lot on 'What do we mean by… ?' and the quality of information available to those doing the exercise. In the competitive commercial world, a word like 'threat' has great meaning and salience. 'Strengths' are easier to gauge in terms of profits, return on capital, intellectual capital, market share and so forth. I am not so sure that these are so easy to assess for a charity, and they are likely to be largely subjective.
- Charities are not in a competitive environment in quite the same way as commercial firms. They are competing for funds and attention but are not engaged in direct competition with other charities. Other differences were discussed in Chapter 3.
- I also have misgivings about 'opportunities' in a non-commercial environment. For a business it means an opportunity to expand the business in some way – for example a new product, or a new market to exploit – with a view to increasing profits or market share. A charity is more about responding to a need and I suspect most working in the sector do not view increasing homelessness, drug addiction or social deprivation as 'opportunities'. I do accept that there may be opportunities to diversify.
- The charity may have many strengths – capable staff, good flow of income, healthy reserves – so lots to put in that box. But is it fulfilling its fundamental purpose? I question whether a charity with lots of 'strengths' necessarily means it is putting those strengths to a good purpose. There is no automatic connection between the two.

- The process forces you to put something in one box when in reality, things might be a bit more nuanced. Is safeguarding, for example, a threat or an opportunity? For the vulnerable it is a potential benefit. For a charity it will require more awareness and training of staff, but where would you put it?
- It does not set priorities. The exercise often generates a mass of suggestions and comments, but it does not facilitate analysing and selecting which options to focus on.

I have taken part in exercises using SWOT – it is popular with trainers, consultants and course leaders – but my colleagues and I have not always found them to be of that much value. Arguments quickly develop about what the various terms mean in the context of a not-for-profit organisation. We end up with a flip chart covered in lots of Post-it notes which don't actually lead anywhere.

I have to say in all fairness, however, that there are many who are keen on the concept and an internet search brings up many pages of advice built around it. Perhaps recasting the matrix around elements such as Purpose, Capabilities, Change and Perceptions might be more appropriate for exercises of this nature in a not-for-profit setting. I have also come across SOAR: Strengths, Opportunities, Aspirations and Results.

CHAPTER 8

Finance

I will move now from information to another key area of interest for trustees, and that is finance. Finance is a key part of a trustee's responsibilities and for many, I suspect, the one that gives them the most anxiety and concern – assuming, that is, they do not have an accountancy background. Some of this concern derives from a sense that they are not qualified enough to question what is put before them, combined with feeling a little baffled by all the numbers. Some trustees will ask a few token questions about some particular figures but often, this part of the meeting can pass by with little discussion. In this chapter then, I want to try and explain what is going on and to try and arm you with some pointers to help you perform this particular element of being a successful trustee.

For the vast majority of charities, there are few problems. They have a competent and honest accountant, who produces the correct figures and who keeps the financial ship afloat. At the end of the year, auditors (if the charity is large enough to require auditing) pick up on a few points, ask some questions which might require minor adjustments; otherwise everything is satisfactory and there is no cause for concern. From time to time, however, problems do crop up and when they do, they can have quite dramatic effects, even causing the demise of the charity. So it is important, as a trustee, to keep a close eye on the financial affairs. Although rare, in the worst case, a trustee can become personally liable.

In Chapter 13, there will be some discussion about issues of fraud and dishonesty.

The Charity Commission provides copious guidance on the role and duties of a trustee. It can be quite forbidding and runs to around fifty pages. A lot is about the proper management of the charity's funds and requiring a trustee to act prudently and with reasonable care and skill. You must comply with the law. It is also important to avoid, wherever possible, exposing the charity's assets to undue risk. You must be clear about the powers the charity has and what it can and cannot do. You must also be clear about its purpose. It is required reading for a new trustee but I would urge you not to be put off by the seemingly relentless list of strictures. I would suggest keeping them in mind and referring to them from time to time or when a particular problem emerges. The Commission has to offer comprehensive guidance.

I will start with a basic principle concerning information which I have already discussed in Chapter 7. This concerns the key distinction between data and information. There is often plenty of data but this is not always turned into useful information. From information comes understanding:

Data → Information → Understanding

This is never more relevant than with accountancy information. With accountancy, the problem can be a surfeit of information rather than a dearth. It is particularly important that, as a trustee, you are gaining an *understanding* of what is happening. If you feel baffled by all the figures, having made reasonable efforts to understand them, then something is wrong. It is not helped by the fact that, quite correctly, the accountant does not feel it is his or her duty to tell you what to do. Their duty is to present the numbers and explain the current financial situation. It is for you as trustees to take the relevant corrective action if this is what is needed. If you and your fellow trustees do not grasp what is happening, then serious mistakes can occur. It is important to stress, however, that there are two parties to understanding: the accountant in presenting the financial information in an understand*able* form and the trustees in trying to gain an understand*ing*.

The basic principles outlined in the previous two chapters are the same and the SCAPS model applies. It is about selecting what financial information is needed, collecting and analysing it, presenting it in a digestible form and finally storing it securely. Most of this chapter will concentrate on the 'P' element – presentation – since this is where many of the problems in terms of trustee understanding arise. It will also discuss the first 'S' element as well – selection – because presenting management accounts is just as important as presenting financial ones.

A lot will depend on how the accounts are presented, and there are rules laid down by the Charity Commission about what accounts are needed for what charity depending on its size. So minimal accounts are needed for the very small organisation with income of less than £10,000 per annum, and there are other rules at £250,000 and at over £1m. Even a charity with an income of over a million can still be a small charity in terms of its size and number of staff. Statement of Recommended Practice (SORP) rules set out how the accounts should be handled. Many accountants use accountancy packages nowadays, which do a lot of the heavy lifting for them. The danger is when the rules of how accounts are presented act to confuse rather than elucidate.

It is likely you will need *management* accountancy information *in addition* to the *financial* accounts to enable you to get a good understanding of what is happening. Financial accounts are for the whole charity, whereas management accounting looks more closely at performance issues within the organisation. You need both to gain an understanding of the financial affairs of the charity. This does *not* mean a huge increase in the amounts of detail such as what is spent month by month on particular costs, e.g. phone bills, postage and stationery, electricity and so on – which I have experienced as a trustee. This can lead trustees to dive into the fine detail and engage in rather pointless debates about these costs. Remember: you are not managing the charity but acting as its custodian.

Where to start? Preparing the budget for the year ahead will follow the work you will have done on the strategy. This answers the questions: Where are we now? Where do we want to be (in a year, say)? How do we get there and what will it cost? This will set out what the charity hopes to do and this process was discussed in Chapter 4. Results from the current year will inform this process and might for example lead the trustees to decide to spend more on fundraising or on aspects of marketing. They may want to research forming a partnership with another charity in the area. They might decide to upgrade the charity's IT or to spend more on training its staff or volunteers. Whatever they decide will form the basis of the budget for the year. I have argued elsewhere that change is ever present in our lives, so if it is proposed to simply carry forward last year's budget with just some adjustment for inflation, then you should be suspicious. This is not a recipe for long-term success.

The question for you is: how do I keep track of what is going on financially? This is in fact both simple and very difficult. In researching this question, it is apparent that considerable guidance is available from the Charity Commission – as previously mentioned – together with a number of accountancy firms who offer help as well. Almost all of it is directed at an accountancy audience and very little is directed at what trustees should look out for. I suspect that if you followed the same trail as I did, your head will spin from the pages of sometimes quite complex or detailed advice. You will not be preparing the accounts yourselves but you do need to be in a position to ask sensible questions, and you do need to be on the lookout for fraud or other malfeasance. So I will try and discuss what you need to consider and be aware of.

WHAT YOU NEED TO KNOW

What are the key things to be aware of and to look out for as a trustee in relation to the finances of the charity? Starting with content:

- Firstly, it is vital to check that the accounts are prepared to a standard required by the Commission and by HMRC (if there is tax to pay). This will depend on the size of the charity and there is copious advice available to help you. If you have a qualified accountant and an auditor then it is highly likely that this is being done correctly. In smaller charities without this level of professional help, it may not be.
- You must receive regular reports on the financial affairs of the organisation (consisting of what, I will come to below). This usually means on a quarterly basis, although some charities meet every other month.
- Financial information should be available before the meeting, not just presented at the meeting itself. This will give time for trustees to peruse it and hopefully, understand what the situation is. It is not satisfactory or good practice for reports, financial or otherwise, to be tabled at the meeting itself, except in exceptional circumstances.
- It is likely that the figures will be presented by the accountant but that does not absolve the CEO from knowing what's happening. It is not acceptable for the accountant to make a statement of some kind, or point out a problem, and for the

CEO to declare, or act, as though that is the first they've heard of it. At the very least it implies there is a communication problem. The CEO has overall responsibility and having a grasp of the financial affairs is a key part of the role.

- The accountant should present key financial statements. What level of detail will depend on the size of the charity, as has been said: the smallest need only have an income and expenses statement as they may have no assets beyond cash in the bank. But a charity of any significant size, one with an office and employees for example, will need more than the basics. The essentials are:
  - An income statement
  - A balance sheet
  - A cash flow statement
  - Statement of reserves

  One of the differences between a charity and a commercial firm is that some of the income it receives is 'restricted'. This might be because it has been given a grant or funds that cannot be used for general expenses, but only on a specific project. It is important to recognise this because at first sight, a charity may have a lot of income and look on the face of it, to the untutored eye, to be financially healthy. But if a lot of the funding is restricted in some way, should problems occur, then those funds may have to be repaid (clawed back).
- A cash flow statement is not always a regular feature in the presentation of accounts to small charities. This is to be regretted since a charity (and other organisations) can be doing quite well but can become vulnerable if it runs out of cash. The organisation has to remain solvent, and to carry on operating whilst insolvent is a crime. It can lead to trustees becoming personally liable. You do need to keep a close watch on this matter

and if a cash flow problem emerges, you may need professional advice from a specialist. The NCVO site has guidance on this. I would add that there is a kind of 'psychological trap' which is important to be aware of. If your charity is engaged on expanding its activities, there is a strong feeling that things are going well. Extra staff might be recruited, a new office may be being opened and there is a general feeling of excitement. It is during this activity that cash flow problems can conceivably crop up. Essentially, it is because money is going out before the income comes in. Additional costs are also being incurred (new IT or extra staff for example). You need therefore to be on guard that the excitement of the growth in activity does not result in the cash situation being overlooked. Another factor about cash flow problems is the suddenness of their occurrence and how little time there can be to do anything about them. In *The Sun Also Rises* by Ernest Hemingway, a character is asked, 'How did you go bankrupt?' The answer: 'Two ways. Gradually then suddenly.'

- A balance sheet gives a snapshot view of the assets and liabilities of the charity and is another vital document which trustees must receive at board meetings. Either as part of this or separately, a statement of reserves is necessary. It is important for you to have a reserves policy. You need to work out what you will need to close the charity and pay all its obligations if it is no longer able to carry on. It will take into account any obligations under a property lease, for example. If there are several years to run on a lease this can be a significant liability. Don't forget also that you may need to refurbish your offices when you quit: another cost. You may hear of something called the 'three-month rule' for reserves. As far as I have been able to determine, there is no such regulation, although typically it is quite a good rule of thumb. With your accountant, you need to work out what reserves are needed if the worst comes to the worst.

- The above concerns financial information – that is, information about assets, liabilities, income and expenditure, reserves and cash flow. You will also need *management* accountancy information if you are to understand what is going on in the charity. This will help you understand more of the workings of the organisation: what's going on 'under the bonnet', so to speak. Some charity boards have nothing of this kind at all, which I do not recommend. What is needed? This question is difficult to answer because of the wide differences between different charities. I can only suggest some options which will depend a lot on the specific nature of your charity.
  - If wage costs are a big element of your charity's expenditure then showing a ratio of wages to income, expressed as a percentage, is likely to be useful. If there is a table showing quarterly or monthly figures this will enable you to see the trend over a year or so.
  - Overheads as a proportion of income is also a useful statistic, again expressed as a percentage and tracked over a period of months or a year.
  - Many charities are involved in fundraising of some kind or another and this is a crucial activity for many. The amount given to charities has declined during the pandemic largely because there were few opportunities for street collections. Also, people have less actual cash about them these days as we move towards a cashless society, and this has combined with fears of infection. There are two suggested ways to track this activity if your charity is engaged in bidding or applying for funding, and that is to show the ratio of funds bid for to funds received as a percentage. This is a kind of 'success rate'.

Another one I have seen suggested but have not experienced being used is the cost of fundraising as a percentage of funds received.

- A ratio keeping track of current assets to current liabilities is key. Called the 'current ratio', it is closely linked to the cash flow report mentioned above in financial reporting.
- Age of debts is also a useful measure. Most should be paid within thirty days or less, so if you start to see more debts appearing with longer periods – thirty days plus – this should prompt questions.
- One other figure which is important, but is not usually reported on, is called the '**day rate**'. This is the cost per day of a member of staff (it can be per hour but I have not come across this in a charity). It crops up particularly if your charity is applying for outside funding. If you are making such an application, then the time element of fulfilling the duties with the funds you are awarded is crucial. The combination of time spent, with the wages of the staff involved, is a significant element in working out the cost. It is not altogether easy. One difficulty is correctly allocating the overheads to the project. In a competitive funding situation – which is the norm – there is a tendency to ignore, underestimate or downplay these costs. Don't forget that people are only effective for part of the time they are working. Time is lost in meetings, training, research, holidays and so forth.
- I would suggest asking searching questions about this topic to satisfy yourself that they have been properly calculated. Have overheads been appropriately apportioned? Was an accountant involved in making the calculation? Has a sum been allocated as a contribution to making a surplus?

How valid are the assumptions of time spent on the project? Is there due allowance for supervisory time?

- Linked to this – although not strictly a management accountancy issue – is a need for a robust system for time recording. In essence, an application for funding will be based on a combination of time spent multiplied by the cost of that time – the day rate. Time sheets are a tedious chore in most organisations but a necessary evil nonetheless. Again, a question worth asking in terms of what system is in place: is it checked and how confident are the managers that it accounts for time spent?

In this chapter I have tried to put across the important principle that as a trustee, you need to have a good understanding of the finances of the charity. Actually, it's stronger than that: it is vital you have a good understanding. Ensuring that the assets of the charity are managed properly and prudently is a key role for any trustee. It is really easy to be swept along by sets of figures presented in such a way as to tell you very little, unless you are an accountant or have some training in the subject.

I have listed the basic information you need to achieve this understanding. You and your fellow trustees do not need sheaves of data about telephone bills, water rates, stationery costs and so forth – you are not the managers. You do need the basics set out clearly and, to hammer home the point again, an indication of what is happening over time. You do need some information percentages or ratios to be presented where this helps the understanding. I must emphasise this point about percentages and ratios. It will help you grasp the essentials of what is happening and to see trends more clearly.

Quite what is presented will depend on the charity and its activities, certainly as far as management accounts are concerned.

But please keep in mind the *vital importance of cash.* Organisations of all types can come to grief if they run out of cash so managing this is truly important. Things can be looking good as far as the activities of the charity are concerned, but if you are not getting sufficient cash in to pay the bills as they fall due, it can all come crashing down in the twinkling of an eye.

If you are not getting the right information, presented in an understandable way, then you do need to raise it with the chair. Do not be shy of asking questions if you do not understand. I wager that there will be at least one other trustee who didn't understand either but was reluctant to ask!

CHAPTER 9

Communications

In this chapter I want to address a key question: what is it we want to communicate to whom? Nine words, simply stated but quite difficult to answer. I warrant that a great deal of time will be spent on this topic – if it hasn't been already – and there will be some tricky arguments to negotiate. The answer will inform and underpin several areas of your work, for example the website and other means of communication. The value of getting it right however is immense. Before reading on: do you think your charity is clear about this? Have you identified your audiences and are you clear about what message you wish to communicate to each of them? Does your website, social media and literature convey useful information to each audience group? Maybe you can put your hand on your heart and say 'yes', in which case this is a chapter you can happily skip through.

The different audiences you identify are likely to require individual messages tailored to them. This reflects the different interests in your charity's work and maybe the differing degrees of knowledge about your area of activity and of your charity. When it comes to communication, therefore, it is unlikely that one size fits all. Yet if you look at many charity websites, social media and literature, that seems to be the pattern. If your charity is involved in housing or rough sleeping, for example, then one of your audiences may be the local authority, the officers of which will know of the problem and will be aware of the various acronyms in use, and so you can assume a high degree of prior knowledge. The general public are not likely to be so well informed on the details of the problem and so the language will be different for them. There will be an absence of jargon and acronyms. Another audience might be funders, current or potential, who might look at your website or Facebook page to get a wider view of what your charity does. They will want to know more about how effective you are, governance issues and how well managed the charity is. Each will come with different interests and different degrees of knowledge.

The first stage is the identification of your audiences. This will of course vary, but for many they are likely to be one or more of the following:

- The public
- A 'professional' audience which might be a local authority, medical, social services, teachers, vets and so on
- Funders, either current or potential
- The people you are trying to help, or potential 'clients', or however you refer to them
- Other

The second stage is to decide *what* it is you wish to communicate to them, *how often* and in *what form.* In addition to the direct messages you want to give your audiences, there will be the question of 'brand'. You will be well aware of commercial brands. We are surrounded by them and almost all your buying decisions will be influenced by your perception of a particular brand. Some you will associate with quality, some with style, and others with price. The important thing is that the brand gives instant recognition and to an extent, helps guide you to a buying decision because of what you already know about the brand's message.

Some people find the idea of branding difficult to swallow. They feel (I say imagine) that their decisions are taken on empirical grounds and they are not influenced by the brand. They are possibly the same people who say they are not influenced by advertising. This may be true in some cases, but in the majority of instances, the reputation of a brand is all that is needed for someone to be attracted to the product or service.

A distinction between charities and private companies is the difference between the *charity itself and the cause which it is promoting.* This distinction is not usually drawn by writers on this topic. People have opinions and views about particular causes and this is likely to colour their view of the charity which may be promoting it. So for example, some people are not sympathetic to drug users. They feel that it is the drug user's fault that they have become addicted. They think it reflects on their lack of self-control, and question why they should give money to a charity when – in their view – it is money wasted. There are other causes, such as homelessness or helping ex-prisoners, where there is sometimes a lack of sympathy or understanding of what the problems are. A negative press does not help with stories of life in prison being like a holiday camp. People on benefits are sometimes cast as scroungers and feckless, so there is unlikely to be much empathy from people who read and believe these stories.

There are three levels to consider. First, the overall problem; second, the cause; and third, the charity itself. For example, to explain the point: something like inequality, which we can see is a problem in the UK. It has increased significantly over the last few decades. A feature of the problem is that people at the bottom of society – the most unequal – have difficulty in being able to purchase sufficient food. Charities have set up a network of food banks around the country to help the hungry.

Each of these aspects will need thought because people's attitudes towards and knowledge of them will vary considerably. Many people are only vaguely aware of the extent of inequality. The statistic that half the world's wealth is owned by a number of individuals who are able to fit into a double-decker bus surfaced in 2019.[56] A book I would recommend at this point for any trustee interested in inequality and its effects is *The Inner Level* by Richard Wilkinson and Kate Pickett. It followed on from their influential book *The Spirit Level.*[57] *Inner Level* discusses a wide range of issues such as self-esteem, meritocracy, attitudes, the effects of inequality on the human condition, and much more. It is useful background reading for any trustee of a charity which is engaged in helping those left behind or who live on the margins of society.

I am a member of the local Amnesty International group and we used to do a lot of campaigning in the street on behalf of prisoners of conscience or for those on death row around the world. We used to get a steady stream of people willing to sign cards or petitions. In recent years, the number has diminished and there has been a small increase in aggressive language towards us. Some of our supporters are less happy to take part in these events because they feel uncomfortable. Attitudes towards charities and their causes have to an extent changed, and a favourable response cannot as readily be expected.

In passing, I would recommend doing something in the street or in the town centre for your charity if you don't do this already. The responses you get are likely to be instructive. It is important in this exercise that you *listen carefully* to the comments people make about your cause or your charity. Try and avoid, if at all possible, engaging in arguments (I know, it can be extremely difficult). Gently correct any factual errors but listen: then listen some more.

Misapprehensions, lack of knowledge or awareness, as well as possible hostility, can be useful indicators of what people truly feel about your cause. You might almost call this market research. You may well be put on the spot in trying to explain to someone in a few words what it is you do. Sometimes called the 'elevator test', it is being able to explain to someone what your charity does in a few sentences: the idea comes from chatting to someone between a few floors in a lift. Remember: if people have the wrong idea about what your charity does and whether it achieves anything worthwhile, whose fault is that?

Another useful suggestion is to seek funding from one of the supermarkets which gives out tokens for customers to pop into a box for one of three charities. This seemed to stop during the pandemic, but it might resume in the future. Where I live, Waitrose and Tesco did this and again, it is a useful test of how the public views your charity or the work it does. People take only a few seconds to decide, briefly reading the words or just reacting to a cause they are familiar with. I suggest the knowledge gained is worth more than the relatively small sums gained. Having observed these bins over the years, I'd say it is causes linked to animals and children which usually do well.

YouGov carries out research in this area, and the list of the top twenty charities is instructive.[58] Five are animal charities and six are medical ones.

Ten years of austerity, with the Covid-19 pandemic as well, has left many people struggling with their finances. Those concerned about their own finances and how to get through to the end of the week are not likely to have a benevolent attitude even to those worse off than themselves. This attitude to giving and helping others surfaced in the decision by the Chancellor of the Exchequer in November 2020, to reduce the money available for foreign aid from

0.7% to 0.5%. The government won a vote in parliament on the decision in July 2021. The decision was popular among the public and a YouGov survey showed that two-thirds of the public were in favour.[59]

BRANDING

Branding does not feature prominently in discussions and meetings that charities have. If you are a trustee already, how many times has the subject been discussed in meetings you have attended?

There is a feeling that 'branding' is something for commercial firms who are trying to sell cola, cars or trainers. There is a sense that it is linked to various dubious or unsavoury business practices such as pretending a product is 'green' when it isn't. Its link to marketing can give rise to worries about manipulation. It is also felt that it shouldn't be necessary for a charity to engage in this kind of activity. There is a belief that firms do because they are trying to sell, for as high a price as possible, something that costs a few pennies to make. But, some might say, our charity is engaged in good works helping the disabled/the poor/drug addicts/the homeless/distressed animals and so on, so what need of a 'brand' and how would it help us? Why spend a lot of money on a logo and a new brand image when the money would be better spent on the cause itself? Also, we don't want to look too posh, as it might give the impression to those who fund us that we are spending their money on tarting ourselves up and not on the cause.

There is considerable literature on branding, its importance and significance, especially in the commercial and business world. Few could argue with its importance in those settings. We buy a brand of car because it suits our lifestyle and the performance and service is good. We will often buy another model of the same brand, and another, for some considerable time. Branding has a big influence on our buying decisions – just look at the food items in your store cupboard or fridge, the clothes in your wardrobe, even the toothpaste you use. Brand provides reassurance. If you buy a Heinz soup, you know what you will get in terms of quality and consistency because you have bought Heinz products many times before.

A lot of branding is about segmentation – that is, firms seeking to subdivide markets into reasonably homogeneous subunits to which it can direct its marketing effort most profitably. It reflects in part the fact that consumers have become more discerning and want products and services which match their aspirations and lifestyles. A brand helps them do this. A brand is 'a complex multidimensional construct whereby managers augment products and services with values and this facilitates the process by which consumers confidently recognise and appreciate those values' (Helen Stride).[60]

The literature extols the virtues of branding, and there are entire books and many journal articles devoted to different styles and techniques. It might seem natural that these techniques and ideas can transfer across to the not-for-profit and charitable sectors and I do admit that the notion of branding is relevant to the sector. However, this is an area where a direct and unthinking transfer is not at all straightforward.

A rather more sceptical view of the subject is provided by Naomi Klein in her book *No Logo*.[61] She explores the history and some of the negative aspects of the move to branding in the commercial world. One aspect is the creation of brand values, which enables firms to detach the production process and move it overseas and in particular to parts of the Far East. There is evidence of widespread use of sweatshops and labour abuses. The brand becomes a thing in its own right and considerable effort and resources are expended to promote and develop it.

If we look at commercial branding, several things are evident:

- The value is in the brand, since nearly any firm can make the product itself. Many firms can make jeans, trainers, whisky, paint, toothpaste or cars. For a company to maintain its position in the marketplace it has to create, advertise, support and build a brand. When we, the consumer, go to a store or online, it will be the brand which will catch our attention and it will play a major part in our decision to purchase that model or that product.
- Branding is often about selling a lifestyle, since we usually want something which we think will enhance our wellbeing and quality of life. The product will make us feel or look good, save time or provide some other benefit.
- Brands will often link to well-known celebrities in the pop, sport or acting worlds. George Clooney is currently promoting Nespresso, for example (summer 2021). The hope is that their fame and celebrity will rub off onto the product itself and create a feel-good factor.
- Brand awareness focuses on the brand itself rather than how or where it is made. The consumer is invited to accept the values of the brand rather than focus too much on what is actually being purchased. There is, in other words, a kind of detachment.
- Creating value in a brand – which in the case of famous brands can run into many millions of pounds or dollars – can be used as a means to avoid tax. The brand is part of schemes of transfer pricing in which intangible costs like patents and copyrights are transferred between companies and subsidiaries to enable profits to end up in a low or zero tax jurisdiction like Bermuda.

- Once a brand has created value, this can be used to expand operations into new markets. Virgin is an example of a brand which has expanded into media, an airline and healthcare. Oh, and space travel.

This is only a brief summary of commercial branding and I have tried to pick out some of the key elements. How does this compare with a charity or not-for-profit seeking to develop a brand of its own? The first thing to note is that the act of developing a well-known brand name requires a huge investment, the level of which is not available to a small charity. Bigger charities can, but the majority of charities and not-for-profits cannot[62].

A second point of difference, I suggest, is that a charity's brand is rooted in what it does. It cannot, like a commercial firm, detach itself from the cause it is pursuing. The charity is the cause and its reputation will be built on how effective it is at tackling or alleviating it. I cannot, for example, think of a charity which has used its brand to expand its operations into wholly new fields. They nearly all 'stick to the knitting'. To a large extent this is due to restrictions arising from their charitable status and in the way their purpose is defined. Another perspective centres on a charity's values. Stride argues that a key issue for charities is that their values are non-negotiable and that this is what distinguishes them from the corporate sector.[63]

When you buy a product or service, you receive something tangible for the money. Whether it be an item of clothing, a book or a bag of groceries, you have given someone money and in exchange, get something back. Even if it is intangible like an insurance policy for your car, the element of exchange is there. When a member of the public donates to your charity they get nothing. You collect the money and your charity does something with it for someone or something else. This is one of the differences between the public and private sectors I spoke about in Chapter 3.

People when buying are able to judge value, quality, delivery and so on before they make their purchase. Or at least they think they can. When they give to your charity they cannot do this. This means they can only judge you on your name, what they know about the cause, word of mouth concerning your reputation, or some other motivating factor. A huge amount of trust is involved. Clearly the merits of the cause are a factor. If they believe homeless people are only homeless because they are feckless drug addicts or out of choice, they are unlikely to donate. This all points to the importance of branding because in a way, it's all they've got to go on.

Another point of difference is the question of ethics. Naomi Klein and others have discussed the vexed issue of commercial firms' exploitation of people and even entire countries in pursuit of profits. Low wages, poor working conditions and abusive labour practices are widespread. This kind of activity is not open to a charitable organisation. Indeed, when Oxfam staff were found to have hired prostitutes in Haiti, there was a huge scandal. The essence of a charity's brand is that of trust and integrity. There is an expectation that a charity will act with virtue and honesty, an expectation that does not seem to apply to commercial firms.

With these observations in mind, what should the key factors be in a brand for a small charitable organisation? I suggest the following six principles:

- **Affinity**. A supporter or donor must broadly agree with the purpose or cause the charity is pursuing. They must be able to think 'I agree that [the cause] is right and I want to help.'
- **Recognition**. People must be able to recognise the charity or its cause. The recognition may be incomplete – confused

even – but nevertheless it must lead someone to think 'I recognise this charity [or cause].'

- **Trust**. You must be able to reassure the public or donors that you are essentially trustworthy and in particular, that the money they give you will be spent wisely. They will also want to know that most of the money will find its way to the cause itself and not disappear in expenses and salaries. You want them to think 'I believe my contribution will do some good.' Included in this trust element are matters such as the fair treatment of staff, and the absence of bullying and racism.
- **Giving hope**. This matters because some of the causes that charities get involved in are so big that there can be a feeling – even by people well disposed towards the cause – that it is too daunting for a small charity to make any difference and that it is in essence a 'lost cause'. It will be important therefore to convey a sense of hope that something *can* be done. You want to avoid the belief that 'However much I give to this charity, it could not make a realistic difference.'
- **Understanding**. Linked to affinity and to recognition, this is conveying an immediate sense of what it is you are trying to do and what you hope to achieve. It may be done with an image, a story or some other means to convey that understanding. You want the donor to say to themselves 'I know what they are trying to do.'
- **Values**. The core values of your charity have to be either evident or at least consistent with your messages and image.

Finally, I want to come back to the essential – vexed even – issue of the attitude of some of your staff and volunteers to the whole question of marketing and branding. As I have argued above, elements of commercial activities – tax avoidance, environmental damage, the use of sweatshops and anti-union activities, etc. – taint the notion of branding. Staff may feel that branding makes your charity just like these commercial companies. By thinking in terms of a brand and adopting some of the techniques, is there not a risk, they think, that potential donors, supporters and well-wishers will consider us to be no better than some rapacious firm charging huge sums of money for a product cheaply made in a sweatshop in Indonesia?

I do not think these ideas and beliefs can be dismissed lightly. After all, they contain a measure of truth: there is exploitation; firms are engaged in large-scale tax avoidance activities; huge chunks of the Amazon are being felled. Branding is being used to conceal or distract from some pretty unsavoury activities. The values of a charity are non-negotiable, as I have argued.

While this is true, there are good brands as there are firms which behave responsibly, treat their employees well and respect the environment. 'Brand' is a word in its own right and using it in the context of your charity does not mean you are the same as the worst of the commercial companies. The purpose of your brand is to convey the positive things your charity does, as set out above. Indeed, as far as the public is concerned, the word will not appear.

There will be those who think the intrinsic value of what you do should be sufficient: what need of this branding nonsense? Well it might be. They worry that we will be seen as too commercial. But you have to point out that there are hundreds of worthy causes all jostling for attention. Some of them will have strong brands and powerful recognition. Your charity exists in a competitive marketplace with all manner of causes looking for attention. You often only have a moment or two to make an impression or gain someone's attention. Brand recognition is key to that.

It is vital however that you give thought and devote time to these objections and beliefs. To leave them unresolved is to risk disenchantment and perhaps resentment. It will be important to convince doubters that a good brand will make the work of your charity easier. Fundraising will be easier because of better recognition, understanding, trust and the other aspects listed above. In short the benefits will have to be explained.

Despite these practical issues, there will still be those who have moral qualms about adopting commercial means to promote a charity. They almost feel it in their bones: it just isn't right and shouldn't be necessary. This can be a hard belief to shift. We are all possessed of a set of core beliefs about a wide range of things; some amount to prejudices.

Two things to note here. Firstly, it is common for people to link 'branding' with a logo and secondly, some may believe that the cause the charity is engaged in is so intrinsically powerful and obvious that branding is simply not necessary. Charity brands are not easily explained by definitions that focus on a name and logo alone; they are more closely linked to causes and beliefs.[64]

Your charity is in a competitive marketplace in common with all the other causes. There are thousands of other charities with hundreds of causes being promoted and those charities which do have successful brands achieve enormous success in attracting funds. Since how much people and organisations give to these causes is finite, the piece of the cake you are likely to get, without a brand strategy, is going to be less than it might. It really is as simple and as brutal as that. The sad reality is that, with the occasional exception, people give on the basis of emotion, recognition and empathy. It is all done in a fraction of a second. I mentioned the boxes at the exit of some supermarkets and I suggest spending a few moments observing how people decide. You will notice they take only a few seconds to make their choice. Few read the piece of text describing what the charity or cause is about. It is done quickly and because they have a feeling for the cause or recognise the charity or cause concerned.

One of the things you may have to do, therefore, is convince fellow trustees and the senior staff about the importance of branding. There may well be resistance for the reasons I have noted. Stand by for the comment 'we are not selling cornflakes'. Stand by for resistance because of cost. Isn't it better, they might say, to spend the money on doing something useful rather than waste it on this branding nonsense? You may have to explain that although what you do is valuable and needed, there are lots of other causes which are valuable and needed. You may have some pretty literature and leaflets, but are they read? If people do not recognise the name of the organisation and it does not have an emotional impact, the charity is unlikely to succeed.

I accept it is a lot more difficult for the small local charity to crack this nut. It is difficult for commercial firms as well, despite having an expensive consultancy to help them. The decision of Standard Life Aberdeen to rebrand themselves 'Abrdn', which was ridiculed by many, is such an example. Many of the examples I came across researching this chapter are of major charities who can afford consultants and design experts to reshape their brand, image and marketing. Macmillan for example – a very successful charity doing valuable work helping cancer sufferers – had an income in 2018 of £236m and spent £65m in fundraising.[65] It received £133m in donations and £80m in legacies. It can well afford to spend money on brand development. For smaller charities – who are the great majority – it is a lot more difficult and, because the results are likely to be uncertain, harder to justify. If you are to succeed in the marketplace, however, you do need to attend to your brand.

You and your colleagues will need to consider the changed climate that charities exist in today, and I don't just mean the pandemic.

I referred in the introduction to the various scandals that have hit the sector, for example Oxfam and Kids Company. These have left a mark on the sector as a whole. It has left the public slightly less trusting of charities than they once were.

The starting point when considering your charity's brand is the basic purpose, usually expressed in the mission statement. This has to be crystal clear and expressed in as few words as possible – in other words the 'elevator test' I spoke about above. This, or a version of it, will be expressed in the strapline of your charity. It has to explain to someone not knowing what your charity is or does, what you do. From experience, I can say achieving this is extraordinarily difficult. There are people who worry that a short sentence or phrase will not capture the range of things you do. Others will worry that it is misleading. Whatever the reasons, it is usually a challenging exercise but it has to be done.

From there it is a matter of developing the communications plan and, dare I mention, thinking about the logo. Few can afford a design studio and it may seem an easy task but, unless you have someone who really is good with graphic design and is a dab hand at Gimp for example, then the results can look amateurish. A problem might be the name of the charity which, if it is long or contains several words, can be difficult to put across. I mentioned the Macmillan charity earlier: a nice simple name. But if you set up a charity today and just called it something like Macmillan, what would it mean? The fact is that they have spent considerable time, expertise and effort to promote the name so that when you see it, and the associated design and typeface, you recognise it and you have a good idea of what it does.

Nearly all the advice on offer stresses the need to focus on the emotional aspects of what you do. This is good as far as it goes but it deals with the cause, not the charity. With an increase in scepticism about charities, the brand does have to engage at some point with the charity itself, its probity and ability to deliver. People need to be reassured that the money is going to the cause and that it will make a difference. It is the case that the general public does not always appreciate the overheads a charity has. When they give a pound, they hope and perhaps expect that it will go to the cause, all one hundred pennies of it. There is no simple answer to this. As you will recognise if you are a trustee already, any charity has costs. Even if staffed entirely by volunteers, which a small organisation may well be, there are still costs to be met. A survey by Ipsos MORI for the Charity Commission in 2010 (before several of the scandals) found that donors not knowing how their money was spent was a reason behind lack of trust in some charities.[66] A poll by Populus in 2020 found that trust in charities had increased but had not reached pre-2014 levels.[67]

The need therefore is to convince people that you can do something and that you are effective. You have convince them both about the cause and that your charity can do something about it. This is about describing results and what you have done. Stories are an important part of the equation.

This is where, in fact, a small charity does have something of an advantage. Being small and probably local can be a powerful plus in persuading people to give or contribute. Some people are a little wary of the large charities, some of which I have seen described as 'bloated'. They may suspect that too much money is going on executive salaries. I do not generally subscribe to this view and, size for size, chief executive salaries of large charities are not overly generous – nevertheless, the perception persists. If your charity is tackling a local problem which people can understand and with which they can empathise, they are more likely to be sympathetic.

Research by nfpSynergy, which advises charitable organisations, says that the four important factors which encourage giving are[68]:

- The charity is clear about what donations are spent on (56%)
- Learning about the impact which the charity has (47%)
- Positive stories about the charity in the media (37%)
- Case stories about individuals that have been helped (33%)

In thinking about how to put yourself across, it is well worth keeping these points in mind.

A common problem with small charities is too much information. This may seem a surprising comment in view of the fact I have spent two whole chapters talking about nothing else. This was, however, information that you, the management and your fellow trustees need to manage the charity. Although this information will be useful as part of the communication exercise and your brand, it must be used sparingly. People are not generally persuaded or influenced by statistics unless they have some dramatic quality. Statistics rarely have the ability to engage people at the emotional level. There is huge suspicion about statistics and just about everyone knows the quotation 'lies, damned lies and statistics'. So one or two numbers can be helpful and informative but a lot of them is likely to confuse.

Presenting the numbers is worth a brief comment. Spurious accuracy can be counterproductive. If the statistic (whatever it might be) is 69.3%, for the sake of an example – well, you might be that accurate, but it is likely you are not. If the statistic was taken a month or a year later would it still be 69.3%? Probably not. It is much better to say 'around 70%' or approximately 70%'. It might even be better to say 'nearly three quarters'. Remember that there are people who suffer from dyscalculia as well as those who have difficulties with data and statistics generally.

Another related point is that people respond more if there is a single identified beneficiary rather than a group. Statistics on the scale of the problem have little effect, it has been found[69]. There are problems with the public's attitude to advertising the effectiveness of the charity which can paradoxically have the opposite effect[70]. This is to emphasise the difficulties charities have in breaking through and to repeat the points made in the introduction to this book that charities are not the same as businesses. People are giving less to charities and one reason suggested relates to the scandals which have taken place. The state of the economy also plays a part.

There has been a lot of interest recently about 'contagion' and its effect on people. It may seem an odd word to use as coronavirus is still present in the world, but it does have a wider meaning. One recently published book, *Under the Influence* by Robert H. Frank,[71] explores how the environment in which we live influences our behaviour. Frank cites various experiments which show how strongly we are influenced in our beliefs and behaviours by those around us.

Considerable research and literature exists on the issue of giving and why people contribute (or not) to charities. Unfortunately there are no simple answers. Every piece of research I looked at seemed to offer a different cluster of factors. Issues of emotion, familiarity, localness, contagion and feeling good are some of the points researchers and others list. This makes giving simple advice rather difficult. There will also be variations between causes. Everyone knows about cancer and almost everyone knows of someone who has suffered or died of it. It is no accident therefore that three of the top ten charities are involved in some way in trying to tackle the disease. Animal charities are popular – at least in the UK – and a charity dealing with dogs is in the top ten.

So how do you go about developing a strategy on communication and branding?

These suggestions are designed for a small charity not able to afford sizeable sums to engage consultants or design specialists. They are likely to be mainly DIY with a bit of help here and there. The steps are in brief:

- Ensure commitment of your fellow trustees
- Be sure about the mission
- Know as much as you can about what people think about your charity and your cause (which may be different)
- Consider what message you want to give to what audience
- Are you seeking funds from the public, the corporate sector or the public sector (local authorities, the Lottery for example)?
- Remember the staff and keep them involved

ENSURE COMMITMENT

I have put this first because as I have already noted, there is little point in spending time – and maybe some money – in working on a plan for this if people are not committed. If the belief that 'we are not selling cornflakes' is the prevailing point of view among your fellow trustees or senior staff, then you are unlikely to make any progress. If they believe their key duty is to be custodians of the charity and its finances and not to promote the charity or its cause – a kind of defensive posture – then you will have work to do.

There has to be an acceptance of the need for the charity to develop a communication plan which recognises that different audiences need different messages. There has to be an acceptance that brand is important and how people perceive you and your cause is a vital consideration. It also has to be recognised that although you regard what you do as important or even vital, the public may not share that view or might think other causes more worthy of their money or support. Some may actually oppose your work, for example helping the homeless, people released from prison, or drug users. In short, there has to be a degree of hard-headedness and self-awareness.

There are some who dispute the value of branding even in a commercial context. They claim not to be influenced by marketing, promotional activities, advertising or brands. They claim never to look at TV adverts and make all their buying decisions based on a dispassionate analysis of competing products or services. Rubbish! I am sure that like me, you have friends and acquaintances who swear blind that they are not in the least bit influenced by advertising.

What to do if there is a stubborn denial of these points? If the charity has been around for some years and has not seen any need for this kind of activity, what can be done? What sometimes happens is that charities gently decline. This is where the information and analysis of the numbers comes in. If you are able to look at annual reports going back five years or so, then it is easy to work out the income and the surplus over time. What about the reserves? If these show a slow decline then the charity could be heading for a crunch point. This could be a rent uplift or the end of a lease. Or a key member of staff leaves and you find that replacing them is more expensive than you thought.

Jonathan Spencer runs a charity called Charity Checkup and lists seven reasons for failure. His first point is that trustees do not think clearly about the support needed to sustain their charity. Other factors include the lack of a marketing plan and a lack of awareness of external changes. His list can be summed up as trustees not getting a grip. One of the problems of a slow decline is that when the crunch point does come, the charity may no longer be in a fit state to respond. Some trustees are likely to disappear quite quickly, as will key staff. All of a sudden, there's a crisis. These problems can arise because there is complacency among the trustees – and possibly the senior manager as well – which leads to a lack of seeing things as they are. If this complacency seems hardwired into the board, then you may have to consider your position as a trustee. Something called 'founder syndrome' can be a related factor here. Someone sets up a charity to right a wrong or tackle a particular issue which has grabbed them. The charity grows but gets to a point where the founder thinks it is getting out of his or her control. More time is spent on governance and management issues than doing what they were set up to do. Resistance to further growth can be an outcome because they feel it will only make matters worse. Founder syndrome takes many forms but it often means the founder has, sadly, outlived their usefulness and can become a threat to the future of the charity.

Securing commitment is therefore the supremely important first step. After some basic financial analysis to set out how the charity has performed financially over a period of at least five years, the next thing is to look at other performance such as how many people have been helped. You may find that this data is unavailable. Going back to the earlier chapters on this topic, collecting and analysing performance information is often not carried out in small charities. They are heavily concerned with today's issues, not peering into the past. As I said in Chapter 6, understanding trends is key. If you can get this information, then seeing how the charity has performed over a reasonable timescale will be useful.

Thirdly, what is going on in the outside world? Change is so fast now that the original purpose of the charity may well be eclipsed by other organisations, economic change or another charity moving onto your pitch. The way you are managing your charity may also need to change again because of technology. One thing Covid-19 taught everyone was that it was possible to meet online, rather than drive half an hour or so to meet at a fixed place.

So putting these things together: the financial trends, the performance information and what is happening in the outside world should reveal that the charity cannot stand still. Hopefully, these arguments should be sufficient to convince enough of the trustees of the need for change. To repeat, there is little point in going further if the prevailing attitude of your colleagues is reluctance.

MISSION

Being clear about your mission and expressing it in as few words as possible is the first – and a difficult – step. It should do at least two things and possibly a third: one, say what you do and two, for whom. It might also say how. Aim to get the main purpose in at the start. So for example:

> *The [...] Youth Centre provides an environment where young people can learn and practice leadership skills and focus on ethical decision making. The [...] Youth Centre is able to reach at-risk young people and offer much needed care and support. For these aspirations to become reality however, it is essential that the youth centre is seen to be firmly rooted within the life of the wider parish community, and that wherever possible, young people are provided with the opportunity to participate in the life of that parish community. Through the programmes, activities and ethos of the centre, the leaders guide and support young people and act as mentors and role models in their personal, social and spiritual development. The programmes that the centre provides will create opportunity for the young people to develop into mature and responsible adults who will play an important role within their communities and wider society.*

This is in my view too long, even much too long and is probably written by a committee of people all keen to ensure everything is explained. Perhaps '*Helping at-risk young people to learn leadership skills and ethical decision-making in a community setting*' might be a little better and quickly explains what it is they do. A quick search of mission statements with a search engine brings up a number of examples which are sometimes suggested to be good ones. It might be an idea to print some of these off and display them during the debate about yours. The results are often interesting because what are put forward as good examples can often be pulled apart by your colleagues as too vague, all things to all people, too long or not being entirely clear about what it is the charity does. A kind of momentum of criticism can build up with some statements being torn to shreds! This can help with writing yours because the bad points of the examples can inform your efforts. This process does work quite well.

So where do we start? I suggest the first question to answer is 'What is the purpose of having a brand and what do you expect it to do?' That's two questions really but they are closely linked. The answers are likely to be along the following lines:

- To make your charity stand out – so in one way or another, when people see e.g. 'Brown's Charity' (a made-up name) they know what it is and stands for
- To help with recognising the cause you are promoting
- To convey to your audience that you are reliable and have integrity
- To convey to your audience that if they offer help or money, it will go to the cause and only the cause
- To convey your values

So essentially it is about recognition, integrity and personality. This is what you have to convey in your branding. How is this done? The means you have to achieve this are:

- Your name – that is, the name of the charity
- Design, colour and typography
- Illustrations, photos or videos – that is, visual content
- Words and messages

These are the essential tools at your disposal. Starting with the name, ideally it should be as short as possible and give some clue as to what you do, although it has to be said that many well-known charities give no clue of what they do in their name – I have mentioned Macmillan earlier. A major charity local to me is Trussell Trust, the food bank people, and there is no telling what they do from their name alone. The Dogs Trust on the other hand is – how can I put this – about dogs. Some charity names are acronyms. This satisfies the brevity point but may not convey much. If there is no vowel in it, it can be hard to say.

In working on communication and branding, it is worthwhile knowing something about what the public thinks of your charity and the cause you are espousing. Thomson Reuters divides these causes into thirteen types.[72] One of the principles of marketing is knowing your customer and in this context, customer means those who might be persuaded to give money or other resource to your charity. The Institute of Fundraising and YouGov both have survey results of a general nature.

HOW TO GO ABOUT IT

Up to now I have written in general terms about some of the principles and problems, and you may be getting a bit confused about all this talk of missions, branding and communications. What does it all mean in practice? How do you, as a small charity, go about this whole process of making your charity known and recognised in the local community and perhaps wider afield? I cannot, of course, know all the ins and outs of your particular charity, so this method does have to be used in ways that suit your organisation.

There is no single answer. There is no definite right or wrong way, which does make the process a difficult one. It is subject to judgement and the ideas of one person against those of another. Nevertheless, it is a worthwhile exercise and ultimately, it can be revised and changed again – although you want to avoid changing it too often, if only for reasons of cost.

I cannot overstress the importance of involving and engaging staff and volunteers in this process. Volunteers especially receive no reward other than the satisfaction of carrying out the charity's objectives. Typically, staff in small charities are not paid fortunes and often belief in the work they do is an important motivation. If they feel that this will be compromised by the proposed changes it will have a demotivating effect. Some may have migrated to you from commercial organisations, where they have suffered from a surfeit of management speak and gobbledygook delivered by bright-eyed consultants. If what you propose reminds them of that, they might react negatively.

I go into more detail on this important topic in Appendix A, with a suggested 'how to do it' framework. This area of work is likely to involve trustees and it is desirable for that to be so.

In the next chapter I want to move on to the sometimes vexed question of marketing. For many working in charities, they feel the answer to their woes is better marketing. Well, it can be …

CHAPTER 10

Marketing

In this chapter I shall be parting company with some other writers on the role and significance of marketing for not-for-profit organisations and charities. Many of the texts and much of the advice assume the techniques and skills employed by commercial and profit-seeking firms are capable of being employed by charities more or less as they are. It is sometimes difficult to distinguish these texts from those which fill the business and marketing sections of bookshops, designed to advise commercial organisations. That marketing is an important component in the charitable sector is unarguable. The techniques, methods and skills however are a different matter and cannot in my view be used in a straightforward way. The techniques need to be selected carefully and often need to be adapted to suit the world in which a charity operates.

I spent some time in Chapter 3 discussing the differences between profit-seeking and not-for-profit organisations. I argued that a charity is working ultimately for its own extinction: it is working to reduce and ultimately eliminate poverty, disease, animal cruelty, threats to the environment or whatever cause it is engaged in. The basic principle of a transaction between two parties does not exist in the same way. A charity seeks funds from someone to help someone else. Whereas a commercial firm and its customers are about self-interest, a charity is about helping other people or things. The giver of funds will receive no tangible benefit or reward from the help they provide.

Many charities cannot select who they help within their chosen area of activity. They must endeavour to help all stray dogs; they have to help the homeless wherever they may be found; they must help all drug users. There will be limits according to their funding and resources but they do not vicariously ignore parts of their client base. Marketing texts for firms, however, speak of 'segmenting' their markets – that is, dividing a market up in some way and selecting those parts of the market which are likely to be most profitable. I question the concept of applying segmentation in the context of charitable organisations.

There are many charities on the other hand whose focus of activity is, for example, promoting good health, stopping smoking, promoting better mental health or reducing dependence on drugs. These charities are interacting directly with the public and in particular those whom they seek to help. Commercial marketing techniques are a useful guide in these cases and Gerard Hastings in his book *Social Marketing* provides many examples and case studies.[73] The subtitle to the book is 'Why Should the Devil Have All the Best Tunes?' and it argues that the techniques of the commercial marketing world can be used to promote good causes, just as they can be used to persuade us to 'eat Big Macs, smoke Marlboro and drive SUVs'. For this type of charity, concepts of segmentation, market research and marketing plans based on a mix of activities are very relevant.

There is also a moral or ethical dimension. A seller of cars for example will be obliged to offer a gas-guzzling car as part of its line-up if that is what customers want. Shops can sell cigarettes (except to minors) despite their health risk. Likewise alcohol.

There are many organisations offering gambling and there has been an explosion of gambling sites on TV. Charities on the other hand operate in a different moral universe. Public expectations are such that they have to operate ethically and be seen to be doing so.

Perhaps the biggest difference is the fundamental principle of success for a profit-seeking firm – namely, find out what the customer wants and seek to provide them with that at a profit. Charities are about satisfying needs rather than wants. So a charity like Alcohol Change for example is not opposed to alcohol but, in their words, 'we are for a future in which people drink as a conscious choice, not a default'. [74] This is clearly a moral position and recognises that alcohol gives pleasure to many but if abused, can cause problems. It is likely that the people they deal with, if they are addicts, would want more alcohol. A similar problem exists with gambling firms.

There are three things to consider in relation to charity marketing, three 'levels' if you like. The first is the *issue*. This is the fundamental problem which underpins your charity's activity. It may be poverty, homelessness, inequality, cruelty to animals, a disease, the environment or some other problem that motivates you and your colleagues to try to do something to help. The next level is the specific *cause* you are set up to tackle. So if we take poverty as an example, then one aspect of that is that some people do not have enough food to eat. The third level is your particular charity, since you will not be the only one set up to do something about the cause.

Each of these three need to be considered. If you are raising funds from the public, either directly or using online methods, the people you are asking will have a range of knowledge, opinions and beliefs about these aspects. So looking at this example, we might see:

	Attitudes towards:
The issue of poverty	• Some believe that poverty is the result of laziness and lack of willpower[75] • Only a third of the population think the government should redistribute more • Some assume people are poor because of drink or drug problems
The cause: a food bank	• Public attitudes to the need for and use of food banks generally show sympathy for the plight people are in[76] • 64% are concerned or 'extremely concerned' • The study concludes that there is no need to convince people of the need for food banks • Analysis shows that people's charitable help shows society's failure not our generosity • Some criticism by right-wing newspapers: 'Politically motivated scaremongering' and use of food banks by the 'underserving poor'[77] • Also political critics such as Iain Duncan Smith MP
The charity itself	This is where you would need to consider what public attitudes are to your particular charity

This is only a brief analysis but from it, we might conclude that the public's attitudes are somewhat ambivalent, but have become more understanding and sympathetic over the decade or so since food banks have become a feature of our society. Your charity will be completely different (unless you are a food bank that is!). The public in general are not that sympathetic to the poor as a class and many think it is the poor person's fault that they are in the position they are in. If they only stopped drinking or got themselves a job, they think, they would no longer be poor. On the other hand, there seems to be an understanding of *food* poverty and the need for government to do something. This could be connected to the fact that poverty has always been with us and seems insoluble. Food banks on the other hand have only appeared in the last decade or so and are therefore a relatively new phenomenon. They have also received a great deal of coverage in the media. Media critics do not seem to have dented the public's overall sympathy for food banks and their awareness of the need to help those who cannot gain sufficient income to feed themselves.

Clearly, one conclusion you might draw from this is to concentrate on *food* poverty rather than poverty in general, where you might not be so successful and public attitudes are harder and less sympathetic. Many think it a responsibility for government to tackle this issue and by inference, it is not for a charity to do so. The point I want to get across is that individuals' attitudes to – in this example – poverty are nuanced. This will inevitably impact on their propensity to donate.

In 2020 we witnessed some extraordinary events surrounding the Manchester United footballer Marcus Rashford. There was a high degree of food stress during lockdown and many people who had lost jobs or had been furloughed were struggling. Children, who would at least have got one meal at school, were facing inadequate levels of nutrition during the holidays. Rashford initially teamed up with a charity called FareShare[78] to deliver food parcels. He then decided to write an open letter to the UK Government urging them to end child poverty and in a very short passage of time, the government changed its mind and began offering free school meals in the summer holidays.

A point to note is that there are a considerable number of charities helping children and trying to tackle food poverty in one form or another. But it took the actions of a footballer to bring the matter to the nation's and the government's attention in a way that made a significant difference.

For these reasons, I argue that the core principles of marketing are not straightforwardly applicable and need to be chosen and used with care. I have separately argued that seeking the help of people with a marketing background, gained in a profit-seeking environment, needs also to be undertaken with care.

When we talk about marketing in the context of charity, what do we mean and how does it apply? Most charities are engaged in one, two or three of these activities:

1. Doing things the state does not do or has stopped doing
2. Doing things which are not commercially viable, principally because the clients are too poor or too few
3. Trying to change attitudes or policies, primarily for the benefit of the poorest or most vulnerable

As an operation, it is in addition:

1. Raising awareness of the cause it is engaged in
2. Raising awareness of the charity itself, i.e. its brand
3. Trying to recruit volunteers and helpers
4. Raising money
5. Trying to improve the problem it was set up to tackle

A useful starting point is to look at what forces are acting on a charity, and one technique from the business world is Michael Porter's Five Forces Model. He suggested that a firm was acted on by a combination of new entrants to the marketplace; the threat of substitutes; buyer power; supplier power; and rivalry among firms. Clearly, this does not read across to a charity in a simple way but nevertheless, it does give a pointer to an approach. For a charity the forces acting upon it are:

1. Funder pressure
2. Public perceptions
3. Legal and governance issues
4. Recipient pressure
5. 'Competition' from, and between, other causes

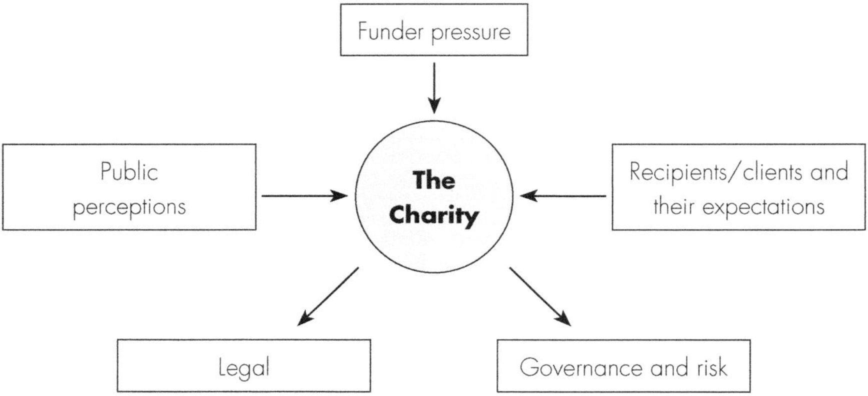

Fig 3 Forces acting on a charity (after Porter)

FUNDER PRESSURE

Many charities now undertake work for public organisations such as local authorities, or seek money from funders such as the Lottery. These create obligations on the charity to perform work in a particular way. In a sense they become a contractor to the funder. The charity seeks funds to carry out a particular piece of work, and inherent in the relationship is that the charity does that work and reports on its success or otherwise. I once worked for a regeneration partnership and part of the work was giving grants to a range of mostly community-based organisations. From time to time – thankfully rarely – money we gave for a particular project was used by them to carry out a quite different one without telling us. On a handful of occasions, we had to seek a return of the funds – called 'clawback' – and this was painful for everyone concerned. The problem was that the recipients did not recognise the obligation to do what they had set out in the proposal to us. They were engaged in a good cause, so surely this was enough? Sadly, it doesn't work that way.

Seeking funds from the public represents another pressure. Many people are experiencing economic difficulties and their capacity to contribute is less than it might have been. Some think that 'charity begins at home' and are less likely to contribute to a cause which has no salience for them.

PUBLIC PERCEPTIONS

Another aspect to the question of funding is the attitude of the public, especially if your charity is involved in street collections which many are. The public are fickle and attitudes can change rapidly. Earlier in the book I spoke of the change in attitudes towards charities following the various problems and scandals surrounding Oxfam and Kids Company. Some charities are popular and attract considerable funding. Charities involved in cancer research, children and animal welfare have little difficulty in fundraising. A 2018 YouGov survey found that in the top twenty of the most popular charities, four were involved with children, four with animals and three cancer – that is, more than half were within these three categories. They are all worthy causes of course, but if your charity is not engaged in any of these activities, it is that bit harder to make an impression.

Another issue is the question of how much money goes to the cause and how much towards administration. People have firm views on this and expect most of their money to go to the cause, regarding money spent on administration to be wasted. Similar attitudes are evident around wages and salaries paid to those who work in the sector.

Both these aspects reflect a pressure on a charity to perform in a particular way and represent a force on it.

LEGAL AND GOVERNANCE ISSUES

I do not propose to say much about these, not because they are unimportant – quite the opposite – but because considerable advice exists elsewhere on the Charity Commission site and in organisations such as NCVO. They are a significant factor, however, and to an extent limit what a charity can do.

RECIPIENT PRESSURE

Some people who are helped by charities are in many respects the same as a customer of a profit-seeking business. It is a fact that people have become more demanding over the past few decades. They have become used to speedy deliveries, discounts and bargains, plenty of choice, guarantees and other aspects of consumer power. Some of this attitude has crossed over to the charitable world and represents a force charities have to deal with. It is linked to the first factor, funder pressure, since the people receiving the service may well be aware that the charity has to perform in certain ways and meet various targets.

COMPETITION

Although charities are in a sense in competition with one another, it is not something that is particularly noticeable, in contrast to commercial operations. However, they do compete for money and as with the 'perceptions' point above, some will find it harder to win a donor pound than others. As I mentioned above, some causes are more popular than others which means the less popular ones will have to work harder to make themselves visible.

How do you start the process and look at how your charity is marketing itself? To start with you will need to do a situation analysis. There are a number of techniques for this but the main point here is to look at the environment your charity operates in and the fitness of your charity itself. There is little point in devising grand plans and strategies if you are in no fit state to carry them out. You need to be solvent, with adequate reserves, and to have a reasonably stable team of people. There should not be any pressing problems of a serious kind which overhang the charity.

Externally, a useful technique from the business textbooks – and an example where business techniques do come in useful – is often referred to by its acronym; STEEPLE (sometimes PESTLE). As noted previously, this stands for Social, Technological, Economic, Environmental, Political, Legal and Ethical. It represents a useful set of questions to ask about your charity and how it relates to the environment around it. The central question is: what changes have taken place which affect your charity and how it operates? Legal changes are fairly easy to see: a law is passed or new regulations come in which directly affect you, your sector or the people you are trying to help. Others are less easy to see, such as ethical considerations. These can change quite slowly and almost invisibly. The environment on the other hand has recently moved quickly up the political spectrum, partly due to the activities of Extinction Rebellion who have been campaigning actively in pursuit of their objectives.

These changes can affect how people view your cause. It may be positively, with increasing concern and interest, or it may be negatively as people become less interested or have moved on to something new. You need to take a critical look at each of these issues as they affect your charity and ask if they impact on what you do and how you do it. Are the changes sufficient to necessitate a serious change of approach or even a change in strategy?

This exercise is something that trustees are almost certainly to be involved in, and the use of an outside moderator is something to be considered. You need someone to guide the discussion and ideally interject ideas and suggestions you should be considering.

THE 7 Ps

One marketing concept which has stood the test of time in the commercial world are the 7 Ps (which started life as 4 Ps). They are: Product, Price, Place, Promotion, People, Process and Physical evidence. These do not translate exactly to the charity sector (except where they are carrying out commercial activities, as in the case of a charity shop) so they need to be adapted.

Product. Charities usually provide a service unless they have a trading arm (not really the subject of this book). We have to bear in mind though that in commercial terms, a product is exchanged for money as between a buyer and seller. As we saw in Chapter 3, a charity operates somewhat differently in that it takes money from A to help B, someone quite separate whom A is unlikely to know or meet. There is no direct exchange.

Price has little relevance since the money gained from funders or the public is used to help someone or something where money does not exchange hands. It is of relevance for those charities that run commercial operations, such as charity shops, to raise funds.

Place. A firm does not always have a choice when place is considered. They have to go where the customer is or where the customer demands. If I want my house to be painted, the firm has to come to me to do it or they don't get the job. Similar principles apply to charities, although that is not always the case. There may be a question of where a service is supplied based on convenience, price, security or access (for people with disabilities, for example).

Promotion. Clearly the service needs to be promoted and this is a matter for the charity to consider. It is closely linked to communication, discussed in Chapter 9.

People. This was one of the Ps added in recent times and recognises the significance of the people in an organisation. For a charity there is often the question of volunteers. In this context, how these staff and volunteers interact with the people being helped is vital. Volunteers are rarely motivated by money; the desire to help is nearly always their primary if not their only motivation. They are motivated by the results they achieve. Sometimes, motivation can come from the approval of peers. In some ways this makes managing them easier although there can be problems from overenthusiasm. Staff, on the other hand, do have legitimate financial concerns: they have to eat and pay the rent, the same as the next person. But people who work for not-for-profit organisations almost always have strong motivations around the cause of the organisation.

Process. This refers to the whole business of making sure the right person, who is properly trained, is in the right place to do the right thing. It is often an area of weakness with both businesses and charities and can be a Cinderella. It requires organisation and often great attention to detail. It will also, nowadays, require IT which is secure and meets GDPR regulations. It sometimes suffers from lack of attention from managers because it is seen as administrative and hence can slip below the radar. As was mentioned under 'people' above, the chief motivation of staff and volunteers is to help the recipients of the charity, and this can lead some to feel that the mechanics of the organisation and its systems are an activity of lower importance.

Phones that aren't answered, messages not passed on, people being in the wrong place at the wrong time are just some of the problems that beset some businesses and charities and can have damaging effects on their reputations. Cutbacks have led some charities to reduce the money available for training their staff. You notice this with stale websites because no one knows how to update them, and confusion when you phone because the person answering does not know how to access the diary on screen. It is an important area and neglecting it can have significant consequences.

Physical evidence. At first, an odd-sounding one, but this is the business – linked to branding – of how you carry on your activities, which link to your ethics and your values. It can impact both positively and negatively. People are very sensitive to the issue of how charities use their funds – more so after some of the scandals which have afflicted the sector in recent years. Donors want to know the money they give is spent wisely; they do not like to see flamboyance or signs of excessive spending.

Few giving to charity will have read the accounts and actually know how much is spent on salaries and overheads or the reasons why. The only evidence is what they see when they interact with your charity – the 'physical evidence', in other words. I was truly shocked once when I went to a meeting at the offices of a national charity in a south-coast town and arrived at palatial offices with panoramic views of the harbour. A FTSE director can be paid millions and be paid more millions in bonuses and may pay little in the way of tax. This is more or less accepted. A charity cannot do this.

An important consideration therefore is the 'look' your charity has. It is ultimately a subjective process. Do you convey trust, or efficiency? Does your brand express what you are and what your values are?

I know that some reading this will feel that this is a bit of a fool's errand. You might argue that your charity does excellent work helping children/the homeless/the environment/people with debt. That may indeed be so, but I am suggesting that people have very short attention spans and make decisions exceedingly quickly and largely based on emotional factors. This is discussed in some detail in Daniel Kahneman's book *Thinking, Fast and Slow*. He discusses the two types of thinking, which he calls System 1: operating more or less automatically and quickly, with little or no effort or sense of voluntary control; and System 2: effortful mental activities.[79] Think of your own buying and shopping decisions. You might be someone who carefully weighs up all the options, studies them on the internet and makes a fully researched decision before buying. Or you might be someone who sees something in a shop window or on display, thinks 'I like the look of that' and decides to buy. Most of our choices are made quite spontaneously and based on a range of emotional factors. Giving to a charity is similarly based, I suggest, on quick emotional judgements – and the look, as well as the cause itself, is a factor in that fairly instant decision to give or not to give.

Presence. Earlier, I suggested 'price' had little relevance as far as a charity was concerned, for various reasons. A factor that I *do* think important is 'presence', which happily begins with a P. By this I mean it is important for most charities to be recognised and known for what they do – that is, they have a *presence* in the society within which they operate. It is a key element of branding. This is something more than marketing and manifests itself in things like being approached by local media when a topic close to the charity's activities is being reported on. Some of the national charities are often quoted or interviewed when something comes up in their area of work – I am thinking of Liberty or Shelter for example. Do your local media organisations come to you when something relevant to your work is going to be the subject of an article? Are you recognised when the name of your organisation comes up? Are you included when there is some kind of exhibition being mounted locally? Or did you discover it was on by word of mouth and hastily try to get an invitation? At present, Extinction Rebellion is the organisation immediately thought of when the question of climate change is discussed. But what about the other organisations that beaver away on this topic?

To achieve presence is part of the marketing and communications plan, but it is also down to the mindset of staff and trustees. They need to recognise the importance of being 'seen' and how having a presence is a vital component of your charity's success.

The issue of presence matters in respect of political matters. Charities cannot of course be party political. The work they do is of political consequence, however, and in my view they should be listened to and taken account of more than they currently are. The fact that they are not is, in part, due to the reticence of charities – sometimes under the mistaken impression that they are not allowed to speak out. In the introduction I said that charities often pick up the pieces left over or undone by local or national government. When funding for services is cut, it is they who help the homeless or provide food for the hungry. Yet too often their voice is unheard. At election time, the airways are full of politicians, pundits and assorted experts arguing about this, that and the other policy or manifesto promise: seldom is a charity representative given space or a hearing. When for example did you last see a charity person on the BBC's *Question Time* or *Newsnight*? There are countless 'vox pop' interviews with members of the public. Yet all the arguments, the tax policies, austerity and the spending priorities, result in thousands experiencing stress which, as I have said, ends up at the door of some charity or another.

I have mentioned the Trussell Trust before – the food bank charity founded here in Salisbury – and in an interview in the *Guardian* its chief executive, Emma Revie, speaks of the tension in running a charity like hers. They now give out 2.5 million food parcels (year to April 2021), a third more than the previous year. Yet the article refers to her reluctance to apportion blame for the 'years of freezes and benefits not keeping track with the cost of living, a significant reduction in the value of working-age benefits, the five weeks claimants have to wait before receiving any universal credit, "pushing them into debt and pushing them into food banks"'.[80]

The Charity Commission has given clear advice on what charities can do in relation to campaigning, and the guidance is worth reading closely.[81] It makes clear that political campaigning 'can be legitimate and valuable activities for charities to undertake'. It must however 'be in relation to its charitable purposes'. A charity can 'campaign for a change in the law'. A charity cannot support a particular party or politician. It is clear therefore that charities can make their voices heard if they follow the rules laid out. I think it a pity that the experience that they have garnered, often working in challenging sectors and seeing the results of government policies at first hand, is not more widely shared. The reticence shown is regrettable.

I suggest that trustees think carefully about whether their experience of dealing with problems and stress should be more widely shared and publicised. Their knowledge of these issues can be an important contribution to informing the public about the real state of affairs in their sector.

PUTTING IT TOGETHER

We are in a position to look now at putting these ideas and principles into some kind of order and sequence of actions. The following diagram sets out the issues discussed in this section:

A situation analysis: What changes, if any, do you need to make? What changes have taken place in the environment which affect your charity? The STEEPLE analysis.
What are the main objectives of the charity? Which of the following is it/are they? 1. Raising awareness of the cause it is engaged in 2. Raising awareness of the charity itself, i.e. its brand 3. Trying to recruit volunteers and helpers 4. Raising money 5. Trying to improve the problem it was set up to tackle
Decide on the strategy. Is it still the right one? Does it need to be revised?
The 7 Ps of marketing (adapted): • Product (service) • Place • Promotion • People • Process • Physical evidence • Presence
The communication plan: What do we need to communicate to whom?
The marketing plan: • Our brand • Key messages • Measurement of effectiveness
Feedback: How is it all working? How can we improve? What needs to change?

Fig 4 The marketing process

The plan will require implementation. Seeking outside help might be an option. Having someone to facilitate your discussion is likely to be useful. They will keep you on track, prompt questions and perhaps challenge assumptions. It is not usually the sort of activity which can be done in one day so there will the question of cost to consider. The activity will be unfamiliar to most of the board, which is a point in favour of outside support and encouragement. I do not think having a marketing specialist is absolutely necessary. What is needed is someone to keep you on track through the thinking process I have set out above.

What is important though is staff involvement. One of the perils of medium-sized charities who appoint someone with 'marketing' in their job title, is the belief that it is they 'who do the marketing'. The function becomes detached from the mainstream work of the charity and is devolved to that person. This is bad practice on several counts.

Firstly, it is everyone's function to represent the work of the organisation, to be an 'ambassador' for it. So although the majority of staff and volunteers do not have 'marketing' in their title, they are nevertheless representing the charity at several different levels, at meetings, in public events or with individuals. As far as the majority of people are concerned, it is the front-line staff who 'are' the charity and from whom they will gain their impressions of it (good or bad). Since staff and volunteers are coming into contact with a range of people and organisations, they should be a source of ideas and information which is likely to be of use for the social media platforms and the website. It is vital therefore that all staff are engaged in the marketing activities. This is a point you should look out for as a trustee. If it seems that the only person involved in marketing activity is the person with 'marketing' in their job title, it might be worthwhile mentioning the above points.

The matter of the website and other social media will be a feature of the marketing discussions. Most charities have such a presence now and it is very likely that your charity has one already. They are easy to set up these days and programs like WordPress and GoDaddy, for example, are easy to use and need only minimal IT skills. *PC Magazine* gives advice and other suggestions. It is not all straightforward, however. Setting up the site is one thing, populating it another. You will no doubt come across websites where nothing seems to change from one month to the next. It's Easter and there is still stuff about Christmas being featured. An event held two months ago is still being advertised.

Securing material – whether it be stories, events, activities or 'think pieces' – is surprisingly difficult, I have found. Your charity may be doing brilliant work and making a real difference in the field in which you are active, but is this reflected on your website or Facebook page? Is there a steady flow of information and stories about your work to interest the public or other followers? Thought not. If there is, then you can skip forward a few paragraphs. If – as is quite likely – the site shows little sign of change from one month to the next, then stay with me.

I run several websites and getting people to submit material is not easy. I know others who say the same thing. We are told about interesting conferences that people have been to, fascinating meetings attended, inspiring talks listened to, or significant help given to someone. A few words for the website? They rarely appear. Why this should be I am not sure. Speculatively, it is because people are naturally reticent about writing something that the world will see. It may also be because of a natural shyness: they may have written essays and the like at school or university but these were not for public consumption. Another factor I have experienced is that people are very reluctant to write about matters concerning the people they are dealing with because of confidentiality. This is of course understandable and perfectly proper. They do not want to reveal sensitive matters about an individual and in fact, a local charity can find anonymising a story quite difficult. To breach confidence in this way is quite wrong. British reticence is also at play – we simply do not like, as a nation, to blow our own trumpet.

However, for a charity promoting a cause, acting as a bridge between the media and the cause is an important element of their work. Assuming your charity is involved with people in some way, then you will encounter in your work individuals who are experiencing problems, distress or deprivation in some form. Bringing this to the attention of a wider public should be given serious attention. Making this connection between an individual and a journalist can achieve significant results.

How do the management tackle this? I have to be honest and say 'with difficulty'. I and others have struggled to winkle out contributions with only limited success.

The first step is to ensure that there is a belief – a culture even – within the charity that telling the world what you do and what you have achieved is important. In the commercial world they say 'if you don't tell, you don't sell'. Hiding your light under a bushel is not really an option for any charity, especially not in the current climate. This has to be hardwired into the organisation from the CEO downwards. Unless this is the case, nothing else will succeed. On a related note, contributing to the marketing and communication efforts of the charity should be part of the job description of *all* staff and volunteers. What sometimes happens is that the job falls to someone whose principal role is marketing or managing social media and the website. They will depend on staff keeping them informed and providing the material: if they are not getting this input, then their task is akin to making bricks without straw.

All staff meetings should have, as a standard item on the agenda, something about what successes or newsworthy things staff and volunteers have come across or achieved in their work. Getting people to express this as a matter of routine should help to encourage them to volunteer ideas. Once one does, it can act *pour encourager les autres*. Once in a while, this can yield something that is worth wider expression, either on the website or for the annual report or as a press release. On the question of staff meetings, it is worth considering: where does this question of stories sit in the agenda? It is often the case that these meetings are taken up with a lot of staff matters, casework discussions, problems with IT and various other matters one might collectively call 'domestic'. They are important to the people concerned, of course. Once all this is done, there might be a request for any stories or things worth wider promotion. Unfortunately, if this comes towards the end of the meeting (which has already overrun), people are anxious to get away, papers are being gathered and some vague promises are made to 'see if I have anything' and off they go. I suggest that this needs to be nearer the start of the meeting and given a degree of weight by the manager or CEO.

The person putting forward the success may themselves be reluctant to take it any further, but the management can perhaps ask someone else or even recruit someone from outside to do the legwork of turning it into usable copy. In fact, having someone from outside is a good idea in itself, as it will help to make it accessible to the general reader and make sure jargon is kept to a minimum.

A word about photography. I was once asked to prepare an annual report and needed to illustrate the publication with some photographs. I secured a supply from around the organisation, none of which I was able to use. They were either little more than snaps, or were undated and without adequate description of when and where they were taken, nor whether permission had been obtained from people in the photos. The digital files had never been catalogued so couldn't be found. I do suggest thinking carefully about photography and doing so throughout the year. It is no use, if your need for photography is in June, say, trying to get a photo organised for an event which took place in February. Something about trees with leaves and people wearing short sleeves doesn't look right. Everyone, it seems, has a smartphone these days and they do take good-quality images. Getting a well-composed picture however is not a skill everyone has. I also suggest that unless you really do have a keen and capable amateur on staff (or known to you) with proper kit, you should seriously consider using a professional. You get what you pay for. Good photographs just look so much better than snaps.

What then do you do as a trustee? You are not after all managing the show, so the things I have suggested above are not for you to do. Your role is to ask questions along the above lines. Is there an item in the staff meetings concerned with marketing, capturing stories and using them in the work of promoting the charity? Do all staff see it as part of their role to promote the charity? Is there a plan to photograph projects/events through the year and is it being done properly and professionally? You need to keep an eye on the website and social media to see that there is a regular flow of material and they are being kept up to date. Asking about this will often bring up some of the problems I have discussed above.

FUNDRAISING

A key concern for virtually all charities is the issue of fundraising, which has become more difficult in recent years.[82] There are so many competing causes and so many important issues in need of funding that it is a daunting task for small charities. Not for them the advertisements in a national newspaper or the series of professionally created TV advertisements that the major charities can afford. A small charity does have one advantage – a big one – and that is its localness. An acquaintance of mine, who is a trustee of a major charity, said they were aware of resistance because they were national in scope. There is perhaps a perception that big national charities have big overheads to match, a not altogether fair assumption.

For trustees of a small charity, the issue needs thinking about at the strategic level.

- The first point, which I have already discussed, is the attitudes of the public and funders towards your charity, and I have made the point of distinguishing between the cause and your charity itself. Understanding this will help in crafting a plan or marketing campaign.
- What is your message? This has to be crystal clear because in some situations, you may only have a few seconds of someone's time. I have discussed the donation boxes at the exit of some supermarkets and how shoppers only devote a few moments in deciding which box to put their coins into.
- How is your brand strength? Is it recognisable and does it convey, in words, images and the name itself, a strong message? A key concern nowadays is reassuring people of your effectiveness and that the money is going to the cause itself. It will be important to provide a statistic which says 'X% of our funding goes to the [cause/activity]'.
- Where actually do you propose seeking money from? There are three main sources: the public (and do not forget bequests), companies large and small, and statutory bodies such as local authorities and the Lottery. There is conceivably a fourth and that is a commercial enterprise of some sort and arranging

to gift any profit to the charity. Charity shops are a common sight in this regard. With a company, it may not be money but help or expertise which can in fact be very helpful. Remember that nearly all firms will want to gain a benefit to themselves from giving. It might be reputational or it could just be part of their Corporate Social Responsibility programme. It will be advisable to think: what can we offer this firm?

- If you are seeking funding from a statutory body or a trust, then the application must be properly put together. This can be an opportunity for a trustee – or several of you – to make a contribution to the process. It is a bit like an exam really: you have to answer the question put, especially if it is in the form of an application form. Frequently nowadays there are word counts, so concise prose to explain what you do, the project and other matters in 200 or 300 words is essential. It will be important to read their guidance and the focus of their funding. Does your proposal address this?
- Online forms, crowdfunding, Facebook and various apps now enable giving money at the press of button or a finger on a screen. Do not forget that we are rapidly moving towards a cashless society – a move speeded up during the pandemic.

I now want to move on to the vexed topic of meetings.

CHAPTER 11

Meetings

When you flicked through this book and saw the chapter headed 'Meetings', did you inwardly groan? As you turned to this chapter, did you do so with a heavy heart? Meetings have a bad press and much of the guidance on websites starts negatively. They are seen as a necessary evil, sometimes even an *unnecessary* evil. They are to be got over as quickly as possible, with considerable attention paid to how wasteful they are of participants' time. There is a growing literature suggesting stand-up meetings (literally held standing up), mainly for the morning get-togethers in software firms. I might be wrong, but I suspect most staff in software firms are in their twenties and thirties and well able to stand for a one-hour meeting. Meetings are seen as wasteful, time-consuming, repetitive, too long, unfocused and altogether a bad thing. A blot on the organisation's landscape. I could end the chapter here.

You might be surprised to read, therefore, that I think that meetings are overall a good thing. You read that right: 'meetings' and 'good thing' in the same sentence. I do not deny that they can be too long, too unfocused and all the other things people have said, but, despite that, I think the benefits often exceed the cost and the disadvantages. In this chapter, in addition to singing their praises, I do want to set out how to try and make the best of them and what you can do as a trustee to help make them a success.

Before going any further, I should say that many reading this will have had plenty of experience of meetings, good and bad. I suspect that in all honesty, they may not derive much from this chapter. My experience is with commercial firms, a quango and in two local authorities (as well as several charities and not-for-profits subsequently). The character of meetings was slightly different in each. Whether they are different in type is hard to say. One local authority held their meetings in public and this is significantly different from a meeting in private. If there are differences I would say the key one is the character and ability of the chair. This matters more than the type of organisation.

Why do I think meetings are a good thing? The first point concerns the fact that we are social creatures. We actually enjoy contact with others, especially those with whom we have a degree of affinity. It was a common refrain during the pandemic lockdown period in 2020, how depressed people became at their forced isolation. Not seeing someone else in the flesh affected many people in quite serious ways. Various means of communication using meeting software such as Zoom, Webex and Microsoft Teams helped people to speak to others and to maintain a degree of visual contact. People could send emails, use the phone and even write letters. But none of this, including the use of virtual platforms, equalled actually meeting others and speaking face to face.

There is copious advice on how to run a good meeting. Many are of the type 'X rules for a successful meeting'. Nearly all the advice is about increasing their efficiency and their effectiveness, and making sure they don't go on too long. I don't doubt the value of much of this advice and bits of it I will repeat here. It all seems to derive, however, from a belief that meetings are wasteful and inherently inefficient. The assumption is that they detract from the real work that people do in their offices or in front of their screens.

So anything which can be done to shorten them must necessarily be a good thing.

I suspect that much of this advice is intended for commercial organisations. Certainly some of the language used has a 'corporate' feel to it. It is perhaps another example of how the commercial and not-for-profit worlds are somewhat different in their outlooks and ways of doing things. I suspect one of the reasons why so much advice is based on minimising time in meetings and making them as efficient as possible is because it is prepared for commercial firms, who have a powerful incentive to act this way because they need to make a profit. Time is also important for a not-for-profit enterprise, but perhaps the imperative is not so great. It is perhaps one of those differences I discussed in Chapter 3.

Regarding meetings as potentially 'a good thing' and as an activity of value, I suggest, provides a slightly different perspective. So the meeting goes on a bit too long and finishes twenty minutes after it should. If a meal lasted twenty minutes longer than intended, would you regard that as a poor do? If a social do lasted twenty minutes longer than expected, would you not think that a measure of how enjoyable it was? There is nothing wrong with an efficiently run meeting with everyone making perfectly timed and brief contributions. If efficiency trumps effectiveness and inhibits people from making their contributions, however, it might not be such a good thing.

The critics of meetings sometimes argue that they can be replaced by various electronic methods. It is more efficient for people to speak electronically rather than travel miles to make contact physically, they argue. The increase in home working during the pandemic seemed to show that work could be done without the need for continuous travelling about. This is undoubtedly true and the number of meetings can indeed be reduced by these means with the consequent savings of time and expense. But ultimately, nothing can replace the pleasure and satisfaction to be derived by meeting in person.

What do we mean by meetings? They come in all shapes and sizes, from Monday morning get-togethers which can last a matter of minutes, to fully fledged board meetings which can take a while longer. As a trustee, it is the latter which will mostly concern you and it is those on which I want to focus. If you have had experience of meetings before becoming a trustee, then this chapter will probably not tell you much, but not all trustees come from that background and so may be less familiar with board-type meetings. I hope the observations which follow will be of use to those people.

What is the point of a board meeting or other meeting of trustees? Understanding this is the first step to getting it right and having a useful one. I would list the following points:

1. **Morale.** You may not see a fellow trustee from one meeting to the next and although emails may pass between you, and meetings may be held electronically, actually meeting your colleagues personally is not just useful but it should also be pleasurable. This is a point which seems to be missing from those who are dedicated to advising on how to run super-efficient meetings which last not one second longer than is necessary. You are a group of people who have volunteered to help in some charitable cause, and meeting together should be a valuable experience in its own right.
2. **Motivation.** A second and linked purpose is a reaffirmation of why you are all doing this work. This is unlikely to be an agenda item but during the course of the meeting and examining and discussing the work of the charity, you should

gain a sense of why you are there. This is something more than the mechanics of the meeting – the discussion of its finances, progress with the strategy, funding, staff issues and general progress – but something almost metaphysical. A feeling that it is all worthwhile and that you are playing a part in it.

3. **Progress.** Moving on to more down-to-earth purposes, one is to check in on progress. It is useful to have meetings which act as a kind of marker in the year. Something agreed at the last meeting might have an action of 'by the next meeting'. Although some of this can be done without the need for people to congregate, a meeting enables progress to be seen in the round. More importantly, if there are problems or progress hasn't been made, then it is an opportunity for trustees to hear the reasons why from the horse's mouth, so to speak. It is a bit like a jury: actually hearing what the reasons were can be crucial. Hopefully, this should not be a regular occurrence, but from time to time, it must need to take place.
4. **Exchange of information.** I have discussed information earlier in two chapters on the subject, so I will not go into too much detail here. But as I have said, it is important for a trustee to receive information in digestible forms, to see trends explained and for some information to be presented in graphical form or as charts. In the last chapter I stressed the importance of receiving it before the meeting. It is essential that the management are acting on what is revealed and the CEO should take ownership of it.
5. **Discussing ideas.** If there is an idea which is ill-formed and someone wishes to discuss it and get a view from others, then a meeting is often the best way to do this. It can lead to other suggestions and yield additional help, like contacts. People are often more comfortable with commenting in a meeting format

because they can hedge their observations and soften them if they disagree with the idea. There is a natural reluctance to make negative comments in a written format like an email. Sending out an idea which others are reluctant to comment on, possibly with good reason, might not elicit any responses and so not move the idea on.

6. **Taking stock.** The sixth advantage of a meeting is the ability to take stock – that is, viewing progress with the strategy and with specific projects or funding applications. Although a lot of this can be done outside a meeting in the form of schedules and reports, it is not an exact science and it does merit some general discussion.
7. **Management of change.** 'If anything is certain, it is that change is certain. The world we are planning for today will not exist in this form tomorrow' (attributed to Phil Crosby). We live in an ever-changing world and your charity has to recognise that and adapt accordingly. Change has to be acknowledged, its implications discussed, and what needs to be done debated. It is the kind of topic best discussed in a meeting.
8. **Sensing problems.** Finally, you have the opportunity to see the whites of the management's eyes. Hopefully, everything in your charity is as it should be and the reports give a true and fair view of what is happening. But if there are problems, hearing it from the management's mouth is worth a great deal. You can get a sense that things are not quite right even if you do not know what the problem is. This direct physical contact is important. We do have within us an innate sense of being able to spot someone dissembling or not quite telling the truth. This can only be achieved in a face-to-face situation such as a meeting.

I have put these points forward as some of the benefits of meetings; they still need to be managed. Take item 5 for example: discussing ideas. I suggest that a meeting is an ideal format for this purpose because of the contribution others around the table can make to the idea. What can happen, though, is people can just turn up with and launch into what might be a 'pet project' or a wild idea which has just come to them. A meeting can quickly descend into a kind of sea of chatter with everyone speaking at once and frankly no progress being made at all. It still needs a degree of discipline and good chairmanship. A chair can suggest that before an idea is brought to the board, a trustee runs it past him or her first and seeks to have it as an agenda item. Ideally, of course, a paper should be written and circulated beforehand. My own experience however is that it is extremely difficult to achieve this with many who sit on these boards.

A board paper comes in three forms: for *information*, for *decision* or for *discussion*. Whichever form it is should be clearly marked at the top so that fellow board members know which one it is. A paper for decision should ideally have the recommended decision(s) at the top of the report. Anyone reading this with a civil service, public sector or large firm background will be familiar with these procedures. Trustees who do not have this kind of background may, however, not be. It is also useful in such a paper to set out what the options are and the reasons for *not* choosing the ones which have been rejected. The aim should be to give trustees all the relevant information, such as costs, relevant background, timescale, and management implications, together with a discussion of risks and how they will be mitigated. If there is more than one option, explaining why one has been chosen and others rejected is desirable. And don't forget, 'do nothing' is often an option to be considered.

Those reading this with the sort of background I have just explained will be familiar with all this, but if you are new to meetings, then attending one where papers are not presented and where nearly everything is verbal might lead you to think it is the normal way of doing things. It isn't, or shouldn't be, and I suggest that for any matter which is at all complicated and where there are several options, you might like to gently suggest a paper setting things out as preferable.

There can be a tendency for a member of staff to turn up with a problem – either a written report or as a verbal presentation. Trustees, having digested what the problem is, can begin to make what they feel are helpful suggestions, only to be met with rebuffs such as 'we tried that, and it didn't work', 'we cannot do that (for some reason)', 'it's not practical' or some other comment. I do not think it is acceptable for staff to do this. Quite apart from the waste of time, if the options were too difficult/impractical/have been tried before, why wasn't that in the report?

Which brings me to the whole business of boards and how they work. I have mentioned the considerable quantity of published advice, some of which I will come to later. Firstly, I want to discuss some of the recurrent problems with meetings which can have a profound effect on their effectiveness and in turn, on the effectiveness of the charity itself.

GROUP THINK

One of the most pernicious issues with meetings is what is called 'group think', which was put forward as a concept only as late as 1972.[83] Irving Janis suggested it was a particular risk when a group was under some kind of stress. It occurs because members of the group – in this case a charity board – refrain from disagreeing with what appears to be the consensus. They go along with the majority view even though they may have severe misgivings. They value conformity over disagreement. It comes about for a range of reasons, one of which is the desire to achieve a decision quickly. This results in a kind of rush to conclude the discussion where no one wants to be the one who raises an objection.

There are a number of examples in history and one often cited is the failure of the 'O' rings on the *Challenger* mission, made famous by Richard Feynman who was asked to investigate what went wrong. It transpired that many scientists had their reservations about the use of this material and its tendency to brittleness in conditions of extreme cold, but they suppressed their doubts because of the need to progress the project.[84] The result was disaster when the rocket blew up, killing the crew on board.

Other examples are described in Chapter 17 of *The Blunders of our Governments* by Anthony King and Ivor Crewe, among them being plans to introduce a poll tax in the 1980s.[85]

How then do you and your fellow trustees avoid the group-think trap? Here are some suggestions:

1. Recognise that it is a dangerous trap and one that is easy to fall into. An official is quoted by King and Crewe saying, 'Everyone agrees. So we must be wrong.'[86] This does not mean disagreeing for disagreeing's sake, but if what is being discussed is complex, hard to define and with a degree of uncertainty, then unanimity can be a sign of group think.
2. It is important that the chair of the meeting (who might be the chair of trustees) does not disclose their position on the project at the outset, only doing so some way into the discussions. This is particularly so if the chair is a forceful character. Achieving this can be difficult of course, such is the nature of characters

like this. But if he or she can be persuaded to adopt a neutral position, then it will enable all trustees to have their say without feeling they are treading on toes or on hallowed ground.

3. The chair should expressly ask if there are those who have contrary views or doubts and invite them to contribute. This should be a normal part of being a good chair in any event. Appointing a 'devil's advocate' can also be a good idea.
4. King and Crewe specifically warn against PowerPoint presentations.[87] For one thing, they 'privilege the presenter' and have the effect of discouraging critical discussion and analysis. They encourage group think, they argue, and are a 'dangerous instrument of persuasion'. They might have added that they have a deadening effect on the audience – 'death by PowerPoint' is a common experience, especially where the presenter stands with their back to the audience reading off the screen. Their very sophistication and slickness gives a sense that everything is cut and dried. Nobody likes to interrupt such presentations whereas in a presentation without it, they might do.
5. In Daniel Kahneman's bestselling book *Thinking Fast and Slow*, previously referred to, he discusses the conduct of meetings and encouraging independent judgements: 'A simple rule can help: before an issue is discussed, all members of the committee should be asked to write a very brief summary of their position. This procedure makes good use of the value of the diversity of knowledge and opinion in the group. The standard practice of open discussion gives too much weight to the opinions of those who speak early and assertively causing others to line up behind them' (p85).

It does take courage to be the one to speak out when there is a rush to consensus. If you are a new board member, this is also difficult because as the 'new boy or girl' there can be a feeling of nervousness. As the new person, you will still have an outsider's view and this is quite likely to give you some insight into the problems being discussed.

The problem of group think usually occurs because basic assumptions are not challenged. There can be a kind of institutional inertia. If the starting point is wrong, it is hardly surprising that the end result is too. It is also difficult because ensuring it doesn't happen needs action by the chair, whose responsibility it is to ensure that all opinions are invited and respected. It can take some encouragement and cajoling to draw the more reserved members out to express their views. Group think is undoubtedly a powerful force and ultimately the cause of many problems and disasters within organisations.

If there is pressure to run an efficient meeting and to get through the agenda by some fixed time, then this is likely to add to the problem of group think. If you and your fellow trustees feel this pressure and the clock is being watched as the meeting progresses, this will act as a disincentive to put forward a dissenting view and hold up the proceedings. A giveaway here is a chair who takes off their watch and props it up in front of them. There is nothing wrong with good time management and an efficiently run meeting, but if it becomes a fetish then there are real risks that mistakes can be made in the rush to finish on time. If, in the rush to finish, there is not time to discuss a topic which you feel is an important one, then I suggest asking for a paper to be presented to the next meeting. I am not a fan of agendas with times allocated to each item.

MANAGING MEETINGS

A key theme in the advice about running a good meeting is to be clear about why you are doing so – its purpose and objectives. In some cases there may a single purpose and one agenda item: a meeting to decide on a particular project, for example. Typically, meetings have a series of purposes: to review progress, to allocate tasks, discuss staffing issues and so on. The agenda will be its purpose.

On the question of agendas, the composition of what is discussed is worth a little reflection.

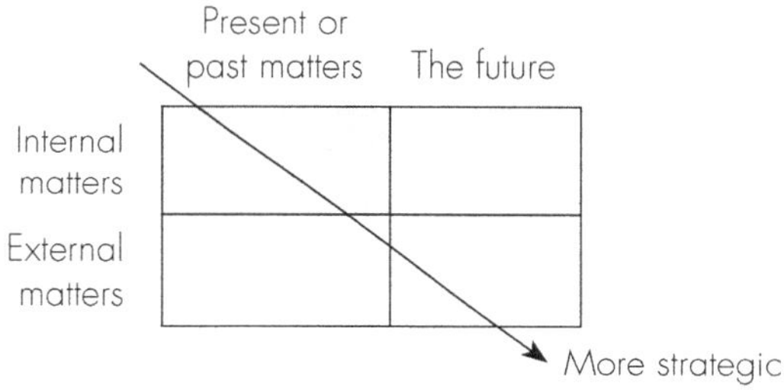

Fig 5 Components of an agenda

The diagram shows an agenda broken down into four elements: internal and external, present (or past) and future. In broad terms, the more future and external the matters to be discussed are, the more likely they are to be of a strategic nature. If the agenda is all about the present (or past) and internal matters, it will be less strategic. I have to be honest and say it is not a perfect fit, but I suggest it as a guide to looking at the agenda and the meetings you go to. A board of trustees should be focusing on the strategic so should be spending time in the bottom right of the diagram. If your meetings are all in the top left, you are right to be a little concerned.

> *'Change is the law of life, and those who look only to the past and present are certain to miss the future'* – John F. Kennedy

Linked to this is continuous improvement, which I will now discuss.

The Japanese have a word for this – '*Kaizen*'. It is one of the reasons we buy so many of their products, such as cameras and cars. It is something that charities could learn from even though they are not making a product. There are likely to be activities which you are doing on a repetitive basis even if – like organising a conference – you only do them once a year or so. A key question to ask – after holding an event (or running a training seminar, organising a conference, or whatever it might be) – is 'If we were to run this activity again, what we would do differently and what could we do better?' These questions often do not get asked. Worse, when the event is repeated, people have forgotten some of the key issues and repeat the mistakes for a second time.

I have never been that clear on why we do not do this more regularly, but wherever I have worked, this reluctance to review projects in the light of experience is rarely methodically undertaken. It might partly be not wanting to be seen to criticise the organiser. If the event went well with only a few minor hitches, people are keen to praise the organiser for a job well done, and suggesting improvements might be taken as detracting from the praise. There is a risk the organiser sees it as only 'carping'. Yet it is rare that something, however well done, cannot be improved. If the event did not go as well as planned, there might be a desire to 'put it behind us' and move on to the next thing. Dwelling on a failure is not something people wish to do. Whatever the reason, the process of rigorously reviewing projects and looking for possible improvements should be an established part of a charity's management. If this cannot be done at the time (for reasons of tact or otherwise), then keep a private note of possible improvements for a later date or when the project is repeated.

Perhaps a way of avoiding embarrassment or causing wounded feelings is to review every element of the project, rather than concentrating on the parts that went less well. This method provides plenty of opportunities to say 'that went well' or 'that was especially successful', thus avoiding hurting the organiser's feelings.

It is also vital to write it all down so that there is a record for the future.

Meetings are a vital part of the culture of the charity you are part of. They should be enjoyable and fruitful. If you do not look forward to attending yours, I suggest something is wrong.

ELEVEN POINTS FOR A GOOD MEETING

Bringing all this together, I suggest the following eleven points which will contribute to good and effective meetings:

1. **Preparation**. Reports are prepared and distributed to trustees about a week before the meeting takes place. There will be the occasional exception (typically, illness or genuine urgency).
2. **Reports**. All reports should be marked 'For decision', 'For information' or 'For discussion', as explained above. This will help with the decision-making process. Some kind of **action** should result, certainly from decision items.
3. **Purpose**. There should be a clear sense of purpose, which will usually mean reference to the work or the strategic plan. It should answer the questions 'What are we trying to achieve?' and 'Are we achieving it?'
4. **Financial reports**. These should contain ratios or percentages, focus on key issues, and discuss solvency and reserves as discussed in Chapter 8.
5. **Management accounts**. In addition to financial accounts, there should be some management accounts, again with ratios or percentages. This was also discussed in Chapter 8.
6. **Information**. There should be a supply of succinct information, showing trends and perhaps some visual information as well. See Chapters 6 and 7, but also Chapter 5 on governance.

7. **Opportunity**. There should be an opportunity to both praise and challenge staff and management. It is natural to focus on problems but remembering to praise staff and volunteers for work done well is important too.
8. **Environment**. An awareness of the outside world, changes taking place and what other relevant charities are doing.
9. **Inclusion**. All trustees should feel able to contribute and not just those with some kind of specialist knowledge. I discuss this in the following chapter, particularly in relation to trustees who do not have any specialist knowledge (relevant to the charity's activities that is). This is also relevant in countering group think.
10. **Trust**. There has to be an overriding sense of openness and trust and that you believe the information you are receiving is honest and straightforward.
11. **Mutual respect**. There must be respect between the members of the board. Views must be heard and opinions allowed to be expressed.

In the next chapter I want to explore some of the issues around being a trustee.

CHAPTER 12

Being a trustee

There are many reasons why people become or want to become a volunteer or trustee of a not-for-profit organisation. One that is frequently cited is to put something back into the community. This tends to be from older people, perhaps those at or near retirement age. Some have a genuine desire to help others. Anger or frustration can be motivating factors, especially at what is seen as an injustice or unfairness. Money is never a reason since by definition, volunteering is unpaid. It is also interesting to note that often trustees do not claim expenses for travel, seeing that as a further contribution to the cause.

Some are able to offer particular expertise. This may be a management skill of some sort, for example a knowledge of marketing, accountancy or human resources. Others have knowledge of the sector in which the charity is engaged. They may have worked in housing or social services, and have valuable knowledge of how things work, key legislation, or processes within a local authority or government.

Some simply want to keep active. Having retired early, they can have a desire to maintain a fulfilling life and be part of something. Some want to volunteer for only a limited or specific amount of time. Other commitments or transport issues could limit what they can do or when they can do it.

This book is focusing on being a trustee which is, in a sense, a specific form of volunteering. It is worth exploring this point a little, because there are many people who might have useful skills to offer as a trustee but who wish for a more 'hands on' role in a local charity. They may have had experience at a senior level within an organisation but feel that they now want to be free of endless meetings and 'management speak' and actually *help* people on a one-to-one basis. There are others who might be able to contribute as a trustee but who feel that they are ill-equipped to do so. Their experience of meetings, budgets and management issues generally might be limited, which leads them to think that they might be a 'fish out of water'. In a larger charity, this might be the case, but for a smaller charity, these technical issues are less intimidating. I would urge anyone who is thinking of contributing to a cause that they believe in or are angry about, to give serious consideration to becoming a trustee and not to be put off by fears of a lack of technical understanding.

There are four key issues to consider when thinking about becoming a trustee. Which charity do you wish to join, and what can you offer them; why do you want to do it, and what time and resources do you have available? I will discuss the first two.

WHICH CHARITY?

For most people this seems to be an easy choice. When talking to fellow trustees and asking them why they joined, the answer is nearly always along the lines of 'I wanted to do something, and the aims of this charity is something that interests me/I am keen about/I have a belief in'. It almost always centres on interest, or feeling an affinity for, or conviction. In my experience it is never about skills such as those I have mentioned. If you are in the position of thinking about doing something, then focusing on an organisation which is engaged in something you believe in, or have an affinity to, makes a lot of sense.

WHAT CAN YOU OFFER?

This is a little trickier. One of the frequent topics discussed at trustee and board meetings is the question of recruitment of a new trustee. This has become an increasing problem and the number of people willing to take on the task has fallen in recent years. It is partly because of the bad publicity that the sector has attracted, but it also may be a result of an increasing perception of the risk trustees face if there are problems. People have less free time as well for various reasons (for example, the need to look after elderly parents), although it remains to be seen if the reduction in commuting and more people working from home following the pandemic might free up more time for voluntary work.

Another issue is the type of person now wanted by existing boards, which are increasingly looking for people with specific skills. These might be accountancy, marketing, HR or related to the sector in which the charity is involved. This can deter those lacking those specific skills who might otherwise make a useful contribution. Of course, people with those skills can and do make valuable contributions to their boards. Relying on these rather narrow issues of specific skills, however, runs the risk of overlooking contributions non-specialists can make. The truth is, a good board should contain a balance of skills and people with specific and non-specific abilities as well. A board comprised of all specialists might not in fact function that well.

So what are these other skills that can be of value to a board? I would suggest some or all of the following:

- **Experience.** I accept this can be regarded as a bit nebulous and that someone who has done the same job for twenty years cannot necessarily claim to have twenty years of experience, just one year repeated twenty times. There will be many though who have done a variety of jobs or held different positions within a firm, who will have plenty of the elusive quality of 'experience' to offer.

- **Judgement.** Another difficult word to define in practice, and only visible when a particular problem surfaces and making a sound judgement comes into its own. A characteristic of someone with judgement is the ability to take into account the various competing factors, analyse them and present a reasoned argument for taking a particular course of action. Such individuals are extremely useful on any board (charity or otherwise).
- **Energy, optimism and enthusiasm.** I have put these three together because they do seem to be present in people as a group of characteristics. Daniel L. Reardon's quote 'in the long run, pessimists may be proved right, but the optimist has a better time on the trip' is instructive. People who bring these attributes to a board are always valuable. They can engender a sense of possibility and of hope for the future. They see glasses half full rather than half empty. They can enthuse and enliven a board.
- **An ability to see the big picture.** This ability to see the scope of things, to see beyond the immediate and to have a kind of inbuilt strategic sense is extremely important. These individuals can be a balance to those who tend to focus on the details. A board without such a person will struggle with strategic issues. I discuss in Chapter 14, on 'Bringing it all together'.
- **Independence of mind.** A lot of people fancy they have it, but it is not always the case. We are all, of course, influenced by what we see and read and by our experiences of life. We are all biased to an extent, however fair-minded we believe we are. But being able to bring a degree of objectivity and not be too taken

in by smooth-talking or simplistic statements is a significant skill. It's an ability to 'see behind' things.

- **An ability to explain or to communicate.** This may seem rather odd but I think it is a very important skill. There are many people who know things. There are many clever people around but unless you can put that into words and carry others with you, the cleverness may go unnoticed or disregarded. How often, for example, have you seen or heard a poor performance from experts who have been invited on to a news programme on the radio or TV to explain a technical or scientific issue? Despite their great learning, some seem unable to put this across in a clear or convincing way.
- **Diversity of experience.** There is a danger of a board being divorced from the lived experience of those the charity is trying to help. A charity dealing with homelessness for example is unlikely to have a homeless individual as a trustee. 'Pale, male and stale' can fairly sum up some boards. A trustee from the black or minority ethnic community will be a valuable addition to most boards.
- **Interested in working in (or as) a team.** Not everyone enjoys this. There are those who find being in a team tedious and time spent chuntering over minor topics frustrating. Others value team working and think that the sum is greater than the parts.

There are other skills of course and, if you have been to many board meetings, you may well have your own set which might differ from those I have selected. The main point I am trying to put across here is that the possession of at least some of these skills and attributes could enable a board member to make a serious contribution to a successful board. Although the specific skills that boards seek are important, these extra ones are too.

I once went on a management course where the week was based around Belbin's theory of teams.[88] Dr Belbin and his team sorted people into nine different types, or 'clusters of behaviour' as he called them. We were given a variety of tests and were grouped according to the cluster Belbin set out. To begin with we did not know how we were individually classified. Where we were in a group with all or most of the types present (we subsequently discovered), we succeeded in our task. When we were reassembled into a different and unbalanced group (without our knowing it) we failed spectacularly to finish – in fact we barely got started. What was astonishing to me was that the dysfunctionality was near fatal: we simply could not make any progress at all. I have to confess to having been somewhat sceptical of these various personality tests and the like, but at least in this case, the results were profound.

Another personality test worth mentioning is the Myers–Briggs Type Indicator – over a century old now – which divides people up into sixteen different types. It is fair to say that this and other psychological tests have a mixed reception, mainly based on a lack of independent validation. I would suggest them as being 'part of the mix' and as a useful guide, rather than as a definitive instruction on how a board should be made up or whom to recruit based on their assessments.

This just emphasises the importance of the make-up of teams. A balance of skills is essential. The key is synergy – recognising that the sum is greater than its parts. A diversity of outlook is also important as this can help counter group think. Crucially, having the mission of the charity foremost in people's minds acts as a kind of glue in meetings. The other component is shared information, which again highlights the importance of this topic. If every trustee has access to the same information in a digestible form, this acts powerfully to bring the board (team) together.

Another issue of importance is the question of diversity. An NCVO research study, *Taken on Trust*, published in 2017, showed that boards did not reflect the communities. They were predominantly white, with twice as many men as women. People from the BAME* community are quite rare on boards. Another point they made was that recruitment was often done informally. The problem here is that 'like attracts like' and boards become populated by people with similar backgrounds, with an increasing risk of group think. There are websites which are designed to help find trustees and having used one, I can report that they do help in widening the net. For one reason or another, all sorts of organisations – from parish councils, to associations of varying kinds, as well as not-for-profit organisations – are finding it difficult to find people to act as committee members, trustees or just serve on committees. When someone does volunteer, they are often greeted with open arms: if they do add to the board's diversity, so much the better. Every effort should be made, however, to increase diversity and it may be necessary to alter meeting times or days to accommodate people who may work unusual hours. Brand is a part of the picture. If you are recognised in the community and stories appear from time to time about your activities, that does help create a climate which might encourage participation.

So to sum up, although technical or specialist skills are important to a board, people with more general abilities or diverse backgrounds can make a valuable contribution and add balance to the team. My message therefore is that if you think you have some of the above abilities (I am assuming you do not have them all – does such a person exist?), then you may well be in a position to make a very useful contribution.

---

* Black, Asian and Minority Ethnic. You should be aware that some people from these communities do not like this acronym.

THE TEAM

I now want to move on to the wider issue of the team itself and how you fit in. The essential role of a trustee is being part of a team. In Figure 6 below, I set out the basic nature of the team and its components. Firstly, the charity or not-for-profit organisation itself, its purpose and its mission in society. The second element is the chief executive officer and his or her supporting management team. Thirdly, your fellow trustees led by a chair. And then there is you.

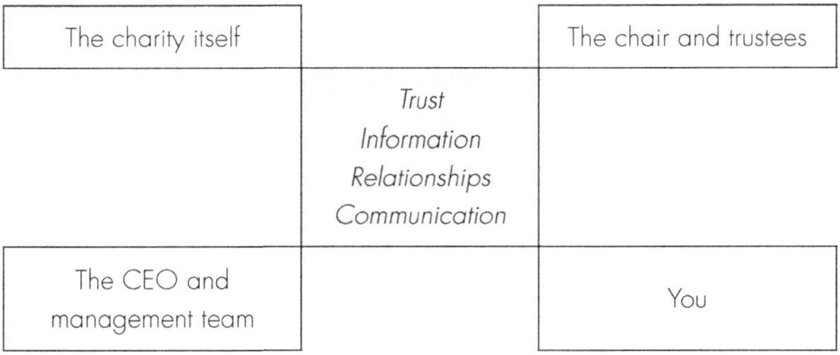

Fig 6 The trustee and the team

I have shown that what links them together and makes it all work involves four key intangible elements. They are *trust*, *information*, *communication* and *teamwork*. For the charity to work and for you to play your part as a trustee, these four tangible elements, linked by the four intangible factors, are what are likely to enable the organisation to survive and prosper. If any one of them does not work properly, or is not present at all, that is likely to lead to severe problems. It is these eight elements that I want to discuss in this chapter.

I will start with you and your role. You need to recognise that, however good you are and whatever your background, you alone cannot make a bad charity good. If one or other of these elements is not working then it will be difficult for you to have an impact. If the CEO is weak, the staff are at each other's throats or the finances are not put together, then it will be unlikely, to put it mildly, that you alone can put this right. You can ask questions, probe the management at board meetings or even contribute advice if you have relevant expertise to offer, but at the end of the day, you are not managing the day-to-day affairs of the charity so there will be a limit to what you can do. Clearly, if you do feel something is badly wrong or dysfunctional, then you will seek to persuade your fellow trustees that action needs to be taken.

One of the things I hope you take away from this chapter is being able to see yourself as part of a whole. The four tangible elements of the diagram have been discussed in previous chapters. Mission and strategy, together with branding, were discussed in Chapter 4. Issues of management have appeared throughout the book. The linking element of information was discussed in Chapters 6 and 7.

I will now look at the intangible factors in turn.

TRUST

This takes many forms but at base, do you and your fellow trustees believe in and have trust in the management of the charity? Do you believe in the information you are getting at the board meetings and at other times? If there is a nagging doubt that what you are getting is selective, sanitised, one-sided or even just plain wrong, there is a problem. Several issues can stand in the way of achieving this trust.

One is the relationship between the chair and the CEO. Let us start with the CEO, who is key to the organisation's success – or otherwise. The perfect CEO has yet to be invented which means that he or she will have a range of skills and attributes but will not have them all. They will have strengths and also weaknesses. The goal of course is not to let the weaknesses become the dominating factor in their performance, which would have a destructive effect on the charity.

The job description of a charity CEO can be forbidding. I remember looking at one for a CEO post we were recruiting for and thinking: is there anyone on the planet who has all these attributes? From managing the strategy, keeping track of the finances, fundraising, managing the team, servicing the board, being responsible for client work, and a host of governance factors, it's a wonder anyone takes on the role at all. At any moment, something or someone can go wrong or a mistake can be made, the result of which could be serious. This can lead to a state of tension if not managed. Many of the activities will be delegated to others but, to paraphrase the immortal words of President Harry S. Truman, the buck stops with the CEO.

The issue of weaknesses in a CEO (or any staff member if it comes to it) becomes a problem if they are unwilling to admit or face up to them. The place for this is with review meetings with the chair. During these meetings, a CEO should feel able to admit that they have areas of their skill set or experience that they may need help with. Facing up to what these might be is half the battle. They are then in a position to see if support, training or mentoring can be of help. It is unlikely there is no solution. Seeking a solution can serve to reduce the stress which can build up in a CEO if they feel vulnerable and exposed.

One thing to check as a trustee is that these one-to-one meetings are in fact taking place. Also, that the issue of competence and support is being discussed. As I have said, the perfect CEO has yet to be invented, so if there is never mention of support, training or mentoring then you need to be a little suspicious. It could be that the weaknesses are not being recognised or discussed. The CEO may be reluctant to admit failings for fear of losing their job. Worse, there may be a dysfunctional relationship between the chair and the CEO. The end result is that problems are not addressed and this can affect the future of the charity. It is an area you and your fellow trustees need to keep an eye on. I should add that, in my experience, the relationship between the two is usually a good one. However, as I mentioned in an earlier chapter, there can be personality and other tensions and this can be a problem, even a serious one.

INFORMATION

I have said enough about this topic in earlier chapters. Information is key to your success as a team since you need to know the basic facts in any discussion and decision making.

RELATIONSHIPS

Good relationships are crucial to the success of the charity, as indeed in any organisation. The first problem is that the board is unlikely to meet frequently, maybe only a handful of times a year. Unlike the staff who will meet each other regularly, board members will come to a meeting once every two or three months and may never see each other in between. It is therefore important that there are opportunities created to rectify this either in formal arrangements such as away days, or informally in a social setting. People are understandably nervous of speaking at a meeting if they are unsure of who the others are. It is much better for the ice to have been broken outside a formal board meeting.

Social gatherings also enable someone to express a worry that they cannot quite articulate – or are reluctant to articulate – in a formal minuted meeting: what is sometimes referred to as 'a quiet word'. I am typing this in the middle of the Covid-19 pandemic and the various meetings I normally attend – together with one in connection with a new project I'm working on – have not happened. They have been replaced with Zoom, Webex *et al.*, which are all excellent in their way, but are simply not the same as a face-to-face meeting. Nor have we been able to have any social gatherings. Elsewhere in this book, I have mentioned the value of meetings and it is interesting that while all my fellow trustees think the electronic meetings are excellent in the circumstances of lockdown and isolation, they all agree that they are not the same as direct contact. Gradually, as time has gone by and new board members have joined, I am in discussion with people I have never physically met.

A crucial part of good relationships is that which exists between the board and the executive, which usually means the CEO. A key word is respect. The advice usually given is that the board should focus on strategic and long-term issues whilst the executive should concentrate on the more day-to-day finances, management and governance, etc. The board should hold the management to account and have an overall responsibility for governance and the probity of the charity.

This advice is sound enough – to a point. The problem is that sometimes a small detail can be crucial and may need to be probed. The devil is very often in the detail. 'Don't spoil a ship for a ha'porth of tar' is a well-worn saying to point out that a small thing can have big effects. (Incidentally, whilst checking the spelling of 'ha'porth' I discovered that it should be 'sheep' not 'ship'. I always thought it meant a small spot of tar to stop a ship sinking. It doesn't – tar was used to stave off flies on sheep. The things you learn.)

So although keeping to the respective roles is important, sometimes a detail can be important and might be something the staff have overlooked. For example, a fellow trustee at a meeting I attended noticed an issue to do with the property and started to ask questions about the lease and what was going to happen at the end. This led to legal advice being sought and what could have been an expensive situation was averted. The staff and the rest of us had not picked this up.

In addition to respect therefore is trust, the subject of the last section. Trust is important because if the trustees are to respect and stick to their role, they have to have trust in the information they are receiving and the fundamental competence of the CEO and his or her staff. This trust will be earned over time.

Of course this is a two-way process. One area important for fostering good relationships is for the trustees to be conscientious in their duties as well. Things like carefully reading papers sent to them before meetings, turning up to meetings, being on time if possible and behaving properly. I have been fortunate in the organisations in which I have served and the behaviour of fellow board members has been good. However, I have heard elsewhere of aggressive questioning of staff, inappropriate remarks, papers not being read properly and other behaviours which can make for difficulties.

Much can depend on how challenges are made. A good board member should challenge the CEO and management from time to time. If they are not acting swiftly enough or if they are diverting time and resources away from what the board consider strategic priorities, then this may need to be challenged. Always the tone should be respectful and if at all possible, in the form of a question. For example, one could ask, 'Are you happy that sufficient progress is being made with X bearing in mind how important it is for us?' or 'Is it possible to make faster progress with Y bearing in mind the end of the financial year is looming?'

A good board should self-assess from time to time. This may take the form of a questionnaire asking board members how they feel things are progressing, and whether they are happy with the performance of the CEO and with the chair and their relationship with him or her. A board member can be delegated to organise this but it is often better for an outsider to be recruited. Answers are kept confidential with a view to enabling members to be candid. Although there is a cost to this, if things are not working and trustees are concerned that everything is not as it should be, then the cost will be worth it. It will reveal issues which are often simple to fix but can have a positive impact on the board's effectiveness. If trustees feel that things are generally going well, then an internal person may well be adequate.

Defining what makes for good relationships is hard to do. When they go wrong, however, it is usually easy to spot. It is rather like an orchestra: the violins may all be playing the same notes but if they are not playing them together, the result is noise.

COMMUNICATION

I have given quite some time to the issue of information, so maybe talking now about communication may seem to be over-egging it. But there is a subtle difference between the two. Information, as you will have seen from the chapters on the subject, is very much about receiving. Information is prepared by the team and presented to the board. Communication on the other hand is more about the relationships and interactions between the provider and the recipient.

Communication can take many forms. It can be written, verbal or visual – for example a video. As you will know from your daily life and experience of work, the manner of presentation, the confidence of the presenter and various visual clues will all have an influence on the message received. Communication is more than just the facts and the information given; it is a whole cluster of factors which can powerfully influence the way in which the information is received. These are closely bound to trust.

In the course of the Covid-19 pandemic, a considerable degree of debate took place about statistics and what they meant and how accurate they were. Professor David Spiegelhalter of Cambridge University was often interviewed about the subject and I watched a presentation he made at the virtual Hay Festival in 2020. The BBC has a programme called *More or Less* which examines particular topics with a statistical slant. Nearly all statistics need a degree of interpretation if we are to make sense of them. Care should be taken over definitions and the assumptions made when collecting and compiling them. All sorts of problems get in the way of the giver and receiver of information understanding each other. One problem is assumptions. The giver might assume greater knowledge than the trustee – if he or she is the recipient – actually has. This might be the case if you are new to the board. Although you have been given an induction and, as a conscientious new board member, you have studied the materials provided and looked at the website, suddenly, during a meeting, you realise you have little idea of what the others are talking about. An assumption has been made about the topic under discussion, its history or its relevance, that leaves you in the dark. Everyone else seems to know what is being said but not you. Remember, when you assume, you make an *ass* out of *u* and *me*.

A factor I have noticed in meetings is that there can be two distinct styles of presentation, especially if it is a verbal one. I call them 'top down' and 'bottom up'. There are people who give an overview of what is going to be said and then go into the detail to fill in the gaps. Others start off in a detailed way like they are slowly building a wall. This latter type of presentation can be difficult to follow because it takes a while before you realise what the crux of it is. Some way into their presentation you suddenly grasp the essential point.

Other problems can include the lack of a report about a topic you think is important. Simply nothing is said, and it can leave you wondering if there is something going on or the matter was separately decided. This leads to the issue of feedback. A key component of good communications is feedback from the recipients to the person giving the report. Questions, comments or asking if one's understanding is correct are ways to do this.

Communications are complex. No wonder considerable research has been devoted to it. If we add in body language, misunderstandings, or reports which are overlong, it can be recognised as a crucial part of the role of being a trustee.

To minimise problems in your role as trustee, I suggest the following:

- An information plan, as discussed in Chapter 6. This will clarify questions of what, when, how, how often and how accurate the information needs to be. The accuracy point is often not thought about. Complete accuracy is seldom necessary and can be costly to achieve.
- Agreement of the board to the content of the reports – the 'what'.
- An agreed format is also desirable so that reports are presented in a consistent way. I mentioned earlier that they should be in one of three types: for action (with a recommendation), for discussion, or for information.
- Do not underestimate your contribution, especially if it is non-technical – i.e. it is not about HR, IT or accountancy for example. I have mentioned some other contributions such as experience and judgement which are often just as valuable as specific technical ones. It can help to add balance to the board.

- As a board, try and ensure that reports and information are provided before the meeting to enable you and your colleagues to read and reflect on them. Verbal and last-minute reports cannot always be avoided, especially if something happens just before the meeting takes place, but on the whole, staff should be prepared in sufficient time. This is more than just timeliness. You want to be assured that the staff are looking at the numbers, not just cobbling them together at the last minute because there is a board meeting.
- The relationship between the chair and the staff and CEO is crucial. If this is going wrong then the charity faces big problems. Any tension may be hidden so keeping an eye out for body language and a lack of agreement is important.
- Make a note of any issue you raise – or indeed that is raised by a fellow trustee – which you think is important, and ensure it is either answered or dealt with, or appears as an item at the next meeting. Do not allow these things just to (quietly) disappear.
- Watch out for important items that seem not to be discussed – the dog that didn't bark in the night (a reference to Conan Doyle's story 'Silver Blaze'). Do not be afraid to ask why it/they are missing. Mostly there will be good reasons, but you may uncover an uncomfortable truth.
- I have kept away from repeating the advice given elsewhere but it is worth looking at advice in this area provided by the Charity Commission, not just in terms of your responsibilities but in respect of important matters such as solvency and governance.

In the next chapter I want to discuss the tricky business of fraud and dishonesty. Earlier in this chapter I talked about trust: it's not always there, and you do need to be on the alert for people abusing that trust and be alive to the consequences if it happens.

CHAPTER 13

Fraud, dishonesty and other problems

No discussion of charities, finance and money issues can ignore the issue of dishonesty in its various forms. From time to time in the local media, instances of this kind of behaviour crop up with a member of staff, or even the CEO, involved in some kind of financial impropriety. I have come across it occasionally in my career, but only rarely, so I do not have a great deal of insight to offer. In Chapter 5, I referred to the Charity Commission's report on investigations where there has been wrongdoing in various charities. In all the cases I have come across – in a business setting, in local authorities and in a not-for-profit organisation – one thing which stood out in each case was inadequate controls, which enabled the perpetrator to carry on for quite some time before someone noticed that stock or money was missing. This common factor argues for proper management controls and for people in supervisory or management positions to be alert to what's going on around them.

Someone I knew was convicted of theft from a charity he managed, having spent years writing hundreds of cheques to himself. It was discovered when the charity ceased to function. He was later convicted of fraud, money laundering and theft. The money should have been going to young people and probably, some kind of check should have been made to ensure they were receiving it. Had any of the trustees conducted a physical check, the fraud in all likelihood would have been discovered much sooner.

One thing that helps is to have a whistle-blowing policy, because it is often the case that work colleagues knew that something was awry but were reluctant to air their views. It is natural for staff to be reticent in this matter: no one wants to identify a colleague, especially if there is a chance of mistake. It is something that might crop up in a leaving interview, which is another reason for holding these.

The sheer range of wrongdoing would require a book all to itself to explain adequately. The Government's advice on fraud and how to prevent it – excellent and comprehensive though it is – is extremely daunting. The Small Charities Guide is very comprehensive.[89] The most important thing for trustees is to be aware that dishonesty can take place and not to assume that it cannot happen within your charity. It can. The scale of it should not be underestimated. One report of thousands of examples puts the average loss at £7,500. Another puts the cost of charity fraud at £2.5bn.[90] Employee fraud in charities amounted to £1.685m per annum – almost certainly an underestimate. It is vitally important that financial controls are in place and that appropriate checks and reconciliations are carried out from time to time.

The effects of fraud go beyond any immediate loss of money or property. If IT kit is stolen it can involve the loss of key data and the risk of breaches of client confidentiality. Retrieving the data can be extremely costly and take a lot of time combing through files to reinstate them. If the fraud or theft becomes public (if the police become involved, for example) there is reputational loss to consider. For a small charity operating in a limited area, this can see a drop in contributions or other support.

The effect on morale can be considerable. The shock of discovering that a colleague has been involved in fraud or theft is often very upsetting. The lost money is often not the most important loss.

There is damage to the charity's reputation. Funders may think twice before donating. A small charity may find it difficult to withstand a quite small loss if their reserves are insufficient to cover it. It has effects on other staff, especially if an investigation reveals it was widely known but no one reported it. It can badly damage the reputation of the CEO if it is shown that controls were lax or warning signs were ignored. The CEO may be obliged to resign which can add to problems enormously, particularly for a small charity. It follows that awareness and proper controls are a vital tool in keeping this risk at a minimum.

There are often warning signs. These can include:

- Vagueness in the accounts and reporting with an absence of key things like a cash flow statement. Questions on the accounts are not properly answered and if they cannot be answered on the spot, promises to inform trustees in a day or so are not kept.
- Not ensuring that the accounts are completed and audited within a reasonable time after the financial year end.
- If you have the trend information suggested in this book, then at some stage, anomalies will occur which will enable trustees to ask appropriate questions.
- Reports and papers are not sent out ahead of meetings to give trustees sufficient time to peruse them.
- There aren't suitable controls on payments with two authorisations needed.

My limited experience is that the people involved did not carry out incredibly sophisticated schemes which required the skills of a Hercule Poirot or Inspector Morse to uncover. For example, I was once responsible for the core funding of a range of charities and would receive their accounts each year. I noticed in one, a curious entry for 'flat rental'. Out of curiosity, I raised it with the local manager and it transpired that it was for the lunchtime 'recreational' purposes of two senior members of staff – one male, one female. And astonishingly, they put it through the books!

A colleague in a local authority noticed stocks of material going down faster than expected. He came back to the workshop one evening to find the lights on and a member of his staff busy using the machinery and stock to run a private business.

When working on a building site – my first proper job – I was told off by the foreman for not ordering sufficient timber and plywood for the shuttering. It later transpired the firm supplying us turned up at one entrance, booked the load in, and drove through to the other end of the site and left with his load intact.

These, and other examples, are not instances of master criminals engaged in highly sophisticated scams, but quite ordinary people seeing an opportunity, and using it to steal or cheat their employer. They got away with it for a time because of lax controls and were often discovered fairly accidentally. Indeed, it is often greed that undoes them. Having got away with it easily once, they go on doing it until someone notices or a chance event gives them away. A supermarket manager and his assistant would ring up a false series of transactions after closing, and pocket the difference. They became quite fast at this with the result that the till caught fire. It was this that led to them being discovered.

IT AND OTHER ISSUES

Computing and IT problems, phishing and other such crimes often come from outside and can easily catch the unwary. These are much more sophisticated and as someone who was once caught by one, I can attest to their cunning. They cost firms, charities and individuals millions every year. They are constantly evolving. They are extremely easy to fall into, with lookalike sites saying you have a credit due or a parcel that cannot be delivered. Click the link and problems can ensue with a download of malware or worse. Loss of data is extremely expensive and as was noted above, has reputational, morale and retrieval costs which can be considerable. People often take great care with locks and keys in protecting their offices, with filing cabinets and cupboards carefully secured at the end of the day. A similar level of care must be taken with data sitting in the computer or on the cloud.

All staff need to be on the alert to this kind of fraud, which can hit anyone working in an office (or at home) at any time. A key point here is honesty: if a member of staff is hit by this kind of scam, they must feel able to 'fess up'.

Years ago there was the carbon paper scam. A salesman would pretend to have had a meeting with the senior buyer and talk airily about having agreed a sale of some 'quires' or other measure which the junior staff did not want to admit they didn't know of. A huge lorry would turn up containing vast quantities of carbon paper. The staff member would panic and arrange for it to be stored out of sight. In the worst cases, the staff member was coerced into buying yet more.

When I was a business adviser, I met someone from an engineering business with an autocratic boss. He placed a large order for various components. Meanwhile the job they were intended for was cancelled. A lorry turned up with the said components at which point the staff member panicked, sending them off for chrome plating to buy some time. He then rented a small factory unit and arranged for the chromed components to be stored there. The firm went bust eventually and the liquidators were mystified by a huge pile of chrome-plated stock with no apparent use, in a factory which had been rented for several years.

Although most of this activity comes from outside, a disgruntled member of staff can cause harm as well. There may not be a direct financial loss, but again, reputation and trust can be badly damaged.

I have included 'other problems' in this chapter title because it is not always dishonesty which can cause headaches. Passwords can cause immense problems. On several occasions, I have known of a staff member leave without telling anyone what passwords they were using. If this is someone like an accountant, it can cause considerable confusion. Have invoices been paid? Have invoices been sent out? How are the staff wages to be calculated? All for want of a password. It is vital therefore that senior staff know what passwords are in use and can give them to the new person.

Individual filing systems are another problem. If there isn't an agreed protocol for how files are to be named and what folders to use, someone leaves and their eccentric system goes with them, leaving colleagues to hunt through file after file to find something.

Altogether, there are a bewildering range of potential problems, which might lead you to wonder if it is safe to set foot in any charity or not-for-profit without risk of some kind of malfeasance. Thankfully, these instances are rare and most charities can continue for many years without serious risk of loss, theft or fraud. The risk is there, however, and having a set of policies, procedures and protocols will act both to deter and, if it should happen, detect anything untoward.

The main points are:

- Be aware that these things do happen, albeit quite rarely. Ask your staff, 'What if … ?'
- Mostly, it is simple stuff, not highly sophisticated fraud. It can be controlled by straightforward procedures and spot checks.
- If it does happen, the effects go way beyond the actual loss of money or equipment. There are reputational issues, morale problems and trust between staff and trustees can be badly affected. Lost data can be costly to reclaim and there may be implications under GDPR if the charity has not shown sufficient care.

- It is a real risk therefore, so it is vital you and your fellow trustees ensure there are policies in place to minimise these risks. One such is a whistle-blower policy since it is often the case that staff are aware, or suspect that something is not quite right.
- Ensure that as far as possible, leavers are interviewed. These interviews can point to things not being right in the organisation.
- Ensure that board papers are available before the board meeting and not tabled in a rush at the meeting itself. Watch out for vagueness or evasiveness. Not all vague answers are automatically suspicious, of course – the CEO cannot know everything – but if a pattern develops then this might be a pointer.
- Ensure that financial reports are complete, as set out in Chapter 8. Is someone reconciling the cash and the bank balance?
- Is there an inventory of expensive kit such as laptops or cameras? If you have serial numbers, it is easier to retrieve these items if staff walk off with them. It acts as a deterrent to taking them in the first place.
- Ensure the charity has up-to-date IT protection and everything is backed up.
- No organisation runs completely smoothly – at least not any that I have ever worked for. There are mistakes, oversights, accidents and plain ordinary cock-ups. So if reports to the board are in the form of seamless and never-ending success, you should be a little suspicious. You should not expect that every little error or mistake is reported to the board – that would be silly and unnecessary – but from time to time there should be sufficient honesty to admit that a mistake has been made.

Just be wary.

CHAPTER 14

Bringing it all together

This book has been about trying to give advice to potential and actual trustees of a small charity or not-for-profit organisation on how to go about their duties successfully. It cannot pretend to be comprehensive but I have tried to focus as best I can on practical issues and to use experience I have gained, both as a trustee of two charities and as a member of other similar not-for-profit organisations, as well as within small businesses, to offer suggestions about how to go about things. The fact remains however that the risks of running a small charity are not that different from those of a large one, and that means there is a lot to take in. If an employee is disaffected in some way, they will take action whatever the size of the charity. If an accident happens, the effects are the same. It does not matter whether it is a little boat or a big ship – it can still sink. Perhaps the only real difference is that a larger organisation can afford good-quality advice to help it stay on the straight and narrow.

The problem can become trying to keep hold of what the big picture is. The Charity Commission explains the fundamental role of a trustee. It explains that he or she is to ensure the charity is carrying out its fundamental purpose; that it is making informed decisions; that actions are taken with integrity and do not conflict with personal interests; that resources are managed responsibly; that actions are taken with reasonable care and skill and that the charity stays legal and accountable. This is sometimes called the 'Director's

Dilemma', which we might change to 'Trustee's Dilemma'. This is discussed in Bob Garratt's book *Stop the Rot* (Greenleaf Publising). How can we (directors or trustees) 'drive our organisation forward, while keeping it under prudent control?' This dilemma is 'complex, continuous and [a] difficult intellectual challenge for every board', he continues. It can result in boards concentrating on the prudential aspects and ignoring the future, which is seen as 'too difficult'. Garratt introduces a useful analogy – that of the crab. Trustees (in our context) can forever be tracking sideways in their quest for good governance and better prudent control, 'scuttling to create more rules and procedures' and either ignoring or avoiding the future.[91]

This is made more difficult for a trustee because you are not managing the organisation, and may only have direct contact on a handful of occasions during the year. You will be relying on a chief executive (or someone with a similar title and role) to inform you of what is happening, and always with a worry that things may be not as they seem and you are not being told the truth. You can be forgiven for feeling a little confused (I hope not just by me) about how you become a 'successful trustee', which this book purports to tell you how to do.

In this chapter therefore I want to try and bring things together and provide a kind of framework of what the whole process looks like. I hope that seeing what the process – and I think the word itself is important – looks like from beginning to end in a typical cycle, will help achieve a holistic view. Figure 7 sets out some of the elements of the process. It is important to note that the process is dynamic. It is really essential to recognise that change is a normal state of affairs and that the future of your charity will depend in large measure on how it adapts to these changes, both internally and externally. These are easy words to write but for many people, change is unwelcome and can represent uncertainty and a threat.

For staff in the charity it can mean their jobs change, not always in ways they might want. It might mean more responsibilities or a complete change of role. So whereas we can quote phrases like 'the only constant in life is change' (Heraclitus), when it comes down to it the reaction in practice can be more mixed. The process of change is time consuming and often stressful for all concerned. Figure 7 tries to pull things together.

Across the top are the key elements of the charity process, starting with the purpose and ending with the outcomes or achievement of its work. Broadly speaking, the process is more strategic on the left-hand side of the table and gradually becomes more managerial as you move to the right-hand side. There is no hard line – no dramatic cut-off point – but as a trustee, issues of purpose, strategy and objectives are where a significant part of your attention should be focused. Matters of delivery, communications and management are the purview of the chief executive and his or her team. Such is the diversity of the sector that there can be no all-embracing rubric, but I suspect this does provide a basis for many charities and not-for-profits.

The second point to emphasise is that it is a dynamic process. It does not start at one end and finish at the other. It is a bit like the Forth Bridge of legend: get to the end and it's time to start all over. Not only that, but it may be necessary to rejig midway through; the recent Covid-19 crisis meant a lot of charities (and every organisation for that matter) had to rethink their work and modi operandi. During lockdown, visiting people, holding meetings, doing street collections and so on became either impossible or very difficult. Demands on some have increased, such as hospices and similar health-related organisations.[92] Many national fundraising events have had to be cancelled. It is likely that many charities have found carrying on too difficult and have given up.

Purpose	Strategy	Objectives	Delivery	Communications	Outcomes
What is our purpose?	Looking at changes: STEEPLE	Setting objectives	Managed effectively	What are we wanting to communicate to whom?	What have we achieved?
Is our purpose still relevant?	Analysing our past performance	Are they realistic but challenging?	Risks are identified and monitored	What are our key messages?	What difference have we made to our cause?
Does it need to be modified or changed?	Should we expand (or contract)?	What are the implications arising from them?	There is adequate governance	What methods will be used?	Are we fulfilling our purpose?
	Strategic analysis	Ensuring they are disseminated to staff and volunteers	Appropriate HR procedures	How good is our brand? Our brand strengths and weaknesses	
	Looking at strategic choices	Preparing a work plan	There is adequate training	Do we need to market ourselves?	
	Making strategic selections	Are the objectives SMART?	There is an information plan: SCAPS		
			Ensure financial probity		
			There is secure IT		
			Morale and motivation is attended to		

Fig 7 The overall process

STEEPLE: Social, Technological, Economic, Environmental, Political, Legal and Ethical
SMART: Specific, Measurable, Achievable, Realistic and Timebound
SCAPS: Selection, Collection, Analysis, Presentation and Storage

Many of the entries in the matrix I have framed in terms of questions or queries. This is to emphasise your role as a trustee, which is in part to ask relevant questions. So maintaining a holistic view of the charity, seeing it as a dynamic process, and accepting and reacting to change are the important points so far. You will only be able to do this if you have adequate information, a point I have discussed in preceding chapters. You will need information about the strategy, financial matters, progress with activities, staffing, funding and relationships.

Since actual management and delivery of the work of the charity will depend on the chief executive, staff and volunteers, this means that the appointment, remuneration, support, appraisal, training and encouragement of the CEO is crucial for you and your fellow trustees to be mindful of. One-to-one contact is usually down to the chair, who will have several conversations and meetings with the CEO within the board meetings cycle.[93] If tensions develop between the two then this can pose problems, even severe ones. It represents a potential weak link between the trustees and the management of the charity. One way to at least discuss this is for the board to meet among themselves for half an hour, say, before the meeting proper starts with the CEO and any staff. You need to discover the source of the tensions which can be, for example, the CEO not performing, an overly dominant chair who is encroaching onto the CEO's 'space', or a plain and simple personality clash. People who become leaders in some form are not usually shrinking violets, so sparks are to an extent inevitable. The problem has to be resolved: leaving it to simmer is not a tenable course of action. It is potentially a crisis in some form for the charity since proving that the CEO is not performing adequately may be difficult (except in extreme cases), so if terminating their contract becomes necessary, this will come at a cost. The risk of a claim for unfair or constructive dismissal will be expensive and time consuming. There will be months of anxiety as it plays out.

If the charity is expanding, this can also pose problems. A small charity which expands can change in character quickly and the CEO needs to become more and more of a manager and learn the difficult art of 'achieving things through other people', which is the best definition of management I have seen. For a CEO who was in at the beginning, or when the charity was very small – and was very hands-on – this change of role can be a difficult one to achieve, largely for psychological and personality reasons. Which brings us to the tricky issue of appraising a CEO's performance.

APPRAISING THE CEO

A CEO should of course receive an annual appraisal in common with other staff and the question becomes, how do you do this? There will be a job description but the nature of the position means the trustees need to ask a range of questions about the performance of the person in this crucial role. How do you assess his or her performance? I would suggest the following – not as a complete list – but those aspects which will give you a good indication of how they are performing:

- How well is the **strategy** being accomplished? This has to be a very important element of the CEO's duties since it is what determines the success of the organisation. The strategy will the foundation of the work plan and how that is progressing will be key to this.
- **Leadership**. A key element and is about leading the team, motivating them and giving them a sense of direction. There are scores of leadership styles and different styles suit differing circumstances. It would be wonderful to provide

a list of 'how to spot a good leader' but I doubt such a list exists. Traits to look out for are composure, openness and a sense of being in control of their own time. The absence of these are relatively easy to spot: a CEO who appears frazzled, discomposed, and seems never to have any time to think is an indicator. Also being able to manage conflicts since these may arise if the charity is stressed in some way or where there is change.

- Linked to this is **emotional stability**. Being a CEO is a lonely job and a stressful one. If this stress manifests itself in a quick temper, irritableness or spending long periods of time secluded in their office it will have a very harmful effect on the morale of staff. They may become reluctant to engage with the CEO for fear of setting off an outbreak of temper. There is also something I have seen referred to as being 'agreeable'. This is not quite the same as trying to be popular, but is about being approachable, pleasant and showing interest and concern about staff wellbeing issues. Staff just need to feel comfortable around the CEO.
- **Being optimistic**. This is an important characteristic. A CEO – who is competent in many respects – but lacks optimism is likely to become a problem over time. It can be extremely debilitating and demoralising for staff. Suggestions are not responded to and there is always a good reason for 'why not'. Of course, not every suggestion *is* practicable but the attitude should always be welcoming and suggestions should always be carefully considered.
- **Managing board relations** well. Providing reports on time, able to answer most questions and not afraid to speak honestly.
- **Team management**, something more than leadership and about the mechanics of managing staff: appraisals being done,

appropriate training being organised, recruitment done well and so forth.

- **Governance**. Having a firm handle on this and managing risks, notifying the board if things are awry.
- **Representing** the organisation. They *are* the face of the charity for many partners or stakeholders so if that is not done well it can be serious.
- **Honesty and integrity** are important for obvious reasons.
- **Being self-aware.** I say this because the perfect CEO has yet to be invented and there are a lot of things to do and get right. Being open with the chair that they need support/training/time off or mentoring is important. The alternative is problems being hidden and unaddressed.
- Willingness to **delegate**. This is as much a personality thing as anything. I have worked for people – as I'm sure you have – who are reluctant to delegate and it is very destructive and inefficient. I used the word 'frazzled' above and failure to delegate properly is likely to be evident here.

A long list. But experience shows that if one or more of the above is not happening, it is noticeable. Reports to the board are missing, late or incomplete. A CEO who appears harassed and is complaining of insufficient time. Frequent changes in staff and good people leaving soon after being recruited. Things just not getting done. These shortcomings are likely to appear during the course of the year not just at the time of annual appraisal. It is not good practice to leave problems until then in any event.

Since the perfect CEO does not exist it is certain that one or more of the above list will not be carried out successfully. What to do? The good news is that if the shortcoming(s) is to do with a lack of experience or knowledge, then training, mentoring or other support (from a trustee possibly) can usually overcome the problem. The representation skill however, is one where – although it can be improved – there are people who are just not good on their feet, in front of a camera or in public setting. They just cannot do it. They may otherwise be a superb CEO but in front of an audience, they crumble. In cases like this, then perhaps a trustee or another staff member can step in. Frankly, it is best to accept the situation and work around it.

A more difficult problem occurs when it is a matter of character, attitude or personality. An unwillingness to delegate for example usually arises from a feeling of insecurity. Another reason is a manager who is detailed focused and is not content with the result but wants to know what is happening at every step. Or they may have little confidence in the team and believe that 'only they' can do the job. Delegating means accepting a degree of risk. Just as you the trustees accept a degree of risk when you delegate to the CEO, so likewise, does the CEO have to accept it. Management is essentially a messy business. Information maybe uncertain, not totally accurate or even non-existent. However carefully made, decisions are often risky and sometimes little more than a best guess. Some find this difficult to handle. They like order and a degree of certainty.

I mentioned loneliness, or as Shakespeare puts it: 'uneasy lies the head that wears a crown*.' Despite being surrounded by people and attending many meetings, some feel this very strongly. Much has been written on this topic and there are strategies for handling it. Loneliness is it must be stressed, a serious negative force so cannot be ignored.

Mentoring can sometimes help or using an advisor to talk through the problem and seek to overcome the shortcoming.

---

* King Henry the Fourth, Part Two.

I must be honest: there are often no easy answers. We all have failings but in a leadership role any one of them can have serious implications.

This problem initially falls on the chair. It is they who are in regular contact with the CEO and to whom it becomes apparent that there is a problem(s). Sharing this (these) with the board raises its own problem since the CEO will be present at the meeting and airing them … well you just wouldn't do it. Having a half hour trustee only meeting before the CEO and other staff attend is the best idea as I suggested above. The chair needs to ensure the board knows the situation. It is vital to avoid the problem of matters coming to a crisis point and the trustees discovering that things have been going wrong for some time and not knowing about it.

Another problem is that since the CEO will be doing most of the reporting to board, and clearly will want to present things in the best light, the impression can be gained that everything is working smoothly and tickety-boo. This can leave the chair feeling isolated. The trustees will think things are going well, unaware of the problems that the chair is grappling with. The chair needs to share concerns on a regular basis and to feel supported if discussions with the CEO become difficult or even fractious.

It is altogether a difficult area. The CEO's performance is crucial to the success or otherwise of the charity. Although staff can and do work round or adapt to shortcomings, ultimately a crunch point will be reached. There are no easy answers as I said above but if the chair is in regular contact, is sharing any concerns with fellow trustees and is open to offer training or other support to deal with particular problems, then disaster can usually be avoided. As a trustees, you need to be alert to the problems a CEO may be experiencing and, as tactfully as possible, try and establish if the chair is alert to them as well.

VALUES AND ETHICS

The question of values and ethics is an area to be aware of. The public expects charities to act ethically and the reaction to Oxfam's activities in Haiti is instructive. There is the legal and there is the ethical – that is to say, you may be able to do something which is perfectly legal but whether it is ethical is a slightly different matter. Codes and legal matters are what the law or the Charity Commission tells you to conform to. There is also a distinction between what you must do and what you should do, as set out in the Charity Commission's *Essential Trustee*. 'Must' is because it is the law; 'should' is because it is best practice.

Ethics is what you *choose* to do. The issue of money, where it comes from and who gives it to you springs to mind in this regard. Receiving funds from an organisation or individual who is 'tainted' in some way, in addition to raising ethical concerns, can also result in bad publicity. There is quite a lot of debate about this. Oil companies' contributions to various charities have caused protests.[94] Recently, the Sackler family – whose company make the opioid drug OxyContin – has come in for some considerable criticism, but they have been major funders of a wide range of charities in the USA. There is often a suggestion that companies use these contributions to sanitise their reputations.

The Chartered Institute of Fundraising cautions against making hasty decisions on this front.[95] The funds may be tainted but the charity has to think of the beneficiaries as well. You may effectively be declining funds which would be put to good use in helping others. It is a very difficult area and trustees need to think long and hard about it. How far do you go? Many commercial firms use labour in the Far East, where abusive practices are not uncommon, to make their products. Other firms go to great lengths to avoid or evade taxes. Some firms pay below the minimum wage. If you sup with the commercial world you may indeed need a long spoon.

On balance, I would suggest a cautious approach, particularly for a small charity. Public opinion is fickle but should the mood be that a company (or an individual) is behaving badly, then the impact on your charity could be critical and last for some time. I commented earlier in this book about the changed attitudes towards charities following the various scandals.

Values are about how your charity behaves, how it treats its people, and its culture. Some matters are of a legal nature, such as treating staff fairly, paying at or above the minimum wage and generally being honest and open in your dealings. There are many things that contribute to making an organisation have good values, that aren't about laws or policies. It is fundamentally about attitude and philosophy – both terms hard to define. I have seen the phrase 'in its DNA' used, which is quite apt. It will include some or most of the following:

- A pride in being good at what we do.
- A conspicuous desire to improve. Instead of a defensiveness about past activities, there is more of a feeling of 'we can do this better' combined with an absence of acrimony.
- Linked to that is being a learning culture – that is, a willingness to acquire new skills.
- A culture of openness. Information is freely volunteered and not dragged out of someone who manifests obvious reluctance to say anything.
- Dealings with people – which includes staff, volunteers, suppliers, stakeholders – are honest and fair.

- Staff and volunteers are involved in decision-making and are listened to, the opposite of what is called 'mushroom management' (which, if you are unfamiliar with the phrase, is: staff kept in the dark with a sack of manure thrown at them from time to time. A word other than 'manure' is often used).
- Staff and volunteers are valued, which shows itself in training, appraisals and general encouragement and support.
- Having a clear set of policies.

Reactions when something unethical happens can be instructive. Being open and transparent can be painful and embarrassing. It can bring short-term problems for the charity in having to admit to what has happened. The temptation may be to play it down or to claim that it was perfectly legal after all, if not entirely ethical. Tempting but almost certainly wrong. You may have noticed that I put the 'having a clear set of policies' last in the list above. That is because I think culture and philosophy are the key drivers. Policies cannot cover every circumstance and in those hard to define areas, it is those factors which can decide the issue.

Not being managers or seeing the staff that frequently, you may feel these matters can be hard to spot. However, if you are on the lookout, they do manifest themselves – for example, in a desire to claim that something was legal if not ethical. I should add that, quite apart from the values argument discussed above, people who are valued by their employers do tend to perform better anyway. On the issue of the 'learning culture', it is useful to remember Revans' Law which states: 'for an organisation to survive, its rate of learning must be at least equal to the rate of change in the external environment'. Reg Revans was a successful management consultant and academic. If your charity is not attending to this issue of learning and keeping skills up to date and relevant to the environment, it risks it long-term survival. 'We cannot afford to train our staff' is simply not an option.

VISION

The start of this chapter focused on the process and the cycle of events from purpose to outcomes. It is important to maintain throughout it all a sense of vision. The strategy is not some mechanical process remorselessly grinding away. I sometimes feel – which I discussed in the chapter on governance – that the sheer process of compliance, reports, risk management performance and delivery can act to stifle people's will. They start to not quite 'work to rule' – that would be to convey the wrong thing entirely – but feel hemmed in, constrained, limited. It is part of the trustees' role to maintain a sense of optimism and vision.

Closely linked to this observation is the behaviour of the trustees themselves. The boards and meetings I go to are fortunately attended by people with a real interest in the health and future direction of the organisation of which they are a member. I have attended – or co-opted to – meetings, committees and like assemblies on the other hand where, to be frank, I have wondered what some of the attendees are doing there. Neither enthusiasm nor much in the way of interest is expressed by them. Apart from a perfunctory question or two, little emotion is evident. If this behaviour is limited to just one or two individuals, it may not matter, but if it is typical of several it can be demoralising for the CEO and any staff present. They prepare material for the trustees and should expect something in return. They seek recognition and support. They are working for the charity sometimes on a full-time basis. There should at least be praise where praise is due. There will of course be matters of concern which are properly brought up. This should not amount to a 'demolition job' however, and I refer back to my last point above about staff feeling valued and being encouraged. Some of the inspiration for people to continue should come from you and your fellow trustees.

BRAND

My final point is: pay attention to the brand. I discuss this in Chapter 10 but I mention it here because how you are perceived by your public is an important part of your effectiveness. In that chapter I suggest that two elements are involved: the cause itself and secondly, your charity.

SUMMARY

The key points in this chapter are mostly about keeping hold of the big picture and a close focus on the purpose of your charity. They can both be quite difficult to do amongst the 'noise' of reports, masses of detail, events and happenings.

Acting legally and according to the Charity Commission guidelines is also vital. It is all about public benefit.

It is crucial to see the strategy as a dynamic process, which in part involves accepting change as the normal state of affairs. Values and ethics are an area to keep in mind. This can be important in relation to funding and contributions, as discussed, and you may need to consider carefully if the source of funds is badly tainted.

The key link between the trustees or board and the staff and volunteers – and the person who is going to actually manage the work of the charity – is the chief executive officer, so looking after their interests is important. Are they equipped for the job? Are they getting the support they need from staff, you and your fellow trustees? Is there a good relationship between the CEO and the chair? If the charity has grown, are they still equipped to do the job?

Be optimistic. It can be good to have a Jeremiah or two on a board – to inject some caution – but if everyone is that way it can demoralise the staff and lead nowhere.

Finally, watch the brand.

For those who like diagrams, Figure 8 shows a summary of this chapter in visual form:

Process
- Being aware of the big picture
- Accepting change as normal
- Being aware of the key role played by the CEO

The Future
- Being clear about the purpose of the charity and its strategy
- Having a vision
- Being optimistic

Information

Responsibilities
- Legal and financial (refer to Charity Commission)
- Being ethical
- Having values

Visibility
- Looking after the brand
- Communications
- Marketing

Fig 8 Key roles of a trustee

CHAPTER 15
Finally

My intention in this book has been to fill what I think is a gap and provide some key advice for people who are thinking of becoming a trustee of a small charity, or who have just become one. There is existing advice, all of it excellent, but you have to hunt around and some of it is quite copious and could be off-putting. Some of the guidance concentrates on the 'what' without going too much into the 'how'. I have tried to get into the 'how' a little in this book.

As I said in the introduction, the idea of writing a guide came to me as I left a meeting of one of the charities of which I was a trustee. I realised as I walked back to the car park that, despite a folder full of reports and statistics and having sat through a two-hour meeting, if someone stopped me and asked me some basic questions about the charity, I would not have been able to answer them. How many clients did we have? Was that increasing or decreasing? How many staff and volunteers did we have? What were our reserves? And so and so on. Simple and quite basic questions which frankly, as a trustee, I should have known.

One of the key messages has been the need to think hard about what information it is you need and the related issue of presentation. I introduced the SCAPS model which sets out the basic principle of *selecting* what information you need; working out how it is to be *collected*; how it is to be *analysed* and made sense of; how it will be *presented*, not just to the trustees but to the managers; and finally, questions of safe and secure *storage*. I also discuss communication, which sometimes gets confused with marketing. It is about thinking: what is it you need to communicate to whom?

I discussed the problem of overlooking the qualitative aspects of information and giving too much weight to facts that can be enumerated and added up. Another problem associated with this subject is being drawn into second-guessing the management. Although I argue for the value of information, properly analysed and presented to trustees to enable them to understand what is going on, there is a countervailing risk of being sucked too far into the details. This is potentially demoralising and ultimately unproductive. Trustees should focus on the strategic and longer term and not try and manage the organisation, for which task they are not equipped. There is a balance to be struck here and I cannot pretend there is an easy answer other than to caution restraint in delving too much into the weeds.

A related frequent problem, with small charities in particular, is trustees becoming involved in the day-to-day management of the charity. It may be because they have a particular skill and this leads them to become engaged in doing work for the charity. This can pose problems. If, for example, a trustee advised on an HR matter which led to a decision being taken to terminate a staff member's contract and the payment of some kind of compensation, other trustees may not have agreed with the decision but felt inhibited because 'one of their own' was closely involved in it. If you are a trustee supposedly concerned with the strategic direction of the charity, then getting sucked into day-to-day management may make this difficult.

There is quite a lot of advice around the concept of trustees sticking with strategic matters and not getting too involved in day-to-day management. I do have a problem with this particularly in the context of a small organisation. I think it can be a little simplistic. If we look at the process of preparing or revising a strategy for the future for your charity, it is not some lofty process detached from the day-to-day. A starting point is thinking about where you are now, what your charity's purpose is and what its capabilities are in relation to changes taking place in the environment and how your charity is perceived. A successful strategy will involve thinking about all levels of your charity. It is all very well thinking of bold, 'blue sky' plans and ambitions for the future, but they will not be achieved if the organisation is not functioning well at all levels. That means efficient IT, trained staff, good managers, a good brand, a clear sense of purpose and so on. To an extent, therefore, trustees have to concern themselves with these matters.

I discuss the importance of *brand*, a subject some trustees and charity staff are a little uncomfortable with. Some feel it is too linked to commercial products and since some commercial brands are tainted by poor behaviour (climate damage, use of low-paid foreign labour or dubious tax activities, for example) they worry that there will be a kind of guilt by association. Branding is not just a series of glossy promotional activities and a fancy logo, but the sum of how you are seen by your audience and the experience they have of you as an organisation.

Since for most trustees, the major part of the contact they have with one another and with the charity is at meetings, I have devoted a chapter to this sometimes vexed subject. I argue that they should be valuable as well as enjoyable: I don't entirely subscribe to the near-universal belief that they are too long, wasteful of everyone's time and should be as short as humanly possible. Yes, they can ramble on – but with good chairmanship, they can and should be productive and the rambling kept to a minimum.

What are the main points which I think will make you a useful trustee and enable you to make a significant contribution to the effectiveness and efficiency of your charity?

In addition to information and communication issues, which I have explored at length, are personality issues. There has to be a degree of optimism from the trustees and the staff concerning the future of the charity. As a trustee, you must not be afraid to ask questions, questions which might at first make you seen naïve or ill-informed. It can often be the simplest of questions which lead to useful insights.

I have argued that qualities such as independence of mind and an ability to see the big picture are valuable attributes in a trustee. These are needed to avoid perils such as group think, or as a foil to a chairperson who may be too close to the CEO or more interested in completing a meeting on time rather than exploring a troubling point in depth.

Not having sector-specific, professional or technical skills should not of itself be a barrier to being a successful trustee. Ideally, a board should be a balance of skills and abilities – some with specific skills, others with more general ones. An ability to take a long view and a wide perspective are valuable attributes.

Having a positive attitude to change is a key characteristic. If change is seen as a nuisance or best ignored, then ultimately the charity is likely to fail. Change has to be accepted as normal and every effort made to adapt to it and seek opportunities arising from it.

I also discussed the tricky issue of private sector involvement, particularly with the appointment of fellow trustees from a commercial or business background. The results are not always straightforwardly good. There are several significant differences between how the private and not-for-profit sectors work, and the grafting of commercial methods onto the latter is not necessarily relevant or useful. I have seen it referred to as 'ill-fitting hand-me-downs'. Private sector involvement can be of considerable benefit for particular aspects – IT and HR spring to mind, where the principles are largely the same. An outside view from someone with experience of strategic thinking can also be helpful. Just encouraging you to think a bit more commercially or in a slightly more 'hard-nosed' way can be a useful stimulus. My main point though is not to assume private sector expertise is necessarily better than not-for-profit expertise, or that it is automatically appropriate, in view of the different worlds they live in. Be selective.

Another key message is that not all of the public will necessarily share the same view about your charity, and they may not be sympathetic to the cause you are supporting. Some causes realise almost automatic and universal approbation: children, animals and seeking a cure for cancer are examples. It is no surprise that the majority of the charities in the top twenty are engaged in these activities. Move away from these subjects and the public can be more ambivalent or even openly hostile. This is likely to affect fundraising and may impact on volunteers' willingness to take part in public events.

My parting message though is to enjoy being a trustee. If all it becomes is a duty or a chore, then the task of adopting an optimistic approach becomes that much harder. If you don't feel you are making a difference or contributing to the cause, it can be unrewarding.

I wish you the best of luck in your time as a trustee.

Acknowledgements

I am indebted to several people who have helped with this book and influenced the style and content. My ex-colleague from the Rural Development Commission days, Chris Brown, changed the direction of the book from the start. Ken Howard, chair of Swan Advocacy at the time of writing, also made useful comments and corrections. My colleague at Wessex Community Action, Peter Hawkins, also made a number of suggestions. I must also thank my wife who suggested many improvements as to style and layout. I want to thank Alan Mitchell especially, who was for several years a fellow trustee of Swan Advocacy, who read two drafts and made a significant number of useful comments, and helped a lot with the structure and content of the book. All remaining errors are mine.

Useful links

This is a list of organisations which are of help or interest to the not-for-profit sector:

Charity Commissions. There are separate organisations for England and Wales, Scotland, Northern Ireland and Ireland. They register and regulate charities in their areas and there is a considerable amount of advice on their sites.

England and Wales:	https://www.gov.uk/government/organisations/charity-commission
Scotland:	www.oscr.org.uk
Northern Ireland:	www.charitycommissionni.org.uk
Republic of Ireland:	www.charitiesregulator.ie

National Council for Voluntary Organisations (NCVO). Champions the sector and volunteering. The site contains a lot of information and support for the sector.

www.ncvo.org.uk

Association of Chief Executives of Voluntary Organisations (ACEVO). Supports leaders of charities and social enterprises in England and Wales. Similar organisations for Scotland and Northern Ireland.

England and Wales:	www.acevo.org.uk
Scotland:	www.acosvo.org.uk
Northern Ireland:	www.co3.bz

Association of Chairs. A membership organisation supporting and helping chairs and vice chairs of charities and social enterprises in England and Wales.

www.associationofchairs.org.uk

Small Charities Coalition. Set up in 2008 with the aim of helping small charities working on the front line.

www.smallcharities.org

Civil Society. News about the sector.

www.civilsociety.co.uk

Third Sector. A lively magazine concentrating on this sector.

www.thirdsector.co.uk

Appendix A

COMMUNICATIONS: HOW TO DO IT

Action	What to do
	Phase 1 – research
Secure commitment	The vital first step. Without it, as discussed, it will lead to a lot of wasted effort. It is probably advisable to get board agreement. To achieve this, a five-year analysis (if possible) of progress is a start.
Define your audiences	You may have more than one audience. It may consist of the public, professional bodies or funders. These main groups need to be identified. Decide what messages you want to convey to each, how often and in what forms.
Ask: what do people know about us?	This is both what they know about you and what they know about the cause – not the same thing. What is their attitude to the cause? Are they sympathetic, indifferent or even hostile? You can find general statistics from people like the Charities Aid Foundation and other similar sources from an online search. A good source is NCVO for this and other useful advice. Finding out what they think about *you* is harder though. Analyse your Website, Twitter and Facebook statistics using Google analytics. If you receive phone calls to an office, be sure to ask how people heard of you and ask what they know of what you do. Use LinkedIn. I have suggested street work and setting up a stall, and listening carefully to what people say can be instructive. Take part in any organised charity events in the town hall, say. Remember: it's not just what they think of *you* but your *cause* as well. At the end of this you should have gathered sufficient information to put together a brief analysis of what people think of you, what they know of you and what they think of the cause you are pursuing. This will inform your communication plan and your brand.

(*Continued*)

Action	What to do
	Phase 2 – planning
Mission	What is your mission and is your existing mission statement up to scratch? • Is it still relevant? • Is it succinct? • Does it say what you do and for whom? Does it, in a few moments, tell someone who does not know you and what you do, what it is you are about and what you are trying to do or who you are trying to help? Form a group and thrash through some ideas. Print off some other charity mission statements from the web and discuss these. What is good or bad about them? Share your ideas or suggested text with the wider organisation.
Branding	Work on your branding. Is the name of your charity still relevant? Could it be shortened or made more relevant? You have only four means to convey your message and your brand: • The name • Use of colour and typography • Use of illustrations and images (moving or still) • Words Does it engage with people's emotions? People engage with causes because they affect their beliefs and emotions. Again, remember the difference between the *cause* and your *charity*. The cause needs to touch them emotionally, as I have just said. But your charity must demonstrate integrity and honesty. This is an area where you may need to spend money on the design aspects. Good design involves flair, skill and some inspiration. The result needs to be simple, have a timeless quality to it, be recognisable and above all, differentiate you from other organisations.

(*Continued*)

Action	What to do
	Phase 2 – planning
Branding	Visual information nearly always helps. You can get good material from agencies and sometimes from Flickr (but pay attention to copyright issues). Unless you have someone in the organisation who is a keen photographer with good kit, do not use amateur material. I think bad photographs do more harm than good. It makes you look amateurish. Paying a professional is often worth the money. Words. You have worked on your mission statement, so it should be possible to develop a simple strapline that says what you do in a handful of words. Stories are often a good way to tell people what you do. If you have someone – or you know someone – who is good with words, that can be a great bonus. It is important to stress in the story, what your charity did to change or improve things. Sounds obvious I know, but some stories are long on description and detail but you are left wondering: 'What did you do?', 'What difference did your charity make?' When you have finished, if you can get an outsider's view, someone prepared to give an honest opinion, so much the better. Finally, carefully check on the legal position with names, copyright and any matters which might impact on your charitable status.
	Phase 3 – delivery
Involvement	Up until now, it has been a small team working on this and hopefully, you will have got a fledgling brand strategy together and a concise mission statement. Before going too far though, you do need to involve all staff, volunteers and fellow trustees. It will be important to avoid the idea that it is a fait accompli. It can be demoralising for staff and volunteers to turn up to be shown material that they have serious misgivings about, only to be told it's too late and it's off to the printers tomorrow. There needs to be a genuine opportunity for input by those not directly involved in the work to date.

(*Continued*)

Action	**What to do**
	Phase 3 – delivery
Involvement	There is a need to explain to them the reasons for the change, the rationale for the changes and decisions made, and the benefits you hope will accrue. Ideally you will have involved them at an earlier stage. You may not convince everyone and people are naturally resistant to change.
Delivery	You now have to put the plan into action. If the alterations are modest and amount to small and relatively insignificant changes, then you can prepare a simple plan and proceed. But if you have made more significant changes, then a relaunch might be an idea, in which case you need to plan backwards from a suitable date. To invite a well-known person to the launch event will help. A budget has to be agreed. It may need a board commitment, especially if changes are significant. If you have agreed on a new logo, a new name or a change in colour scheme, then you may wish to engage a graphic designer to help. There may be talk of using the local college and engaging students in a project. This might work but in my limited experience, it doesn't. The designer needs to be briefed. There are a number of guides online to follow but in simple terms they need to know: • Who you are and what you do. • Who the target audiences are. • What you are hoping to achieve with the redesign. This will be linked to the mission statement. • Something about the message you are trying to convey. Reliability, approachability, integrity, those sorts of things. This will influence colour, design and choice of typeface. • Some idea of the budget. • The range of work you want done – literature, posters, flyers and so forth. • What photography to include. Some will have links to a photographer they can recommend. • Basic details of contact point, timescales and any legal matters.

(*Continued*)

Action	What to do
	Phase 3 – delivery
Planning	I find bar or Gantt charts to be a valuable way of planning a project of any size or complexity (I started work in the building industry). Start with a list of what has to be done, order it and assign durations to each task. Working back from the launch date will give you your chart. This can be done on screen these days and there is some proprietary software. An Excel chart is good enough for this task though, which enables the chart to be exchanged electronically. Make sure you note holidays (national and key staff) and allow for that. Mark key points to act as milestones to check progress. 'If you fail to plan, then plan to fail' is a good saying.
Monitoring	You need to consider how to monitor the success of this work. Larger charities can use external consultants. For small charities this option may be too expensive. There are some simple things you can do to try and keep an eye on how effective it has been: • Check on your social media activity. Is it increasing? • Enquiries likewise. When people phone in, ask them how they heard of you and ideally, what they know of what you do. • In any public forum, ask people what they know of you and what they have seen of your organisation. • A likely purpose is to increase activity and fundraising totals, especially if you rely on the public for some or all of your funds. Is that increasing? • Ask staff and volunteers to note any observations they might encounter. The important thing is to garner as much data as you can and keep a record. If you know what your level of enquiries was before the launch, and you monitor it after, that will give you some kind of measure of effectiveness.

Back to the main point and the distinction between the cause itself and your charity. The cause will be about what the needs are, the problem you are hoping to tackle and maybe a description of the issues. The charity will be about what you are doing to help, and ideally, the successes or outcomes of your work. They link together.

Appendix B

The below is a suggested rubric – and an example analysis – for reviewing external forces on a charity. It is important to try and make it as specific to your charity as possible. I would also suggest only having a small number of impacts: there is a danger in these exercises of 'paralysis by analysis'. Choose only those which are most likely to be impactful. I would also suggest dividing them between 'potential problems' and 'potential opportunities', perhaps colour-coding them.

Factor	**Potential impacts**	**Responses**
Political	• Reduced funding of local authorities	• Diversify our fundraising work • Improve our marketing
	• More liberal attitudes evident (from Social Attitudes Survey)	• Potential opportunity – to keep under review
	• Safeguarding becoming more important	• Revise our policy guidance • Carry out staff training • Modify our website and social media pages
Economic	• People's incomes stretched, affecting their ability to give	• As above
	• Inflation likely to increase	• Monitor staff remuneration more frequently • Keep careful control over cash flow

(Continued)

Factor	**Potential impacts**	**Responses**
Social	• More activity online with impacts on our face-to-face work	• Consider doing more online fundraising
Technological	• Changes in data storage and collection (relevant in view of our diversification plans)	• Research different systems and consider an upgrade
	• Post-Covid meeting arrangements – should they be permanent?	• Consider every other meeting to be via Zoom or Teams
Legal	• New [ ] law will impact on our service • Growth may take us over the Charity Commission reporting threshold	• Set up working party to review and develop new procedures • Seek expert advice on how it will impact on us • Consider whether it is an opportunity for us to expand our service
Environmental	• More awareness of zero-carbon practices	• Ensure we are on target for carbon neutral at the end of the decade • Ensure our literature discusses or explains our environmental policies

Appendix C

These are some example charts and means to express information in as clear a way as possible. Both Excel and Apple Numbers enable charts to be created easily in several different styles. An example is income:

INCOME

	Quarter				£000s
	–5	–4	–3	–2	current
Income	200	178	188	201	190
Direct costs	100	92	100	89	88
Surplus/(deficit)	100	86	88	112	102
%	50	48	47	56	54

This shows five quarters and reduces the information to its basics. Note that the numbers are expressed in thousands as this aids clarity. It shows income and the surplus or (deficit) as a number and as a percentage.

Another matter of concern is overheads and showing them as a proportion of income is often useful:

OVERHEADS

	Quarter				£000s
	–5	–4	–3	–2	last
Income	200	178	188	201	190
Overheads	60	65	77	76	75
O/H to income %	30	37	41	38	39

We can see in this (imaginary) example that overheads have slowly increased from 30% last year to 39% in the current quarter; income has stayed broadly static. It would be an area to explore. This fact however may be hard to see if you are provided with a page of figures with all the overheads described in detail but with no percentages shown.

You can break down overheads further into their main categories, thus:

OVERHEAD ANALYSIS

					£000s
Category	–5	–4	–3	–2	last
Office expenses	30	28	35	30	30
Finance	14	16	10	9	8
Marketing	5	5	6	7	8
Training and hire	1	6	3	4	5
Other	10	10	23	26	24
Total O/H	60	65	77	76	75

Some explanations are needed. The –5 refers to the last quarter of the previous year which, as explained, helps with any seasonal differences which for some organisations can be quite marked.

It is useful to know how many staff you have and also how many volunteers. In addition to the numbers, the staff turnover is potentially useful since, if it starts to rise, this might prompt questions as to why people are leaving. It is also important to know whether they are trained. You may need to consider dividing training between things you *have* to do and *staff development*. Shortage of funds has meant that many charities are not training their staff sufficiently, leaving them short of key skills, particularly in areas of IT or marketing. You need to keep a handle on this because lack of training can mean lower efficiency, staff muddling through and not being able to use, for example, Excel or similar programs.

STAFFING

	Months			
	Jan	Feb	Mar	June
Staff FTE	7	7	6.5	6.5
Volunteers (number)	8	9	9	7
(hours)	24	28	25	21

FTE: full-time equivalent

Staffing levels are usually shown at full-time equivalent or FTE, so that people working three days a week, say, are shown as 0.6.

Fundraising is a continuing problem for most charities, and often the cause of their demise, so again it is useful to keep a track of what fundraising efforts are being made. As a minimum, you need to know how many applications have been made, of what value and to which organisation. A success rate is a useful statistic – that is, the value of successful bids divided by the total of bids made, as a percentage. If you are doing street collections, include how much is collected and how that is changing over time.

FUNDRAISING

	Qtr			
	–3	1	2	current
Applications made (number)	6	3	7	2
(value £'000s)	68	200	45	105
Value of funds received (£'000s)	5	24	0	35
Other fundraising	20	25	15	29
Total	25	49	15	64

In this example, the report is in quarter 3 so a comparison with that quarter in the previous year might useful. Reporting on fundraising is more difficult mainly because of the time delay between applications and knowing the results, which can be considerable.

Another approach is to look at progress compared to what your strategic fundraising needs were for the year, and present these in a graphical form:

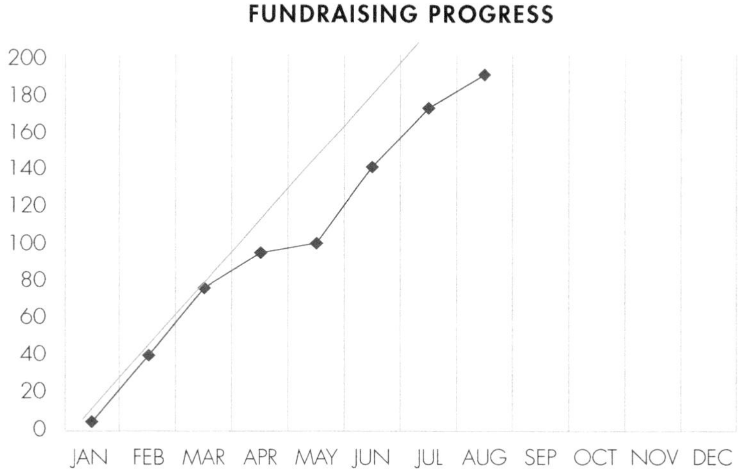

The thin line is the target of £360k shown as a monthly figure, and the heavier line shows progress: in this example, a little behind where you hoped to be. There are lags of course and it might be that a major source of funding is imminent. The graph gives you a clear and visual insight into fundraising progress.

This is some of the information which you are likely to find useful as a trustee. These are made-up figures but they would prompt some questions for the staff in real life. Numbers only give half the story of course – it's the story behind the numbers which is often of interest. I repeat my main point, however: without these numbers presented in a clear fashion, you would not know what is happening and you would not know what questions to ask.

References and notes

1. Various estimates for the number of charities, *viz:* 'How many charities are there?', How Charities Work, https://howcharitieswork.com/about-charities/how-many-charities/.
2. Jesse Norman, *Adam Smith: What He Thought, and Why it Matters*, Penguin Books, 2019.
3. Sheila McKechnie Foundation report, *The Chilling Reality*, explaining the effects of the Lobbying Act 2014 on voluntary and charitable organisations: https://smk.org.uk/wp-content/uploads/2020/08/SMK_The_Chilling_Reality_Lobbying_Act_Research.pdf.
4. Full Fact's article on aspects of lobbying: https://fullfact.org/law/lobbying-act-2014/.
5. The Charity Commission for England and Wales provides a great deal of detailed advice – see 'Charity Commission guidance', GOV.UK, https://www.gov.uk/guidance/charity-commission-guidance. For Northern Ireland, see 'Manage your charity', The Charity Commission for Northern Ireland, https://www.charitycommissionni.org.uk/manage-your-charity/ and for Scotland, 'Running a charity or community group', mygov.scot, https://www.mygov.scot/browse/living-visiting-scotland/charities-volunteering-honours/charity-community-group. The National Council for Voluntary Organisations is another useful source: https://www.ncvo.org.uk/.
6. Herzberg – Wikipedia: https://en.wikipedia.org/wiki/Frederick_Herzberg.
7. J.P. Womack, D.T. Jones, D. Roos, *The Machine That Changed the World*, Harper Perennial, 1991.
8. *Volunteering during Covid-19: Understanding Volunteer Motivations and Experiences*, June 2020. Authors: Jonathan Baker, Laura Baker, Hampshire County Council Insight and Engagement Unit, Dr Debra Gray, Dr Jordan Randell, University Of Winchester.
9. 'Priority areas for research into charities & philanthropy', giving-evidence.com, https://giving-evidence.com/2019/07/02/supply-and-demand/. Charity Futures' *Giving Evidence* suggests limited useful research and considerable unevenness. Charities make little use of it apparently.
10. Stanford Social Innovation Review (USA) 12 Common Criticisms of Philanthropy—and Some Answers (ssir.org).

11. Third Sector report into the Oxfam scandal: https://www.thirdsector.co.uk/oxfam-timeline-haiti-scandal-unfolded/governance/article/1459242.
12. Olive Cooke in Bristol received a huge number of mailings from charities. It emerged that information had been sold or exchanged between charities: https://www.bbc.co.uk/news/uk-england-bristol-35359268 It later emerged that the charity requests may not have been the principle cause of death, her family believed, as she had a history of depression. However, the story made headlines for several days and did enormous damage to the sector: https://sofii.org/article/the-olive-cooke-story.
13. Kids Company report with recommendations: https://www.buzzacott.co.uk/uploads/kids-company-final-for-website_(1).pdf. One factor was 'founder syndrome', which is discussed later in this book and is likely to be more common in smaller charities where the founder is still in place. NCVO points out that there were several factors which made Kids Company unusual: https://blogs.ncvo.org.uk/2015/10/29/three-reasons-why-kids-companys-funding-was-unusual/.
14. *Trust in Charities, 2018*, Charity Commission, https://assets.publishing.service.gov.uk/government/uploads/system/uploads/attachment_data/file/723566/Charity_Commission_-_Trust_in_Charities_2018_-_Report.pdf.
15. 'Helen Stephenson: Public attitudes to charity – and why they matter', Civil Society report, 5 November 2018, https://www.civilsociety.co.uk/voices/helen-stephenson-public-attitudes-to-charity-and-why-they-matter.html.
16. 'Capt Sir Tom 100: Family and celebrities embark on their own "100 challenge"', BBC News, https://www.bbc.co.uk/news/uk-england-beds-bucks-herts-56935334.
17. NCVO statistics on the charity sector (recent): 'Fast facts about the charity sector', NCVO, https://www.ncvo.org.uk/about-us/media-centre/briefings/1721-fast-facts-about-the-charity-sector. A useful breakdown of the different sizes of charities is provided by the Commission: 'Recent charity register statistics: Charity Commission', GOV.UK, https://www.gov.uk/government/statistics/charity-register-statistics/recent-charity-register-statistics-charity-commission.
18. 'Facts and figures: UK charity sector 2018', nfpSynergy, https://nfpsynergy.net/free-report/facts-and-figures-uk-charity-sector-2018.
19. Civil Society report 2019: https://www.civilsociety.co.uk/news/government-needs-to-engage-more-with-charity-sector-says-bond-uk.html. There is some evidence that the government is seeking to engage more with the sector since this report was published – see https://protect-eu.mimecast.com/s/H4QbCD135CWX96wUWz8lY?domain=newsocialcovenant.co.uk/.
20. 'Thousands of British charities may close without support, PM told', *Guardian*, 18 February 2021.
21. Speech by the Chancellor of the Exchequer Rishi Sunak announcing £750m of support for the sector: https://www.gov.uk/government/speeches/

chancellor-of-the-exchequer-rishi-sunak-on-economic-support-for-the-charity-sector.

22. Report by Danny Kruger MP on levelling up our communities. Kruger 2.0 Levelling Up Our Communities.pdf (dannykruger.org.uk).
23. Reductions to local authority budgets explained in a New Economics Foundation report (2019): https://neweconomics.org/uploads/files/NEF_Local_Government_Austerity_2019.pdf.
24. Child Poverty Action Group statistics. https://cpag.org.uk/child-poverty/child-poverty-facts-and-figures.
25. Guy Standing, *A Precariat Charter: From Denizens to Citizens*, Bloomsbury, 2011, pp. 374, 375.
26. Guy Standing, *The Corruption of Capitalism*, Biteback Publishing, 2016. He notes that when the austerity regime began, 'public spending cuts were partially offset by subsidising charities [who were] expected to fill the vacuum'. Charities too were expected to share the burden (pp. 113–14).
27. NPC on the unequal distribution of charities: https://www.thinknpc.org/resource-hub/where-are-englands-charities/.
28. https://www.civilsociety.co.uk/news/charity-sector-faces-60-000-redundancies-due-to-covid-19-warn-economists.html.
29. Tom Clark with Anthony Heath, *Hard Times*, Yale University Press, 2014, p. 119. This book reflected the effects of austerity and anecdotally, there was a big increase in volunteering during the pandemic. How sustained this will be remains to be seen.
30. Guardian article, from 2016 at the time of the scandals, discussing attitudes towards charities: https://www.theguardian.com/guide-to-fundraising/2016/jun/23/charity-fundraising-new-regulator-win-back-public-trust.
31. 'Charities need to focus less on the cause and more on the consumer, say agencies', The Drum, https://www.thedrum.com/news/2018/03/28/charities-need-focus-less-the-cause-and-more-the-consumer-say-agencies.
32. Trust in charities has fallen. https://www.theguardian.com/society/2016/jun/28/trust-in-charities-at-record-low-after-scandals.
33. A Populus survey for the Charity Commission includes this among its findings. Public trust in charities 2020 (publishing.service.gov.uk).
34. Charity Commission statistics giving the breakdown of charities by size: https://www.gov.uk/government/statistics/charity-register-statistics/recent-charity-register-statistics-charity-commission. In September 2018, they show that about 86% of charities have incomes below £500,000.
35. https://www.theguardian.com/society/2019/may/22/andy-haldane-bank-of-england-voluntary-sector-civil-society-technological-age. Haldane argues for a possibly greater role of civil society (which includes charities) in the future, in order to support individuals affected by technological change.

36. Ha-Joon Chang, *23 Things They Don't Tell You About Capitalism*, Allan Lane, 2010. This book discusses and analyses a range of assumptions about capitalism and questions their truth.
37. Charity affairs have a low profile in government: https://www.theguardian.com/voluntary-sector-network/2017/jun/16/new-charities-minister-government-civil-society.
38. House of Commons report into the collapse of the outsourcing firm Carillion. The report found, inter alia, that in the eight years from 2009 to 2016, it paid £554m in dividends, three-quarters of the cash it made from operations. Carillion paid out £33m more in dividends than it generated in cash from its operations. https://commonslibrary.parliament.uk/research-briefings/cbp-8206/.
39. Shelter's website describing the work they do and its results: https://england.shelter.org.uk/what_we_do/our_strategy.
40. Charities not using research to evidence their work: https://www.thirdsector.co.uk/charities-rarely-produce-evidence-philanthropists-look-for-research-says/fundraising/article/1694537.
41. Jamie Susskind, *Future Politics: Living Together in a World Transformed by Tech*, Oxford University Press, 2018.
42. Social Attitudes Survey: https://natcen.ac.uk, and for Scotland: https://www.gov.scot/.
43. History of the Post-it note: https://www.3m.co.uk/3M/en_GB/post-it-notes/contact-us/about-us/.
44. Founder syndrome can be a serious problem, particularly for a small and recently formed charity: Anonymous, '"Founder syndrome": the strong personality crippling my charity', *Guardian*, https://www.theguardian.com/voluntary-sector-network/2017/apr/12/founder-syndrome-personality-crippling-charity.
45. Charities becoming risk-averse: 'Charity leaders too risk-averse and need more courage, says Etherington', Civil Society, https://www.civilsociety.co.uk/news/-charity-leaders-too-risk-averse-and-need-courage-and-moral-compass-says-etherington.html.
46. Charity Commission reports into instances of investigations concerning charities not following the rules. https://www.gov.uk/government/collections/statements-on-live-cases-charity-commission#statements-released-in-2020.
47. Government guidance: *The Essential Trustee: What You Need to Know, What You Need to Do (CC3)*, GOV.UK, https://www.gov.uk/government/publications/the-essential-trustee-what-you-need-to-know-cc3.
48. Mike Eastwood and Jacqueline Williams, *Charity Trustees Handbook*, 3rd edn, Directory of Social Change, 2017.
49. Victor Bignell, Geoff Peters and Christopher Pym, *Catastrophic Failures,* Open University Press, 1977.

50. Interesting research paper on the role of information in charitable organisations, discussing some of the problems which can occur: *Trustee decision making in small UK charities.* Journal of Philanthropy and Marketing, Jeremy Vincent, Jenny Harrow, Paul Palmer, 17 February 2011.
51. The importance of information. This article is for a small business but the principle is largely the same. https://smallbusiness.chron.com/importance-management-information-system-5256.html.
52. Excellent guide to why people volunteer and also stop or never volunteer, by NCVO: https://data.ncvo.org.uk/volunteering/motivations-and-barriers/.
53. Florence Nightingale's contribution to statistics: 'Florence Nightingale: The lady with the data', This Is Statistics, https://thisisstatistics.org/florence-nightingale-the-lady-with-the-data.
54. Doubts about the value of a balanced score card approach to assessing a charity's performance: https://www.thirdsectorlaw.co.uk/content/charity-management-efficiency-and-balanced-scorecard.
55. *Harvard Business Review* article explaining the balanced score card method: https://hbr.org/1992/01/the-balanced-scorecard-measures-that-drive-performance-2.
56. The proportion of the world's wealth owned by a handful of billionaires: CNN report based on Oxfam, https://edition.cnn.com/2019/01/20/business/oxfam-billionaires-davos/index.html.
57. Richard Wilkinson and Kate Pickett, *The Inner Level: How More Equal Societies Reduce Stress, Restore Sanity and Improve Everyone's Well-being*, Allen Lane, 2018; Richard Wilkinson and Kate Pickett, *The Spirit Level: Why Equality is Better for Everyone*, Allen Lane, 2009.
58. YouGov analysis of the most popular charities: https://yougov.co.uk/ratings/politics/popularity/charities-organisations/all.
59. YouGov survey of the decision to cut foreign aid from 0.7% of GDP to 0.5% in 2020, showing popular support from the public: https://yougov.co.uk/topics/politics/articles-reports/2020/11/25/two-thirds-britons-support-cutting-foreign-aid-bud.
60. Helen Stride, 'An investigation into the values dimensions of branding: implications for the charity sector', *International Journal of Nonprofit Voluntary Sector Marketing*, May 2006.
61. Naomi Klein, *No Logo*, Harper Perennial, 2005.
62. Hankinson, Philippa, *Brand orientation in the charity sector: A framework for discussion and research*. International Journal of Nonprofit and Voluntary Sector Marketing, Vol No. 3, 2001.
63. Stride, 'An Investigation', ibid p. 118.
64. https://fabrikbrands.com/ultimate-guide-to-charity-branding/.
65. Macmillan's accounts showing expenditure on fundraising (2019), p. 85 note 9: www.macmillan.org.uk.

66. Ipsos MORI, *Public Trust and Confidence in Charities*, research on behalf of the Charity Commission, 20 July 2010.
67. Populus, *Trust in Charities – Overview of Findings*, June 2020 for the Charity Commission. They also found that fewer people see the current role that charities play as essential or very important. The level of resources reaching the intended recipients remains a number one priority among those polled.
68. NfpSynergy statistics https://nfpsynergy.net/press-release/what-would-encourage-people-give-charity-survey-public-attitudes.
69. Guardian article on why people give to charity. https://www.theguardian.com/voluntary-sector-network/2015/mar/23/the-science-behind-why-people-give-money-to-charity.
70. Policy paper from History and Policy [historyandpolicy.org] which discusses public attitudes to charities. Sceptical yet supportive: understanding public attitudes to charity | History and Policy.
71. Robert H. Frank, *Under the Influence: Putting Peer Pressure to Work,* Princeton University Press, 2020.
72. List of thirteen types of charity: https://uk.practicallaw.thomsonreuters.com/.
73. Gerard Hastings, *Social Marketing: Why Should the Devil Have All the Best Tunes?* Butterworth-Heinemann, 2007.
74. Alcohol Change charity and its policy towards alcohol: https://alcoholchange.org.uk/about-us.
75. View by some Conservative politicians about why there is poverty and it being the fault of the poor: https://www.centreforglobaleducation.com/why-governments-are-blaming-poor-their-own-poverty.
76. Attitudes towards food banks, Trussell Trust report: https://www.trusselltrust.org/2019/10/15/largest-ever-poll-poverty-shows-nine-10-brits-think-hunger-problem-uk-says-trussell-trust/.
77. Article unsympathetic to food banks in the *Daily Mail*. This is from 2014 however and attitudes have changed a little. 'Unpalatable truth about food banks the Left finds so hard to swallow', Daily Mail Online, https://www.dailymail.co.uk/news/article-2579715/Unpalatable-truth-food-banks-Left-finds-hard-swallow-Political-football-undeserving-claimants-shame-genuine-need.html.
78. https://fareshare.org.uk – a charity which believes no good food should go to waste.
79. Daniel Kahneman, *Thinking, Fast and Slow* (Penguin, 2011), p. 20.
80. Sam Wollaston, 'Food bank supremo Emma Revie: "This is the best job in the world – and it shouldn't have to exist", *Guardian*, 31 May 2021, https://www.theguardian.com/society/2021/may/31/food-bank-supremo-emma-revie-this-is-the-best-job-in-the-world-and-it-shouldnt-have-to-exist.
81. Guidance on political campaigning by the Charity Commission: https://assets.publishing.service.gov.uk/government/uploads/system/uploads/attachment_data/file/610137/CC9.pdf.

82. 'Are fewer people supporting charities?', NCVO Blogs, https://blogs.ncvo.org.uk/2019/05/07/are-fewer-people-supporting-charities/.
83. *Psychology Today* article on the problems of group think: https://www.psychologytoday.com/gb/basics/groupthink.
84. Article explaining the problem with the space shuttle and the 'O' rings which failed: http://www.feynman.com/science/the-challenger-disaster/. A further discussion can be found here: https://jessicagrice0129.wordpress.com/2014/10/24/groupthink-reflection/.
85. Anthony King and Ivor Crewe, *The Blunders of Our Governments*, Oneworld Publications, 2013.
86. Ibid., p. 259.
87. Ibid., p. 267.
88. Belbin's theory of teams: https://www.belbin.com/about/belbin-team-roles.
89. CFG Guide to fraud prevention: https://cfg.org.uk/userfiles/documents/CFG%20resources/CFG%20Publication/CF240_SmallCharitiesGuide.pdf.
90. Levels of fraud in charities: Statistics Web_CC_Fraud.pdf (publishing.service.gov.uk).
91. Bob Garratt, *Stop the Rot: Reframing Governance for Directors and Politicians*, Routledge, 2017, pp. 123, 128.
92. Stress on charities as a result of the pandemic: 'Charities in the time of Covid-19', *Philanthropy Impact*, https://www.philanthropy-impact.org/expert-opinion/charities-time-covid-19.
93. Guidance for chairs is provided in *A Chair's Compass*, published by the Cass Business School.
94. Problems around the support given by BP to the British Museum: Marine Tanguy and Harry Phibbs, 'DEBATE: Was the British Museum right to bypass BP as a sponsor for its Arctic exhibition?', CityA.M., https://www.cityam.com/debate-was-the-british-museum-right-to-drop-bp-as-a-sponsor/.
95. The Chartered Institute of Fundraising offers a balanced view concerning accepting funding from 'tainted' sources: 'Fundraising ethics is about much more than sticking to the Code and avoiding "tainted" money', https://ciof.org.uk/events-and-training/resources/fundraising-ethics-is-about-much-more-than-stickin.

Index

C

T

U

V